In
Holy
Service

Also by Cornelis Van Dam

Worship Matters (2021)

In the Beginning: Listening to Genesis 1 and 2 (2021)

Hope and Comfort in the Book of Job (2017)

*The Deacon: Biblical Foundations for
Today's Ministry of Mercy* (2016)

*God and Government:
Biblical Principles for Today* (2011)

*The Elder: Today's Ministry
Rooted in all of Scripture* (2009)

Fathers and Mothers at Home and at School (2000)

Perspectives on Worship, Law, and Faith (2000)

*The Urim and Thummim:
A Means of Revelation in Ancient Israel* (1997)

Divorce and Remarriage (1996)

In
Holy
Service:

Essays on
Office–Personal and Ecclesial

Cornelis Van Dam

Library and Archives Canada Cataloguing in Publication

Title: In Holy Service: Essays on Office—Personal and Ecclesial /
    Cornelis Van Dam.
Names: Van Dam, Cornelis, 1946- author.
Description: 1st edition. | Includes bibliographical references.
Identifiers: Canadiana 20230182879 | ISBN 9781990650048 (softcover)
Subjects: LCSH: Christian life. | LCSH: Christian stewardship.
Classification: LCC BV4501.3 .V36 2023 | DDC 248.4–dc23

ISBN 978-1-9906500-4-8

LUCERNA
CRTS PUBLICATIONS
110 West 27th Street
Hamilton, Ontario L9C 5A1

for Carl and Lisa
in holy service

Table of Contents

Chapter 3
Motherhood: Saved Through Child Bearing

Chapter 4
The Calling of Husband and Father

PART B | ECCLESIASTICAL OFFICES

Chapter 5
Calvin and the Reformation of Ecclesiastical Offices

Chapter 6
Some Aspects of the Office of Minister of the Word

Chapter 7
The Preacher as Teacher: The Importance of Catechetical Proclamation

Chapter 8

Elders, a Treasure to Cherish: A Reformation Day Reflection

Chapter 9

Aspiring, Preparing, and Equipping for the Office of Elder: Is Special Training Required?

Chapter 10

Congregational Involvement in Electing to Office

Chapter 11

The Office of the Church in Relation to Civil Government

PART C | WOMEN IN SPECIAL SERVICE

Chapter 12
Culture and Biblical Authority: A Reminder from Luther

Chapter 13
Prophetesses in God's Service

Chapter 14
Women Serving the Church: Divine Directives and Opportunities

PART D | EPILOGUE

Chapter 15
Retrospect and Prospect

Preface and Acknowledgements

There is currently great confusion in understanding one's identity as a person. Many do not want to know or acknowledge that God created humans, male and female, in his image and after his likeness with a clear identity and with responsibilities to the Creator—responsibilities that go with their God-given creational calling or office. Instead we hear the constant secular clamor that we are to determine our own identity and decide for ourselves what we can and should be allowed to do. In the midst of this morally chaotic state of affairs Christians can become confused.

What does it mean to be a Christian? In a time when many have an identity crisis, it is good for Christians to pose and answer this question. Among other things, being a Christian means that we have an office, an official task from God. Believers are expected to be in his holy service. Actually all people have the obligation to live for God and to serve him since all have been created in his image and after his likeness. But our neo-pagan civic culture has lost its Christian moorings, denied the claims of the Creator, and no longer understands the biblical notion of office. It is only by God's grace that we as Christians may know about God's expectations in terms of the office and calling which he has given us as those redeemed by Christ.

This book is a collection of essays about what it means to be a Christian with an office, an official task from God, as an individual, as a married couple, and as a father and mother. Being a Christian also means being a member of the church of Christ. And so besides the specific office or task the Lord has given to each believer, he has also given special tasks to those serving the church in ecclesiastical offices. It is important that we have some understanding of these offices. There are therefore also some chapters on aspects of the special offices in the church, especially with a view to some current issues.

And so what follows in this publication seeks to remind us of God's gracious expectations for our office and calling as Christians, as those renewed in Christ, as well as restating some of the fundamentals of the special office bearers in the church who are meant to help Christians function as God intended. May this publication be of some assistance for being in holy service in a life of gratitude to God.

* * *

Most of this material has appeared in somewhat different forms in earlier publications as detailed in the appendix. My thanks go to William Gortemaker and James Visscher of Clarion and Diakonia, respectively for permission to reprint material that originally appeared in their publications.

I also want to take this opportunity to thank Dr. Gijsbertus Nederveen and my dear wife Joanne for carefully reading through the manuscript and providing feedback and corrections and Lucerna for publishing this material. I appreciate the careful editorial work of Dr. Chris de Boer which has enhanced the work and the expertise of Bill van Beek in designing the cover, doing the layout, and preparing the material for printing.

* * *

Abbreviations for Bible translations:

ESV — English Standard Version. This version is used unless otherwise indicated.

NASB — New American Standard Bible (1995)

NET — New English Translation (The NET Bible)

NIV — New International Version (1984); NIV (2011) is the version of that year.

PART A

THE GENERAL OFFICE OF A BELIEVER

1 CHAPTER

The Office of a Christian: Its Background, Reality, and Privilege

Many people today experience an identity crisis and ask: "Who am I? Why am I here? What is my purpose in life?" In our secular age Scripture is considered irrelevant for answering such questions. Consequently, cultural forces are battering individuals with doubts and questions about their individuality, place, and role in this world. These attacks on one's person can also impact and confuse Christians about their God-given identity.

In such a context it is good to go back to the biblical basics and remind ourselves what the Lord our God tells us about our identity as Christians. He who has made us and placed us on this earth is the only one who can correctly answer the questions about who we are and why we are here. A key element of our identity as a created being is that God placed humankind on this earth for holy service; that is, he gave our first parents, Adam and Eve, and through them all their descendants a task, an office, to be done so that they could enjoy life to its fullness as God, the Creator, had intended. It is important to realize that we do not determine what our ultimate task and goal in life should be in order to find true fulfillment. The Creator determines all that. Only when we follow his design for our life will we find real satisfaction and happiness.

Let us, therefore, first consider the identity and task that God gave to the very first people on earth, Adam and Eve, next the consequence of their fall into sin, and finally the restoration of humanity to true service to God in Christ.

Introduction

Adam and Eve, Their Office as God's Image

Unlike all other creatures which the Creator made, only Adam and Eve were made in God's image and likeness. God's Word tells us that "God

3

created man in his own image, in the image of God he created him; male and female he created them" (Gen 1:27). Much could be said about this passage, but for our present purpose it is important to note that only human beings had the privilege of being God's image on earth. When God took counsel with himself to make the first humans he said: "Let us make man in our image, after our likeness. And let him have dominion" (Gen 1:26). Humanity's being made in God's image meant that they were to subdue the earth and rule over it (Gen 1:28–30). In other words, Adam and Eve had the royal office of a monarch!

Adam and Eve as God's image were also aware of God's will. Made after the likeness of God, they had been created in true righteousness and holiness (Eph 4:24) and lived in communion with the Lord. It seems that God appeared to them from time to time as he walked in the garden and spoke to them (cf. Gen 3:8–9). Knowing God and his works as his representatives meant that our very first parents were also equipped for the prophetic office. They could be expected to extol God's greatness and, as history moved on, to convey his works and will to the next generation.

Another aspect of Adam and Eve's identity as image and likeness of God was that they were also his children (cf. Gen 5:1–3). Adam is even specifically identified as "son of God" (Luke 3:38). As can be expected of children, they were to love God, their heavenly Father, and to consecrate themselves wholeheartedly in holy sacrificial service. This identity focuses on their priestly task.

So, in terms of their identity as created after God's image, one can say that Adam and Eve were created to function in the offices of prophet, priest, and king.[1] It needs to be stressed that both male and female were made in God's image and had the duty of this threefold office (Gen 1:27).

But Adam and Eve failed to honor their God-given identity as children of God, created after his image. Instead of loving and obeying their Creator, they took from the forbidden tree against his express command (Gen 2:16–17; 3:6) and so placed themselves in the service of the adversary,

---

1   Also see Herman Bavinck, *Reformed Dogmatics*, 4 vols., ed. John Bolt, trans. John Vriend (Grand Rapids, MI: Baker Academic, 2003–8), 2:562.

the serpent. Consequently, they and all their descendants were unable to function according to the identity that God had given them (Rom 5:12). In his righteous judgment God drove them out of the garden. However, prior to doing so God had graciously promised redemption from their sin. He would make a new beginning. Satan, who had come in the form of a serpent, would not have the last word. The serpent's head would be crushed (Gen 3:15; Rom 16:20). The One who would do this and restore the way to the tree of life was the Savior, the Son of God (Heb 2:14). The Creator was faithful to his work of creation and did not abandon it to the evil one.

The Second Adam and the Restoration of Our Office

God in his mercy sent his Son as the second Adam to redeem humankind and to begin a new humanity which does have the ability to do the calling and office which God has entrusted to them. Jesus grew up as a real human being under his earthly parents, Joseph and Mary, slowly maturing to manhood (Luke 2:40). His entrance into his public ministry was marked by John the Baptist, baptizing him. When that happened, "the heavens were opened, and the Holy Spirit descended on him [Jesus] in bodily form, like a dove; and a voice came from heaven, 'You are my beloved Son; with you I am well pleased'" (Luke 3:21–22). He was anointed with the Holy Spirit and so became the Christ (Luke 4:18; Acts 10:38). The name "Christ" is the Greek equivalent of the Hebrew "Messiah" and both names mean "the Anointed One." The Spirit descended on Jesus to equip him for his task as the One who would restore humanity to being God's representative and image as the Creator had intended.

The Son is "the image of the invisible God" (Col 1:15; 2 Cor 4:4) in a manner impossible for Adam and Eve, for Christ is also God (Col 2:9). Whoever has seen the Lord Jesus has seen the Father (John 14:9). "He is the radiance of the glory of God and the exact imprint of his nature and he upholds the universe by the word of his power" (Heb 1:3; cf. 1 Tim 6:16). He obeyed the Father perfectly (Phil 2:8). Yet, Christ was also like us in every respect (Heb 2:17). As both divine and human, he was able to pay for sin (2 Cor 5:21) and restore humanity to its God-given identity and calling. "As by one man's disobedience the many were made sinners, so by the one man's obedience the many will be made righteous" (Rom 5:19).

Christ is able to restore us to the office which the Lord God had originally bestowed on Adam and Eve in Eden so that as Christians we can truly live up to the identity of being God's image in this world. Although all humans are still in God's image (cf. Gen 9:6; James 3:9) and are therefore duty bound to honor God and represent his interests on earth, unrepentant sinners are not able to fulfill this obligation. The original created identity of humanity as image of God has been deeply corrupted. Restoration and renewal are needed.[2] As the apostle Paul put it: "you have to put off the old self with its practices and put on the new self, which is being renewed in knowledge after the image of its creator" (Col 3:9–10). Being a Christian means to be born again and to have a new nature. We cannot do this on our own. Divine power is needed (John 3:3–8).

To put the matter differently, we need the anointing of the Holy Spirit. We need to share in the One who is the Anointed, the Messiah. We need to be "in Christ" and so be called a Christian. Believers are therefore called God's anointed. Paul told the Corinthian Christians: "It is God who establishes us with you in Christ, and has anointed us, and who has also put his seal on us and given us his Spirit in our hearts as a guarantee" (2 Cor 1:21–22). In a similar vein the apostle John wrote to the believers: "you have been anointed by the Holy One" and "the anointing that you received from him abides in you" (1 John 2:20, 27). Christians are those who have been anointed by the Holy Spirit and have been restored to be image of God in this world; indeed, as children of God. As Paul expressed it: "in Christ Jesus you are all sons of God, through faith. For as many of you as were baptized into Christ have put on Christ" (Gal 3:26–27). Those who truly live up to the implications of their baptism as claimed by God to be his children "put on Christ." In him they are a new creation and have been raised to a new life (Rom 6:3–11). The Christian's relationship with the Savior as being "in Christ" is all important. "Put on the Lord Jesus Christ, and make no provision for the flesh, to gratify its desires" (Rom 13:14).

This close relationship, this union with Christ, was expressed by the Savior in the metaphor of the vine and the branches. He said to his

---

2   The Belgic Confession, Art. 14 notes: "Since man became wicked and perverse, corrupt in all his ways, he has lost all his excellent gifts which he had once received from God. He has nothing left but some small traces, which are sufficient to make man inexcusable." *Book of Praise: Anglo-Genevan Psalter* (Winnipeg, MB: Premier, 2014), 504.

disciples: "I am the vine; you are the branches. Whoever abides in me and I in him, he it is that bears much fruit, for apart from me you can do nothing" (John 15:5). It is only in Christ and by the power of his Spirit that we are able to be an image of God in this world and bear fruit. Put differently, when we are in Christ and derive our strength from his Spirit then we can participate in his anointing and be a prophet, priest, and king. Then we honor the task and the three-fold office which the Creator intended for his creation when he made our first parents, Adam and Eve, in his image and after his likeness. The Heidelberg Catechism puts it well:

> Why are you called a Christian? Because I am a member of Christ by faith and thus share in his anointing, so that I may as prophet confess his name, as priest present myself a living sacrifice of thankfulness to him, and as king fight with a free and good conscience against sin and the devil in this life, and hereafter reign with him eternally over all creatures. (Q.A. 32)[3]

Let us explore some of the implications of sharing in Christ's threefold office which he fulfilled and restored to us with his earthly ministry.

Christ and Our Prophetic Calling

In the most basic sense, our prophetic calling is to confess Christ. We may confess him as our chief prophet and teacher who has restored us to our prophetic office, and to do so is a great privilege and reason for much joy. How eagerly the believers in the Old Testament must have awaited the coming of that great prophet, the Anointed One, the Messiah! How happy the angels and the shepherds outside Bethlehem must have been when he came down to earth! How joy filled the church of Pentecost in knowing Christ as the fulfillment of the Old Testament promise regarding the great prophet! To appreciate something of the privilege and joy we may have in confessing him as prophet and teacher, we first need to understand what exactly his task as prophet entailed.

Christ's Prophetic Task

The Heidelberg Catechism beautifully summarizes the teaching of

---

3   *Book of Praise*, 527–28.

Scripture by stating that Christ, as our chief prophet and teacher, has "fully revealed to us the secret counsel and will of God concerning our redemption" (Q.A. 31). He has informed us of our salvation in the most detailed and profound sense possible.

What a momentous moment in history, therefore, when the eternal Son of God became a human being in order to be our chief prophet and teacher. He could tell God's people what he, as a divine being, had heard from his heavenly Father (John 8:26). He could reveal God, the Father, and tell us his plan and intentions as no previous prophet could. Although no one has ever seen God, the Son could make him known (John 1:18). As no other human messenger for God, he could speak the very Word of God. While the Old Testament prophets always said, "Thus says the LORD" and then spoke God's Word, Christ did not have to do that. He simply spoke on his own authority. "Truly, truly I say to you." Indeed, that is all that was needed. Is he not the Word of God incarnate? Indeed, he is. As we read at the beginning of John's gospel: "In the beginning was the Word, and the Word was with God, and the Word was God. He was in the beginning with God. . . And the Word became flesh and dwelt among us" (John 1:1–2, 14a). Christ is the Word incarnate and so Christ could speak with power and authority as no other. Those who heard Christ understood. When Jesus spoke, "the crowds were astonished at his teaching, for he was teaching them as one who had authority, and not as their scribes" (Matt 7:28b, 29). No wonder, for Christ is *the* prophet and teacher—the Word incarnate. What he says is trustworthy and true. Indeed, is he himself not the truth (John 14:6)? The revelation he gives is completely dependable.

Christ's prophetic office also included ensuring the continued proclamation and teaching of the secret counsel and will of God concerning our redemption. He gave the church apostles, prophets, evangelists, pastors, and teachers (Eph 4:11). Through his Spirit, he guided the church to receive from his hand the enduring offices of minister of the gospel (or teaching elder) and the ruling elder (1 Tim 5:17). They are charged to equip God's people in their prophetic task by expounding the Scriptures, teaching the way of godliness, and exhorting them to be faithful witnesses of God's will in their lives. We will discuss these offices later in this book.

In the context of our present discussion, it is important to note that the Spirit of our chief Prophet and Teacher now enables all Christians, young and old, male and female, to engage in their prophetic office. Since the day of Pentecost, Christians may share in Christ's anointing and be endowed with his enabling Spirit for their prophetic task. In this way, Christ restores the prophetic office to us.

Our Prophetic Task

What exactly does our prophetic office entail? It does not mean predicting the future or receiving new revelation as the notion of being a prophet may lead some to believe. Christ *has* revealed everything necessary by his Spirit and ensured its being written in the Scriptures for our benefit (2 Tim 3:16–17; cf. 1 Pet 1:11).[4]

In its most fundamental sense, honoring our prophetic office means to confess Christ with whom we are so intimately bound by the Spirit. If we do so, he will acknowledge us before the Father. If we do not do so, he will deny us before the Father (Matt 10:32–33). Indeed, "if you confess with your mouth that Jesus is Lord and believe in your heart that God raised him from the dead, you will be saved" (Rom 10:9).

To confess Christ implies, of course, that we are familiar with the Scriptures that speak of him. As those with the responsibility of the prophetic office, we will do everything in our power to increase our knowledge of God's Word, including our devotional reading, family worship, and listening to the proclamation of the gospel on the Lord's Day. We cannot do our prophetic task without knowing as much as possible about the Lord Jesus who saved us from our sins and who is preparing us for a life of service now and even for eternity. After all, the Holy Spirit who equips us for our prophetic calling, does so through the Word and not without it. He makes the Word function as a light upon our path, as a source of strength and encouragement, and as a fountain of life (Ps 119:105; Phil 2:16).

---

4 On the cessation of special revelation after the canon of Scripture was complete, see Richard B. Gaffin, Jr., *Perspectives on Pentecost: Studies in New Testament Teaching on the Gifts of the Holy Spirit* (Phillipsburg, NJ: Presbyterian and Reformed, 1979), 89–116; Joel Beeke and Paul M. Smalley, *Revelation and God*, Reformed Systematic Theology (Wheaton, IL: Crossway, 2019), 409–57.

For our purposes, two additional consequences of sharing Christ's anointing as prophets can be mentioned. First, since we are to live our prophetic identity, parents have a special responsibility to do what they can to enable their children to live out their prophetic calling, and second, as Christians we are to discern and respond to the spirits of our time. In the process we may experience something of the joy of being in Christ in our prophetic office.

Prophetic Parents

No matter our age or gender, God expects us to live out our prophetic calling as soon as possible as we grow up. The promise of the Spirit and his anointing has been given at our baptism. As the Reformed form for baptism says: "when we are baptized into the name of the Holy Spirit, God the Holy Spirit assures us by this sacrament that he will dwell in us and make us living members of Christ, imparting to us what we have in Christ"[5] and that includes sharing in his prophetic office. The privilege of the baptismal promises places a holy obligation on us from a young age. It is for this reason that parents take on an enormous responsibility when they have their children baptized. They vow before God and his congregation to instruct their child or children in the faith as soon as possible and to have them instructed.[6]

It is, therefore, essential that parents know the Bible and know God's plans and demands for our life. Only then can parents be prophets and prophetesses to their children; yes, be God's voice as they seek to instruct their children regarding God's desires for their life. Children come to their parents with their issues and questions. According to their prophetic office, parents are to answer such questions to the best of their ability and with the conviction that they are faithful to God's Word. Christian parents who truly grasp the gospel and are energized by the Word and its riches, live prophetically, are steadfast and are not moved by every wind and fad. They are also an inspiration for their children.

Solid prophetic upbringing in the home will go a long way to enable children, teenagers, and young adults to live up to God's expectations

---

5   The Form for the Baptism of Infants as found in *Book of Praise*, 597.
6   *Book of Praise*, 598.

in their own prophetic sharing in Christ's anointing. As members of the church, the Spirit has also been promised to them. They too may experience the joyous reality of knowing that God has laid his claim on them and has a plan for their life. As the young grow in understanding the Word, they too will mature in prophetic insight and be a source of help and encouragement to their siblings and peers. Through the reading and reflection of the Word of God, the Holy Spirit will equip young and old in their prophetic calling.

Prophetic Insight

That calling includes being able to discern and respond biblically to the ungodly spirits of our time. Such discernment continues to be necessary for we live in the last phase of world history when the final day of judgment approaches and Satan gets more and more desperate. World history moved into this final period of time with the outpouring of the Holy Spirit on the day of Pentecost. Scripture calls the age in which we live "the last days" (Acts 2:17). "The end of the ages has come" upon us (1 Cor 10:11). It is a time period when "some will depart from the faith by devoting themselves to deceitful spirits and teachings of demons" (1 Tim 4:1) and when many antichrists appear (1 John 2:18).

For such a time we can be grateful that Christ equips us for our prophetic calling and office. Through the agency of our Savior's Word and Spirit, we may be able to see through the propaganda barrage of Satan and discern truth from lies, right from wrong. Although the devil seeks to confuse the minds of God's children, we can resist and oppose him, going on the offensive. We do not have to heed the father of lies, the devil (John 8:44) and receive instruction from him. We receive our life direction from the divine Word. As those who are "in Christ," we as Christians are not only enabled to understand the Word but also to speak it forthrightly and with authority and to set our lives in harmony with it. The apostle John wrote: "The anointing that you received from him abides in you, and you have no need that anyone should teach you. But as his anointing teaches you about everything, and is true, and is no lie—just as it has taught you, abide in him" (1 John 2:27). The fact that "you have no need that anyone should teach you" does not mean that we no longer need instruction from Scripture. It is critically important that we know and heed the Word. We need the daily reading and instruction from the Word of God and its preaching on the Lord's Day. What we do not need is the false instruction of heretics and deceivers which is the context in which John was writing (1 John 2:18–25). The Spirit will expose the lies and guide us into all truth by our abiding in Christ and his Word (1 John 2:24).

The prophetic voice of Christians against the current predominant post-Christian culture is not welcome. It means that we must be prepared to pay the price of being in opposition to the satanic forces that inspire the decadent sin-tolerant culture of our day. Christians are considered hopelessly out of touch and out of date. But when we have the opportunity, we need to seize the moment and speak up and let our prophetic voice be heard. The Creator knows what is best for his creation and we must let his will for our society be known as he has revealed in his Word as we have the opportunity to do so.

The Ongoing Challenge

Being a prophetic voice is not easy. The opposition is formidable, but we are in Christ, and we may boldly confess his name and promote his honor in today's world. Scripture does not picture an easy time for Christian witness in this final period of world history. "In the last days there will come times of difficulty. For people will be lovers of self, lovers of money, proud, arrogant, abusive, disobedient to their parents, ungrateful, unholy, heartless, unappeasable, slanderous, without self-control, brutal, not loving good, treacherous, reckless, swollen with conceit, lovers of pleasure rather than lovers of God" (2 Tim 3:2–5). With the western world abandoning the Christian values it once had, it is becoming ripe for God's judgment, not unlike the world in the time of Noah (Matt 24:37). In such a context, Christians have a prophetic task to confess their Lord and the biblical norms he proclaimed in all areas of life, be it political, economic, social, academic, etc. Being a prophet or prophetess can involve addressing the issues of the day in different ways: by talking to our neighbors and to our legislative representatives, and by being active in supporting initiatives and organizations that seek to uphold biblical standards in the life of our nation.

Above all, confessing Christ prophetically means honoring him in the day-to-day responsibilities of our Christian walk of life; as parents equipping our children for their prophetic task by educating them in a biblical world and life view, and supporting them in the challenges they face in school and on the job; as teens and young adults resisting the allures of the sins in our current civic culture and confessing that we belong to our Savior. In spite of all the challenges that the prophetic task entails, we may do it joyfully in the realization that we are confessing our Savior, who loved us even up to Golgotha and who lives, guiding his people through his Word and Spirit.

Which saved sinner, who knows his unworthiness by nature, would not want to confess and rejoice in the Savior with whom he is bound as a branch into the vine? After all, as his prophetic voice in this world, we may see reality and the world in the light of his redemptive work. We realize that although we are in this world we are not of it; therefore, we can see beyond any current trials. From his Word, we know that God is sovereignly guiding this world through his Son in such a way that his promises are true for all those who confess him and live prophetically in this world.

Christians will also be affected by the trials that God sends over this world. Indeed, the persecution of Christians in our day is in ways unprecedented in world history. The enormous number of Christians presently being persecuted at one time is incredible.[7] But, in spite of all the sorrow, the Christian hope does not disappoint. Accounts coming from those oppressed for the faith even testify of the joy they have in the Lord and in spite of the dangers they cling to him, profess him, and are a prophetic testimony. May that also be an inspiration for us in the free West to fulfill our prophetic office joyfully in a life of gratitude to our chief Prophet and Teacher.

Christ and our Priestly Calling

As Christians we also share in Christ's anointing as priest. But what does that mean? How do we share in his priestly office in our life on earth? We need to distinguish carefully in answering that question. In this section we will consider three aspects of the priestly office of our Savior and how

---

7   See, e.g., the latest Open Doors report available: "World Watch List 2020" found in www.OpenBoorsUSA.org/WWL.

they relate to our identity as anointed priests in Christ: his sacrificial work, his intercessory prayers, and his priestly work of blessing.

Sacrificial Service

Scripture speaks of the priestly office in two distinct ways. There is, in the first place, the priesthood of all believers by which all are to consecrate themselves to the Lord and his service. Adam and Eve were appointed to that priesthood when God created them in his image and placed them in the garden of Eden. They were to use all their gifts, emotions, and love—their everything—for their holy service to God. In the words of the Catechism, they had to be "a living sacrifice of thankfulness" to God (Q.A. 32) for the many blessings they daily received from their Creator. They had to show by their entire lives that they responded to their Maker's love by loving him in thanksgiving. Adam and Eve however did not do their priestly calling for which God had created them. Instead of showing sacrificial gratitude for God's gracious provision, they listened to Satan and fell into sin. In his grace and mercy, God eventually established a priesthood of atonement.

The provision of atonement is the second way that Scripture speaks of the priestly office. The divine intent to provide atonement was foreshadowed by the LORD's spilling blood and killing animals to provide a covering for Adam and Eve's nakedness (Gen 3:21). As the LORD then provided for their immediate needs in covering their nakedness, he would ultimately provide for their need of the full covering of atonement through *the* sacrifice of the Lamb of God, the Savior.[8] He would suffer nakedness and the shame associated with it so that his people could be clothed in righteousness (Matt 27:35; Isa 61:10; Rev 7:9).

Christ offered himself, not as a sacrifice of gratitude, but as a sin offering to make atonement. Christ thus fulfilled the special Levitical priesthood instituted by God at Mount Sinai. "Christ has offered for all time a single sacrifice for sins . . . By a single offering he has perfected for all time those who are being sanctified" (Heb 10:12, 14). It is obvious that believers cannot share in this particular aspect of the priestly office of Christ. Only

---

8   The Hebrew root *kpr* conveys both the meaning "to cover" and "to make atonement."

the perfect Lamb of God was able to give his life as a sin offering and redeem his people. He had to come down from heaven for this atoning work because no creature could do so. Not only are we as believers totally unable to atone for our own sins, we are also unable to share in this aspect of Christ's priestly work because it is finished. *The* sacrifice for sins has been made once for all.

However, apart from his atoning work, as believers we do share in Christ's anointing as priest. By his priestly work, Christ has restored for all believers the original priestly office that the Creator had given to humanity at creation, namely, the consecrating of one's life to God. The life of our Savior on earth also testified to this priesthood and it is in that priesthood of a life of loving and holy consecration to our Father in heaven that believers may share in Christ's priestly office.

Christ's life of devotion to his Father is an example for us to follow. He came to do the will of him who had sent him (John 6:38). With that single-minded conviction he went to the cross and fulfilled his special priestly calling to atone for our sins, but at the same time he showed the measure of dedication that should have characterized the first Adam and that should now characterize the lives of all believers. One thing must be predominant in our lives: to do the will of Father; to love him in all areas of life with holy devotion. Such consecrated effort to love God above all else is possible because Christ has given believers his Spirit so that we are "in Christ." We can pray to "be strengthened with power through his Spirit" (Eph 3:16). In whatever place or situation the Lord has placed us in this life, as priests to God we may give ourselves, our talents, our time, our everything wholeheartedly in his service. Thus, we can respond to the apostolic call: "present your bodies as a living sacrifice, holy and acceptable to God, which is your spiritual worship. Do not be conformed to this world, but be transformed by the renewal of your mind" (Rom 12:1–2). As the well-known hymn puts it: "Take my life and let it be consecrated, Lord, to thee."

God can rightly expect our priestly service to be a sacrificial one in which we give our everything to the Lord. Anything less is not a sacrifice. God wants us totally, and desires to see that reflected in our life priorities. Not that by our obedience to his call we could earn something of our salvation. No! That priestly work has been done by our Savior, once for all. But as the Lord had desired the first Adam to love him with his entire being, we may give ourselves to the Lord in a life of thankfulness. We are able to do this as those connected and empowered by the Spirit of the second Adam. As Christians, we have so much to be thankful for!

Our sacrificial service therefore also includes offering our thanks and praise to God for his many blessings. As believers we form "a holy priesthood to offer spiritual sacrifices to God through Jesus Christ" (1 Pet 2:5). These spiritual sacrifices are in the first place our praise. Through Christ then "let us continually offer up a sacrifice of praise to God, that is, the fruit of lips that acknowledge his name" (Heb 13:15). The language reminds us of the thank offering of Old Testament times (Lev 7:11–18). But unlike that sacrifice which was offered periodically, the New Testament priesthood of all believers is obligated to a continual sacrifice of thanks and praise without end. We must be "giving thanks always and for everything to God the Father in the name of our Lord Jesus Christ" (Eph 5:20). Indeed, all our prayers are to be done with thanksgiving. "Continue steadfastly in prayer, being watchful in it with thanksgiving" (Col 4:2). Thanksgiving is to color our entire life, also when making prayerful requests to God. "In everything by prayer and supplication with thanksgiving let your request be made known to God" (Phil 4:6). With our constant sacrifice of praise, in prayer and in our everyday living, we confess our Savior and honor our heavenly Father and so give glory to him.

The Book of Revelation reminds us that Christians today are priests to God to whom be glory and dominion forever (Rev 1:5; 5:10). Toward the end of the Old Testament collection of psalms, the emphasis is increasingly on doxology and praise. In the final psalms the note of praise takes over more and more until it reaches a crescendo of hallelujahs in Psalm 150. Our priestly praise will one day climax at the marriage feast of the lamb (Rev 19:1–10).

Priestly Intercession

Another important aspect of Christ's priestly office is his intercessory work. Intercession between God and his people was also a priestly obligation in the Old Testament. The high priest would come into God's presence bearing on his breastpiece the names of the twelve tribes of Israel (Exod 28:11–12, 21, 29). He would enter the Most Holy Place to make atonement with the sacrificial blood, but he would also enter with incense, representing the prayers of God's people (Exod 30:8; Lev 16:12–17; Ps 141:2). In this way he interceded as high priest for Israel. Today Christ, our high priest, intercedes for us as we pray to God the Father. We therefore often pray using the words "for Christ's sake" or "in Christ's name." It is because of his atoning sacrifice that we can enter into the heavenly Most Holy Place (Heb 10:19–22). Our prayers join with his intercessory prayers for us as he pleads our cause as our advocate at God's right hand on the basis of his atoning work (1 John 2:1–2).

Already during his time on earth, the Lord Jesus interceded for his people in prayer to the Father. An example is his high priestly prayer in which he prayed for those whom the Father had given him (John 17:9). He also told Peter: "Simon, Simon, behold, Satan demanded to have you, that he might sift you like wheat, but I have prayed for you that your faith may not fail" (Luke 22:31–32). Christ continues his intercessory work in heaven. This reality is of great comfort. "Who shall bring any charge against God's elect? It is God who justifies. Who is to condemn? Christ Jesus is the one who died—more than that, who was raised—who is at the right hand of God, who indeed is interceding for us" (Rom 8:33–34). Christ's work of intercession is part of his complete salvation. "He is able to save to the uttermost [i.e., completely] those who draw near to God through him, since he always lives to make intercession for them" (Heb 7:25).

Our Savior can intercede for us as one who knows our true needs. He knows what it is like to live as a human being in a sin-filled world, as a young boy, as a teenager, as a young adult. He has experienced it all. "Because he himself has suffered when tempted, he is able to help those who are being tempted" (Heb 2:18). "We do not have a high priest who is unable to sympathize with our weaknesses, but one who in every respect has been tempted as we are, yet without sin. Let us then with confidence draw near to the throne of grace, that we may receive mercy and find grace to help in time of need" (Heb 4:15–16).

The great love and mercy Christ showed in his intercessory work extended to unbelievers, even his tormentors. On the cross Christ uttered an intercessory prayer for all those who crucified him, the Jewish nation, its leaders, and the soldiers. "Father, forgive them, for they know not what they do" (Luke 23:34). As Isaiah prophesied, Christ interceded for the transgressors (Isa 53:12). This does not mean that he overlooked their sin. Rather, the objective of his prayer was their repentance. As William Hendriksen rightly paraphrased Christ's prayer on the cross: "Blot out their transgression completely. In thy sovereign grace cause them to repent truly, so that they can be and will be pardoned fully."[9] God heard this prayer by causing thousands of Jews to believe in Christ after his death when they realized what they had done (Acts 2:37–41; cf. vv. 17–19). Similarly, Stephen prayed for those who stoned him to death: "Lord, do not hold this sin against them" (Acts 7:60). That prayer was also for Saul who supported the killing (Acts 8:1). God's answer to Stephen's prayer therefore included Saul's conversion and his becoming Paul, the apostle.

The intercessory work of our Savior points to our task as those who share in his priestly anointing. In presenting ourselves as a living sacrifice of thankfulness to God, we are not to forget the well-being of all those whom God has put on our life path, including our enemies. Christ commanded us: "Love your enemies and pray for those who persecute you" (Matt 5:44). That is part of our priestly obligation to God. Christ who died for us while we were still enemies, expects us to pray for the salvation of those who hate and persecute us (cf. Rom 5:8–10). Reports from Christians experiencing persecution indicate that such prayers take place, for example, in China where there is continual harassment and oppression. Many Christians pray fervently for their enemies that God may have mercy on them and grant them repentance. Our priestly obligation is the same within our context in the post-Christian Western world.

Those the Lord puts on our life path includes, of course, in the first place our families, friends, church community, and neighbors. As we know or become aware of each other's needs we exercise our priestly calling by praying for each other as Christ prays for us. How encouraging and comforting when children hear their parents pray for them and bring their

---

9   William Hendriksen, *Exposition of the Gospel According to Luke*, New Testament Commentary (Grand Rapids: Baker, 1978), 1028.

needs to the throne of grace. Children can follow the example of their parents and pray for them and their friends. Congregation members pray for each other and neighbors pray for the needs of those in their immediate community, in the case of unbelievers that they may have open hearts for the gospel. When we do that we will also look for opportunities to share the good news with them.

Prayers of intercession also include those for the governing authorities. The apostolic command is still applicable. "I urge that supplications, prayers, intercessions, and thanksgivings be made for all people, for kings and all who are in high positions, that we may lead a peaceful and quiet life, godly and dignified in every way. This is good and it is pleasing in the sight of God our Savior" (1 Tim 2:1–3). Praying for the well-being of those in authority and thus of the society in which we live is a long-standing obligation for God's people. The prophet Jeremiah told the exiled Israelites living in Babylon that it was God's will that they "seek the welfare of the city" in which they now sojourned and "pray to the LORD on its behalf, for in its welfare you will find your welfare" (Jer 29:7). As the Israelites in Babylon must have felt out of place in the pagan culture in which they lived, we as Christians can experience similar feelings in our cultural context. However, the obligation to pray for those whom God has set above us (cf. Rom 13:1) and in this way to seek the welfare of the nation remains.

When we exercise our priestly office as believers with our intercessory prayers as thankful holy children of God, the Lord Jesus Christ is through his Spirit having us share in his priestly office.

Priestly Blessing

Christ, our high priest, blesses. That priestly responsibility also impacts our sharing in his anointing as priest. Before we get to the implications of Christ's priestly blessing for our lives, we need to step back and note that in its most basic generic sense, to bless is to wish the best for someone. When Adam and Eve were placed in a perfect world with no sin their priestly office included that they were to be a blessing for each other. Before the fall into sin, life together was beautiful and they lived up to God's expectation in this regard. With their yielding to Satan's temptation, this situation changed radically. They started finding fault with each other and blaming each other. Harmony was broken (cf. Gen 3:12–13). The mutual priestly service of love and blessing was gone. In order to atone for these sins, the Lord established the priestly service of reconciliation.

Among the tasks that the Lord gave the Aaronic priesthood was the duty to bless the people. Such blessing was possible because of the sacrifices that the high priest offered. Only after Aaron had offered the sin offering, the burnt offering, and the peace offering, did he bless the people (Lev 9:22). "The LORD bless you and keep you; the LORD make his face to shine upon you and be gracious to you; the LORD lift up his countenance upon you and give you peace" (Num 6:24–26).[10] Our great high priest, Jesus Christ, fulfilled the entire Old Testament sacrificial service by offering himself as the crucified Lamb of God. He therefore had a solid basis for giving his blessing when the time came for him to ascend into heaven. When he took leave of his disciples, he led them from Jerusalem out as far as Bethany "and lifting up his hands he blessed them. While he blessed them, he parted from them and was carried up into heaven" (Luke 24:50–51). Our Savior departed for heaven while blessing his disciples. He left his blessing behind, so to speak. He had earned it for us. As Christians we can be assured of his continued blessing as articulated in the apostolic benediction: "The grace of the Lord Jesus Christ and the love of God and the fellowship of the Holy Spirit be with you all" (2 Cor 13:14).

These blessings equip us to be a blessing to those around us—our family, our church community, and our neighbors. With priestly concern we may watch for each other's welfare and joy in the Lord. As those partaking in Christ's priestly anointing, we seek to share the fruits of his sacrifice to all those with whom we come into contact. We can do this by showing love, compassion, and empathy; by sharing the gospel of forgiveness and hope; by praying for each other and those with special needs; by bringing some joy into the lives of the lonely or shut-ins. In so many ways we can be a priestly blessing for others in word and deed and so give evidence of the abiding fruits of the blessings of our heavenly high priest.

---

10 For this blessing see further Cornelis Van Dam, *Worship Matters: Essays on Public Worship*, with a contribution by Arjan De Visser (Reformed Perspective Press; Lucerna CRTS Publications, 2021), 95–106.

Christ and our Royal Calling

Just before Christ left earth for heaven, he told his disciples: "All authority in heaven and on earth has been given to me" (Matt 28:18). Christ is king at the right hand of God in glory (Acts 7:55). How are we as Christians to share in Christ's anointing as king? Such sharing seems so unreal, given our fragile and often vulnerable condition here on earth. To answer that question properly, we need first of all to go back to the very beginning and consider God's expectations for Adam and Eve and the effects of the fall. Next, we need to see how Christ restores us to our royal calling today so that we indeed share in his anointing as king.

Kingship Granted, Lost, and Restored

As briefly noted at the beginning of this chapter, God placed Adam and Eve in a position of dominion over his creation. Humanity, as crown of creation, was made in God's image and after his likeness and was to represent God's rule on earth. After their creation,

> God blessed them. And God said to them, "Be fruitful and multiply and fill the earth and subdue it, and have dominion over the fish of the sea and over the birds of the heavens and over every living thing that moves on the earth." And God said, "Behold I have given you every plant yielding seed that is on the face of all the earth, and every tree with seed in its fruit. You shall have them for food. And to every beast of the earth and to every bird of the heavens and to everything that creeps on the earth, everything has the breath of life, I have given every green plant for food" (Gen 1:28–30).

Literally everything was placed at the disposal of Adam and Eve. They were placed on this planet to rule for the LORD; not selfishly, but as responsible stewards with a view to what is best for God's handiwork, his creation. Only God, the Creator, was the authority above them.

Their task was not easy, but God's Spirit enabled them. Adam exercised his royal power and prerogative by naming the animals which God brought to him (Gen 2:19). By giving creatures their name, Adam designated each their place on behalf of their Creator and in accordance with his intent. It was God's world and kingdom, and humankind was to rule, use, and manage it for the glory of the Creator.

That happy situation did not last. Instead of honoring their royal position under God, Adam and Eve listened to Satan and obeyed his will and so submitted themselves to the allures and temptation of the devil's rule and power (Gen 3:1–7). Rather than being ruler under God, Adam and Eve were now subject to another creature and ruled by him. Satan was now the apparent ruler of this world. He, so to speak, made the world his kingdom.

But the Son of God, the second Adam, came to dethrone Satan and restore God's kingship on earth. Satan, however, also tempted the second Adam and tried to bring the man Jesus under his control. As "the ruler of this world" (John 12:31), Satan offered Jesus "all the kingdoms of this world and their glory" on the condition that Jesus fall down and worship him (Matt 4:8–9). Accepting Satan's offer would have spared Jesus the way of sorrows that lay before him and the excruciating suffering of the cross, but he would have received a world in bondage to sin and death. Unlike the first Adam, Jesus rejected Satan's temptation and dismissed him (Matt 4:10). Christ's mission was to announce and bring about the coming of God's kingdom by defeating Satan. To that end Christ cast out demons (e.g., Matt 12:28) and was ultimately victorious over Satan on the cross. Christ "disarmed the rulers and authorities and put them to open shame, by triumphing over them" by the cross (Col 2:15). With his crucified body as sacrifice for our sins, Christ prevailed over Satan by "cancelling the record of debt that stood against us with its legal demands" (Col 1:14). Satan's power to hold us to our debt of sin was broken. He could no longer accuse those who believed in the Savior. Christ paid for all our sins and so set us free. By depriving Satan of any legal ground for accusations against us, he released us from the bondage of the evil one. The Accuser was thrown out of heaven and Christ was given authority over all things for the church (Rev 12:10; Eph 1:20–23). As head of the church, his body, Christ works for the restoration of the office of kingship to all those who believe in him.

This restoration does not take place in a moment. We are still living in a fallen world full of the evidence of the ongoing power of the kingdom of darkness. Although Christ's victory is sure and the battle against Satan has in principle been won, God's kingdom has not yet come in its full splendor and glory. In the meantime, however, all those who are in Christ and share his anointing are being made a new creation and are being enabled to serve as God's royal ruling representatives in spite of the fact that we are still in a fallen creation. How does this restoration of the office of kingship come about?

To be equipped to exercise authority on behalf of God, we must first learn to submit ourselves to the rule of Christ, the second Adam. We need to be "in him" who truly fulfilled the office of king and so share this office with him. Christ needs to govern us completely. Only in this way will we be free to exercise our office as kings and queens ourselves. Our confessing Christ as king, therefore, includes the acknowledgment that, as our eternal king he "governs us by his Word and Spirit," to use the words of the Heidelberg Catechism (Q.A. 31). This biblical truth cannot be overemphasized. It is, after all, through the Word that our king speaks to us, informs us of our office and calling, and equips us by the Holy Spirit.

When we submit to the Word of God, we submit to Christ our king and listen to his will for our lives. The Word then illumines the path before us and shows us the way we should go through the present darkness (Ps 119:105). We need to be very intentional in placing ourselves under Christ's rule in humble obedience because there is much competition for our loyalty and obedience. Satan still claims this world as his own and he uses every possible means to assert his rule over us. Since we are all prone to sin and constantly need to resist the wiles of the evil one, it is imperative that we are constantly controlled and guided by the Word of God. Such divine control of our life is only possible if we use every opportunity to expose ourselves to Scripture, absorb it, and reflect on it so that it can fill and impact our lives in a meaningful way. Like the psalmist, the Word needs to be our joy and delight so that our happiness is found in doing God's will and not that of the evil one (Ps 119:14, 111, 162). There needs to be a purposeful commitment to obey our Lord and Savior and reject the rule and wishes of the powers of darkness. There is no such thing as being a Christian by default. We need to consciously embrace the rule and kingdom of Christ and reject that of Satan. We do that by placing our entire life under the authority of the Word of God.

It is through the Word that Christ speaks to us and also equips us with his Spirit. Of ourselves we are unable to resist satanic advances and temptations and place ourselves under Christ's rule. But the Spirit enables us by the transformative power of the Word which he uses to give us faith (Rom 10:17). When we read Scripture and have an audience, so to speak, with God, the Word penetrates into the deepest recesses of our hearts and works our rebirth—our being born again in Christ (1 Pet 1:23). Our stubborn selves are softened, molded, and shaped to obedient compliance with Christ's will (cf. 1 Thess 2:13). We are being raised as a new creation and know ourselves to belong to Christ's kingdom. We are then equipped to be rulers in Christ!

Rulers in Christ

Executing our royal office as God's representatives and fighting the evil one is indeed only possible in the power of God. The apostle Paul accordingly exhorts: "be strong in the Lord and in the strength of his might. Put on the whole armor of God so that you may be able to stand against the schemes of the devil" (Eph 6:10–11). We need God's strength because "we do not wrestle against flesh and blood, but against the rulers, against the authorities, against the cosmic powers over this present darkness, against the spiritual forces of evil in heavenly places. Therefore take up the whole armor of God, that you may be able to withstand in the evil day, and having done all, to stand firm" (Eph 6:12–13).

The armor of God consists of the resources that we have by being in Christ. We have the belt of truth, the breastplate of righteousness, the gospel of peace, the shield of faith, the helmet of salvation, and the sword of the Spirit, namely, God's Word (Eph 6:14–17). It is obvious from this metaphorical description that our task is not just to defend ourselves but also to go on the offensive. We have the sword of the Spirit, God's Word, which defeats the enemy. When Christ was tempted by Satan, he responded to each temptation with an appropriate quotation from Scripture with the result that Satan had to retreat and try something else. He eventually left defeated (Matt 4:1–11). When we are acquainted with the Scriptures, the Holy Spirit also enables us to wield the sword of the Word against satanic forces. We need to go into the battle realistically, being prepared to give it our everything so that in God's power we can fight against and overcome sin and Satan. We must not let sin and its passions reign in our lives (Rom 6:12). We must "wage the good warfare" (1 Tim 1:18) in obedience to our triumphant King, the Lord Jesus Christ. Then we experience that "we are more than conquerors through him who loved us" (Rom 8:37).

In spite of all the ups and downs of the spiritual battlefield that characterize our lives on earth, we may know for a certainty that *the* battle has been won. The Lord encouraged his disciples and also inspires us: "Take heart; I have overcome the world!" (John 16:33). In faith, in union with Christ, we too can overcome the world. "Who is it that overcomes the world except the one who believes that Jesus is the Son of God?" (1 John 5:5). The day of the resurrection will be another indication of that triumph. Death will be swallowed up in victory. "Thanks be to God who gives us the victory through our Lord Jesus Christ" (1 Cor 15:57).

With that perspective we may in faith see that Christ rules and is in full control of the world today. In spite of all appearances to the contrary, we know that Christ is in charge. Although those in power today may "take counsel together, against the LORD and against his Anointed," yet "he who sits in heaven laughs; the Lord holds them in derision" (Ps 2:2, 3). In that context, Christians can exercise their royal mandate by seeking to subject not only their lives to the King but also other areas of life as God gives opportunity, such as in education, culture, and the political life of our nation. As rulers in Christ, we will also take a keen interest in God's creation and environmental issues and whether the earth's resources are managed and used in a responsible way. In any case, no matter how much or little the Lord allows us to do in this life, as those who are in Christ we have the privilege of sharing in his rule. As we do that to the best of our ability, we can look forward to a new creation where our royal office will be restored as we reign with him eternally. "If we endure, we will also reign with him" (2 Tim 2:12).

An Awesome Privilege

Being a Christian is an awesome privilege. It means having a direct connection with the second Adam, the One who came down to make possible the work of renewing creation, beginning with humanity! As Christians we may share in the anointing of our Savior as prophet, priest, and king. Christians have a sure identity! In a confused world in which so many are not sure who they are or why they exist on planet earth, Christians may know that they share their identity with the eternal Son of God who became a human being in order to rescue us from our sins and to put us on the path to the new creation! He raises us up to a new life. He embraces us as a brother in the flesh. His redeeming work in setting us apart as holy, and so our sharing in his offices as prophet, priest, and king, means that he is not ashamed to call us his brothers and sisters (Heb 2:11). Indeed, Christ is the first-born among many brothers and sisters (Rom 8:29).

Our identity as participating in Christ's anointing therefore includes our being children of God. Although Christ alone is the eternal Son of God, we may be children of God by adoption (Rom 8:14–17); but children nevertheless with all the rights and privileges. The believers' status as children of God is another indication of God's renewing creation. As the first Adam, created after God's image, was son of God (Luke 3:38), in Christ, the second Adam, we too as believers, restored in God's image, may be children of God. "See what love the Father has given to us, that we should be called children of God; and so we are" (1 John 3:1). The unbelieving world cannot understand this identity because it does not know the Father (1 John 3:1). It is an awesome reality to be children of God. It also means that we are co-heirs with the Son of God (Rom 8:17). We can live in this world with the full assurance that we have a secure identity and purpose in life. As children of God, raised to a new life in the second Adam, we have a task, indeed a triple office from God to be his representatives here on earth as prophets, priests, and kings so that we can be a prophetic voice in our culture, give ourselves sacrificially in holy service to him, and fight against the demonic forces of evil. In this way we may reflect something of his glory, his love, and grace to our family, the fellowship of believers, and to a world lost in sin.

Furthermore, as children of God, the future is bright. The apostle John wrote: "Beloved, we are God's children, and what we will be has not yet appeared; but we know that when he appears we shall be like him, because we shall see him as he is. And every one who thus hopes in him purifies himself as he is pure" (1 John 3:2–3). What an encouraging message! One day we will be able to live up to God's expectations for our life and calling as Christians perfectly.

CHAPTER 2

Who is This Woman?
Listening to Proverbs 31:10–31 Today

When Christians talk about the place of women, especially within the family, the discussion can turn to a consideration of Proverbs 31 and the famous passage about what an ideal woman or wife who fears God looks like. Not a few women who read this part of Scripture find it somewhat discouraging! Who can live up to such expectations as a married woman or for that matter as a single woman? For one thing, it's obvious that this woman of Proverbs 31was wealthy! You could ask yourself: What am I as a wife to my dear husband to do with this part of God's Word? And what if I'm not married? What does this part of Scripture say to me? Is there a message here for me?

Well, there most certainly is. In the space available in this chapter, I am going to touch on some highlights to try to show the challenges and encouragement this passage gives God's people, and especially how this applies to believing women. As needed, we will also listen to other passages from the book of Proverbs that help us understand God's expectations for women today.

This last section of the book of Proverbs is a unit; indeed, it is an acrostic, that is, it is a piece of literature in which each couplet starts with a letter of the Hebrew alphabet in sequence. The first couplet begins with the first letter of the Hebrew alphabet, the next one with the second letter, and so on. By the time you get to the end of this section, all the letters of the Hebrew alphabet have been used. This acrostic feature underlines the unity of this passage. This entire section, Proverbs 31:10–31, is concerned with one topic, the woman mentioned at the beginning (verse 10). One could, therefore, say that this section of Scripture is literally the A-B-C of what it takes to be an excellent wife or woman (the Hebrew word can be translated either way) according to God's expectations.

The Question

The woman of Proverbs 31 is introduced by way of a question: "An excellent wife/woman who can find?" Literally it says: "A woman of strength [*hayil*] who can find?" Virtually every modern translation downplays the force of the original text. The word used to describe this woman is a word used for "power, might, strength." It is even used with the meaning, "army" and sometimes with the meaning "wealth." But the basic meaning is "strength, power." She is a "woman of strength." This strength can be evident in "physical power, military might, practical competencies, or character." This strength or power can also show itself in wealth. (People with lots of money can have influence and power not available to the poor.) But the basic meaning of the word is strength.[1] As the context indicates, in this part of Proverbs the strength of this woman is in her solid character that shows itself in the various descriptions of her activities. For that reason, translations often render: "excellent wife" or "wife of noble character" and similar renderings.[2] But let us remember that literally it says: "woman of strength" or "of power."

"A woman of strength, who can find?" This is a challenge because such a woman is rare. The expected answer to this rhetorical question is either that such a woman cannot be found or that it is at least very difficult to find one. Put another way, the woman here described is the ideal woman, the perfect one, so to speak. Where is such a perfect woman to be found who can handle all the things that this passage brings to the fore? Where is that woman of whom it can be said "many women have done excellently, but you surpass them all" (Prov 31:29)?

If we step back from Proverbs 31 for a moment, and consider all of Scripture, then from a New Testament perspective, a perfect woman, one who can at least make a beginning of what is all recounted in Proverbs 31, is a person who has been gifted, renewed, and empowered by the Spirit of

---

1 The quotation is from Michael V. Fox, *Proverbs 10–31: A New Translation with Introduction and Commentary*, Anchor Bible (New Haven, CT: Yale University Press, 2009), 891, 547–48, also 916-17; also see David J. A. Clines, ed., *The Dictionary of Classical Hebrew* (Sheffield: Sheffield Academic Press, 1993–2016), 3:213–15.

2 Adele Berlin, Marc Zvi Brettler, and Michael Fishbane, eds., *The Jewish Study Bible* (New York, NY: Oxford University Press, 2004), 1497–98.

God. After all, only the Spirit of the living God can hope to renew a woman so that she functions as God had intended Eve to function. Put differently, only the Holy Spirit can make a woman a person of strength according to God's design. Only the Holy Spirit can incline the heart completely to the service of the LORD in the true and humble fear of the LORD and so give true wisdom. Only when one is so equipped, is one able to handle the many tasks and duties that belong to being a woman. It takes true godly wisdom. After all, that is what the book of Proverbs is all about—the fear of the LORD is the beginning of wisdom.

And so, what we have here in Proverbs 31 is a picture of a woman as God intended, a woman who is, therefore, equipped and renewed by his Spirit, the Spirit of wisdom. That is why, near the end of this passage, much is summarized in verse 30 with the words: "a woman who fears the LORD is to be praised."

Now this truth is encouraging and gives hope to Christian women. What is normally impossible for us as fallen human beings, is possible in the renewing Spirit of Christ. Although this passage speaks of women who have husbands in the first place, this passage certainly has application to single women as well. The Spirit also recreates and renews single women to God's standards.

Let us consider this passage and see what God's Word here tells us about the place and task of women. God's Word does that by being very practical and taking us into the nitty-gritty of daily life as experienced in ancient Israel. Remarkably, God used a woman, the mother of King Lemuel (Prov 31:1), to bring about this part of his revelation about being a God-pleasing woman. The teaching of this mother was meant, in the first place, for her son, King Lemuel. He is traditionally identified with Solomon (lit. Lemuel means "devoted to God"), but there is no certainty about his identity.[3] He had to know the worth of a woman pleasing to God. The instruction of the mother of King Lemuel is now part of God's revelation so that every believer can be aware of God's ideal woman and wife.

---

3   Solomon seems to have had more than one name. E.g., in 2 Sam 12:25 he is called Jedidiah "loved by the LORD." So to have him called Lemuel, as another name of endearment reflecting God's grace in his life, is as such not impossible. See further, K. Kim, "Lemuel and Agur," in *Dictionary of the Old Testament: Wisdom, Poetry and Writings*, ed. Tremper Longman III and Peter Enns (Downers Grove, IL: IVP Academic, 2008), 427–31.

A Helper Fit for Him

It is noteworthy that one of the very first things that is said about this ideal woman or wife is that "the heart of her husband trusts in her" (Prov 31:11).[4] This is so because, as the next verse puts it: "She does him good, and not harm, all the days of her life" (Prov 31:12). This woman's life is completely devoted to her husband and his well-being. Her chief concern in life is to be of help and assistance to her husband. And is this not what God had in mind when he presented the first man, Adam, with his wife, Eve? She was made with the express purpose to be "a helper fit for him" (Gen 2:18). And so, this woman of Proverbs 31 is there for him "all the days of her life!" Not just on sunny days, but also when there are tensions, worries and hardships.

Proverbs 31 indicates that when a woman gives her all to her husband to help him in every possible way, then the results are amazing. He is able to fully develop his gifts and also make a difference in the community. Because of the support his wife gives him in so many areas, he can assume positions of leadership. With her contribution "she empowers her husband to provide leadership for the entire land."[5] As verse 23 of our chapter tells us: "Her husband is known in the gates when he sits among the elders of the land." Because of his wife's dedication to be as much help to him as possible, he is able to sit in the council of the elders. He has a good name, an excellent reputation.

The message of Proverbs 31 is that his wife's being such a helper fit for him has a lot to do with this man's success. He does not need to worry about all the things his wife so capably handles. In other words, she, the woman, the wife, makes a name for her husband by her contribution as his wife. If a wife wants to encourage and help her husband to take positions of leadership in the church, the first step, according to Proverbs 31, is to be a helpmeet for him in the most comprehensive sense of the word.

---

4   "Outside this verse, Scripture condemns trust in anyone or anything other than the Lord." Jo Ann Davidson, "Women Bear God's Image: Considerations from a Neglected Perspective," *Andrews University Seminary Studies* 54 (2016): 39.

5   Bruce K. Waltke, *The Book of Proverbs: Chapters 15–31*, New International Commentary on the Old Testament (Grand Rapids: Eerdmans, 2005), 522, 529.

Now it is possible that a gifted man who has a less than ideal marriage, might still rise in public life. That's true. But the context of Proverbs 31 clearly links the wife's help to his success. As a current proverb puts it: "Behind every successful man is a great woman." Not always so, but there is some biblical truth to it. The same goes for the world outside marriage. Women who give their all to their task, for example, as a secretary or whatever function they may have in a company, can do enormous good by doing their job wholeheartedly and so freeing their boss or supervisor to excel in his or her responsibilities.

When the wife is truly a helpmeet for her husband according to God's creation ordinance then there is reciprocation. "The heart of her husband trusts in her" (Prov 31:11). He has complete confidence in her as his equal in the marriage with the gifts specific to her. Whatever he can, he leaves in the care of his wife without unjustly overburdening her. He can give her all kinds of responsibilities because they are equal partners in the marriage. As created in God's image, women also have their responsibilities.

Indeed, women need responsibilities to flourish and to use to the utmost their God-given gifts. And look at the responsibilities this husband gives to his wife! He gives her the charge of the entire household. She does not say, I do not really have a job because I am only a homemaker and work at home. She does not look down on housework. No, she capitalizes on the possibilities her husband gives her in being in charge of domestic affairs. She makes the most of it!

With her gifts she could have taken the easy way out and become lazy and self-indulgent. But no, she assumes her responsibilities and takes ownership of her task. She gives leadership in buying the necessities of life, rising early in the morning and working until late at night. As funds allow, she even gets into business dealings, buying a field and planting a vineyard. It is all for the husband and the family. Their interests and welfare dominate her life. Consequently, we read in Proverbs 31:28, "her children rise up and call her blessed; her husband also, and he praises her."

In view of her being such a tremendous and equal partner in the marriage, one can think of the words of Adam: "This . . . is bone of my bones and flesh of my flesh" (Gen 2:23). Man and wife run the family together—each with the task God has given them. They are of one mind and purpose. "Bone of my bones and flesh of my flesh!" This wife truly fulfills God's creational expectations for her. Charm and beauty are less important. "A woman who fears the LORD is to be praised" (Prov 31:30).

Reflecting on all her responsibilities makes one realize that there are more applications for us today.

Spreading her Wings

This woman makes the most of the possibilities and women and wives today may do the same, keeping in mind the biblical priorities, including as wives being a helpmeet for their husbands. Let us just pause for a moment at what this woman of Proverbs 31 all does.

She is not afraid to seize the opportunities that present themselves. She is a business woman. "She seeks wool and flax and works with willing hands" (Prov 31:13). It is possible that she finds this suitable material to make clothes for her household from her husband's farm; but it is more likely, given the context and the words used in the original, that she goes out to the market to purchase it. After all, she's an active woman, not just in her home but also outside of it. "She is like the ships of the merchant; she brings her food from afar.... She considers a field and buys it; with the fruit of her hands she plants a vineyard" (Prov 31:14, 16). Besides her primary task of being a help for her husband in the home and for the immediate domestic affairs, she goes beyond her homemaking and also enriches the family with her labors outside the home. As we read in Proverbs 31:22 and 24, "She makes bed coverings for herself... She makes linen garments and sells them; she delivers sashes to the merchant." And while she is prosperous, she does not forget the poor, but is generous towards them. "She opens her hand to the poor and reaches out her hands to the needy" (Prov 31:20).

It is a remarkable fact that all these business and humanitarian dealings in and outside the home by a wife is in Scripture not just permissible, but to be applauded. These are good activities. This wife is held up as "excellent," a woman of strength and power; an ideal wife, a perfect life companion. As mentioned earlier, a woman with such gifts is rare. "Who can find someone like that?" (v. 10), the text of Proverbs 31 asks.

Yet, it does happen that women with such gifts exist. God can raise up godly women, renewed with the Spirit who have extraordinary gifts and true wisdom. Although it is not for every woman, it can also happen today that such women of strength run an immaculate household and at the same time are busy outside the home as well. Such outside work can involve helping her husband in his business, whether on a farm or in an office. But such outside work can also mean that she has the gifts to run her own business on the side, as the woman in Proverbs 31 does without shortchanging her husband or children. As Christians, we should exalt and emphasize the place of a mother, a home-maker, and so being a helpmeet for her husband in domestic affairs. But Scripture also teaches that a woman's gifts can also be used beyond the home as well without jeopardizing her primary responsibilities. She has not neglected to benefit the home. In the case of Proverbs 31, this benefit includes the financial rewards of her endeavors.

In this connection we can also think of another biblical example, Lydia of Thyatira who was a trader of purple goods and whose heart the Lord opened to the gospel (Acts 16:14). She and her household were baptized (Acts 16:15). We do not read anything about her husband and so she may have been a widow, or she may have been a single woman. It is also possible that her husband is simply not mentioned because he did not become a Christian. In any case, she had a household and if she was indeed single, she had dependents and servants living with her. She is therefore a New Testament example of a woman who had business gifts and ran what must have been a very costly enterprise for purple dye was extremely expensive in antiquity.[6]

Christian women today can have the same freedom as the woman of Proverbs 31 and Lydia of Thyatira, as long as the necessary priorities are met. If the gifts are there, and the opportunities present themselves, women are free to exploit them and so benefit from their labors. The Bible does not know of a so-called glass ceiling barrier that has to be broken for women to succeed in the world of economics and business. The woman of

---

6   See Aaron Devine and Karelynne Gerber Ayayo, "Lydia of Thyatira," in *The Lexham Bible Dictionary*, ed. John D. Barry, et al. (Bellingham, WA: Lexham Press, 2016).

Proverbs 31 is in charge of all kinds of business dealings. She undoubtedly has male employees or perhaps slaves under her. She tells them what to do. She, a woman, is in charge. That is the whole tenor of Proverbs 31 in characterizing this woman. Indeed, another example of this is Abigail who also had male servants who obeyed her (1 Sam 25:19).

There is a remarkable passage that characterizes the woman of Proverbs 31: "She dresses herself with strength and makes her arms strong" (v. 17). She is described as men are often described in Scripture when they are to undertake arduous tasks. The first part of verse 17 literally reads: "She girds her loins with strength." This is a powerful metaphor to prepare for difficult action such as for battle (Jer 1:17) or running long distances as quickly as possible (1 Kings 18:46; 2 Kings 4:29). It is even used of God who "has girded himself with strength" (Ps 93:1 NASB).[7] So to describe a woman as girding her loins with strength says something about her being an equal partner in the marriage and also made after God's image.

As can be expected, this woman of strength is certainly no slouch. "She rises while it is yet night" (v. 15); "her lamp does not go out at night" (v. 18). She does all kinds of menial tasks. "She puts her hands to the distaff, and her hands hold the spindle" (v. 19) and makes bed coverings (v. 22). She's not afraid of work. She will do whatever it takes; whatever she is called to do. In the process, she entered the economic and business world without hesitation and had a position of leadership and authority. Though married, she had the gifts to combine her domestic responsibilities with her business opportunities.

Such a combination is rare as the question that opens this section of Proverbs indicates. "A woman of strength, who can find?" (Prov 31:10). It is therefore good for us now to go back to one of her primary tasks as a woman who is married and has children, namely her responsibility as a mother. After that, we will consider further what Scripture speaks of the place and gifts of women who are unmarried and go through life single and ask what God expects from them.

---

7   The Hebrew term used in Prov 31:17 is *hgr* while in Ps 93:1 it is *'r* but the meaning is the same.

Task as Mother

One of the most important tasks for married women with children, besides being a helpmeet for their husband, is to be a mother for their children. An extremely important duty that both husband and wife share is to educate their children in the fear of the Lord. Already at the beginning of Proverbs we read: "Hear my son your father's instruction, and forsake not your mother's teaching" (Prov 1:8). Similarly, we read elsewhere: "My son, keep your father's commandment, and forsake not your mother's teaching" (Prov 6:20). The importance of the education children receive in the home by both parents cannot be overestimated. The home is the bedrock educational institution. Here the foundations are laid for the rest of the child's life. Mothers therefore have a very important role, yes a critical task. After all, a mother has a very special relationship to her child or children. That special bond can be used for training the children in the fear of the Lord. A good thing to remember in this context is that what is most necessary in raising children is not to have them obey a set of rules (important as that is), but the important thing is that you reach, touch, and mold their hearts. God said, give me your heart! (cf. Prov 23:25–26).[8] That goes beyond mere outward obedience. Parents cannot make a child's heart to be godly, but God does use parents, and perhaps especially mothers with their special bond and greater exposure to their children, to enable children to love God and give their hearts to him.[9] Also with respect to education in godliness she is to be a helpmeet to her husband.

It is important to note how the teaching aspect is brought out in Proverbs 31. "She opens her mouth with wisdom and the teaching of kindness is on her tongue" (v. 26). The phrase "teaching of kindness" is difficult to translate because the original Hebrew term here translated as "kindness" is very rich and full of covenant overtones—faithfulness, loyalty, goodness, kindness. Now the word translated "kindness" does not mean covenant but the term certainly "characterizes the relationship that exists between covenant partners." One translation therefore renders: "She opens her mouth

---

8   The parents are God's representatives. The proverb says give the heart to the father or mother, but this refers to their being in place of God as parents. See, e.g., Waltke, *Proverbs 15–31*, 260.

9   Helpful comments are found in Paul David Tripp, *Awe: Why It Matters for Everything We Think, Say, and Do* (Wheaton, IL: Crossway, 2015), chapter 12 (Logos edition).

in wisdom, and covenantal instruction is on her lips." That pretty well captures the essence of her instruction. After all, every instruction in the fear of the LORD is covenantal. Her words are not just kind. Such an understanding of this passage is far too superficial. They "are kind by flowing from the covenant between God and his people."[10] The context does not immediately associate this instruction with her children. The text simply says: "She opens her mouth with wisdom, and the teaching of kindness is on her tongue" (v. 26). One gets the impression that she is full of God's will for her life and talks about the LORD and his mercies most naturally and so instructs her servants and above all, her children. She *lives* the covenant and shows it to all around her. Her covenant relationship with God is the very essence of her life.

It is not always easy for parents, and now especially the mother, to imprint in her children the wisdom and ways of the LORD. Yet, it is perhaps especially mothers who have the most educational influence on their children while they are at home. She, after all, is with them the most and as an old proverb has it: give me a child for the first five years and I will have him or her for life. Indeed, Scripture says: "Train up a child in the way he should go; even when he is old he will not depart from it" (Prov 22:6). Children may not always appreciate it when they are young, but under God's blessing, as they get older, they are most grateful for the instruction they received. Indeed, in Proverbs 31:28 we read: "Her children rise up and call her blessed!"

When children are endued with a love for the LORD and his agenda for their lives, then they start to take responsibility in seeking to live according to his will. With all the ups and downs typical of our world of sin, children who have had the seed of the gospel firmly planted in their early life, will by God's grace, not be able to forget their identity, namely that they are children of God! And if children, then heirs of all his promises (Rom 8:17).

It is the glory of mothers that they are usually God's daily instruments to instill in their offspring a sense of the privilege of belonging to God. Mothers can imprint on their children something of the glory of car-

---

10   Tremper Longman III, *Baker Commentary on the Old Testament: Proverbs* (Grand Rapids, MI: Baker Academic, 2006), 547.

rying God's name in their lives as a consequence of their heavenly Father's placing his name on them, and claiming them for himself at their baptism. With that realization comes a sense of responsibility to offer oneself as a sacrifice of thankfulness to the Lord (Rom 12:1). In other words, there will be a desire to use one's gifts for God's glory. That will help determine their priorities and their eventual calling in life.

Under God's blessing, children with that sense of identity and privilege, will use their gifts not rashly but consider where they can best use their talents to God's praise. That might be in banking, in fixing cars, in selling real estate, in farming, in becoming a teacher, doctor, or lawyer—whatever! It can also mean considering the ministry as a possibility. Good office bearers, be they deacon, elder, or minister, received their first education for the office in the home and most probably by mother. That is where they learned the meaning of loving and serving the Lord and giving of oneself to him. It started in the kitchen and living room. That's where the foundation of a life of service to the Lord begins. That is where the desire to give leadership in the home and in church is born. And so, as Proverbs 31 puts it: "a woman who fears the LORD is to be praised!" And so also "her children rise up and call her blessed; her husband also, and he praises her" (v. 28).

Single Women

Proverbs 31 ends with the words: "a woman who fears the LORD is to be praised. Give her of the fruit of her hands, and let her works praise her in the gates" (vv. 30–31). This is also true of single women. If the Lord God is the center of our life, whether female or male, then we are truly equipped to be engaged in our office and calling.

In our day there is much talk about women in ecclesiastical office. This is not the place to enter into that discussion. But the point I want to make is that much of this debate about women in office makes it seem as if women have nothing to contribute to the life of the church unless they are ordained in a special office. But nothing could be further from the truth. Scripture has clearly reserved ecclesiastical offices to men only, but this restriction in no way limits the contribution that women can make for the well-being of the church.

With respect to women who are not in the married state, there are many opportunities to use the gifts which God has given to them. They may not have a family of their own so to speak, but they belong to the family of God, the church, in which we all find our home with the brothers and sisters in the Lord. Whereas the married woman has her first attention on the nuclear family, those who are not in the married state know their identity as belonging to the larger fellowship of the saints, the family of God. The apostle Paul characterized the church as "the household of God" (1 Tim 3:15). Within this larger family, women, especially single women or widows or divorcées, have many opportunities to use their gifts.

Proverbs 31 speaks of the ideal wife, but much also applies to single women. For example: "she opens her hand to the poor and reaches out her hands to the needy" (Prov 31:20). There are many diaconal labors that women can undertake in the family of God and thus help the male diaconate leadership by freeing up some of their time.[11] Deacons can ask gifted women to give unofficial assistance to the deacons in situations where it would be desirable and more appropriate to have feminine help. An office bearer may encounter a problem where such help by a sister in the congregation would be most effective when issues best understood by another woman are involved. For example, a widow who has the necessary gifts (cf. 1 Tim 3:11) can help in follow-up visiting and encouraging those who recently lost their husband and are now widows as well. Another example, if a dysfunctional family or marriage is open for help, an older godly female can train a young woman to be a good wife and mother (Titus 2:3-5). When it comes to diaconal help, there are many ways that mature women in the church who have the necessary skill and time can assist office bearers and so support them in their leadership position.

A church has considerable freedom in engaging the help of women in the diaconate. A church can leave the matter of female help to the discretion of the office-bearers or a consistory can appoint certain qualified women to assist the deacons as needed. 1 Timothy 3:11 suggests that women of the congregation help the deacons. These could be the wives of

---

11 For what follows, see Cornelis Van Dam, *The Deacon: Biblical Foundations for Today's Ministry of Mercy* (Grand Rapids: MI: Reformation Heritage Books, 2016), 128–29.

deacons or simply gifted women in the church. Also, a consistory can decide to enroll widows according to the criteria of 1 Timothy 5:9. The point is that women can and should use their gifts for the benefit of the church. Just because they are not in an ordained office, does not exclude them from serving the body of Christ.

Biblical examples such as the women ministering to Jesus come to mind as well. In Luke 8, for example, we read of women who provided for Jesus and his twelve disciples out of their means (Luke 8:1–3). They supported him in whatever ways they could and someone like Mary Magdalene stayed faithful to the Savior and was also present at the crucifixion (Matt 27:55–56), saw where Jesus was laid in the tomb, and participated in anointing his body (Matt 27:61; 28:1). Another woman, Joanna who is also mentioned by name, was the wife of Chuza, Herod's household manager. In other words, she came from high society and probably had financial resources with which to help Jesus. Our Savior also honored women who so faithfully served him. At his resurrection he appeared first to Mary Magdalene (John 20:11–18). Also, the women who ministered to Christ were the first to proclaim the gospel of the accomplished resurrection (Luke 24:1–10).

There are numerous examples of women using their gifts in a complementary and supportive role in the New Testament church under male leadership.[12] Women were involved in evangelistic activities. Actually, as just mentioned, they were even the first ones to spread the gospel of the resurrection since Christ appeared to them first (John 20:11–18; Luke 24:1–11). Their efforts for spreading the gospel continued after that. Priscilla and Aquila taught Apollos privately about the faith (Acts 18:26). Euodia and Syntyche were women who labored side by side with the apostle Paul (Phil 4:2–3). Scripture does not tell us exactly what they did, but it is obvious that Paul was very thankful for their labors. Another woman that Paul commends is Phoebe, a servant of the church at Cenchreae (Rom

---

12 See on this topic Van Dam, *The Deacon*, 77–92; Thomas R. Schreiner, "The Valuable Ministries of Women in the Context of Male Leadership," in *Recovering Biblical Manhood and Womanhood: A Response to Evangelical Feminism*, ed. John Piper and Wayne Grudem (Wheaton IL: Crossway, 1991), 209–24; K. Deddens, *De Dienst Van de Vrouw in de Kerk* (Groningen: De Vuurbaak, 1978), 39–43.

16:1). Precisely what her service for the gospel involved we are not told. We are informed that "she has been a patron of many and of myself as well" (Rom 12:2). Most probably she provided material support for Christians and hospitality for visitors, a service that seems to have been recognized by the church and so she is called its servant. The apostle Paul also mentioned other women in Romans 16: Mary, "who has worked hard" for the church, Tryphaena, and Tryphosa, "workers in the Lord" (Rom 16:6, 12). And there is also Persis "who has worked hard in the Lord" (Rom 16:12). We are not told precisely what work these devoted women did, but it probably involved helping the apostolic work and the witness of the church in whichever way was possible for them.

Women today can also support the work of the church in numerous ways: serving on committees, providing hospitality to visitors, helping church plants and mission posts with their personal witnessing. They can also be engaged in organizations like pro-life groups, political action organizations, and the like. Of course, occupations like teaching in elementary or higher levels also has an enormous impact for the cause of Christ. One can think of many more examples.[13]

In Conclusion

Scripture speaks very highly of the place of women, married or single. Women can have enormous influence for good: mothers in the home nurturing their children in the Lord and those not married or empty nesters helping and supporting the church in its manifold work of promoting the gospel.

There is a striking passage in Proverbs 31 at which we should pause in closing. "Strength and dignity are her clothing, and she laughs at the time to come" (v. 25). A woman pleasing to God is strong in the Lord, has dignity, and greets the future with laughter! What are we to make of that? This woman greets each new day with joy: new opportunities, new possibilities! She is upbeat and trusting and does not burden herself needlessly with worry about the future. Each day is a gift to be greeted with joy!

---

13 See also chapter 14 of this book.

Women can greet the future with laughter for, ultimately, the reason is that God's promises are sure. In Proverbs 31 it is especially the mother, the wife, who can do so. Parents can often worry about the future of their children and fret how things will develop. But, if we are faithful in our task and calling, we can greet the future with joy even if the world around us issues gloomy predictions. Women, married or not, who are recipients of God's promises of which they are reminded every time a baptism is administered in church, can face the future with a peace that is beyond understanding. They can rejoice in the Lord and his work in their lives.

CHAPTER 3

Motherhood:
Saved Through Child Bearing

On my early morning power walks I sometimes see young mothers carrying their bundled up sleepy infants to their cars to take them to day care so that they can go to their place of employment. Married women face a lot of pressure in our society to get out of the house and have their own career, as if being a nurturing mother is not a worthy vocation. Too often in our current secular culture, motherhood and children are regarded as inconveniences that somehow needed to be managed but are actually peripheral to one's personal goals in life. Consequently, one gets the impression that motherhood and receiving children does not appear to receive the recognition and honor that it enjoyed in previous generations.

Yet, the Bible says that "women will be saved through childbearing" (1 Tim 2:15). How are we to understand that?

The Biblical Position of Women Denied

The current secular culture is very individualistic. One's personal goals, aspirations, and the quest for "self-fulfillment" trump all else. Needless to say, this environment presents challenges to us as Christians. Are our priorities always counter-cultural in this respect? Each situation is different and also Reformed mothers, although they would wish otherwise, may in some circumstances and for different reasons need to leave their infants and the comfort of their home. My comments are not intended to condemn such choices but simply to raise the issue of the current disparagement of motherhood and the role which God ordained for married women who have been blessed with children.

It is not fashionable these days to suggest that God ordained different roles for men and women. In a politically correct world, no distinction is to be made. In 2015, Canada's Prime Minister, Justin Trudeau, prided himself in having appointed to his cabinet an equal number of men and women, as if one's gender is the critical qualification necessary for the ability to serve in government. The erosion and, in a sense, the negation of the created differences between men and women are ultimately Satanic, for such efforts are an affront to God's distinctive creation design of male and female, both physically and psychologically. One of the consequences of not accepting God's intention for the basic roles of male and female is the undermining of the family unit as biblically defined with the husband normally being the breadwinner and the wife being the nurturing mother, if the Lord grants children. This order is reflected in the Reformed marriage form in which the husband's duty is to "work faithfully in your daily calling, that you may support your family and also help those in need." The wife's duty is to "take proper care of your family and household."[1]

Now Satan has been around a long time, and this is not the first time that he has sought to subvert the proper role of husband and wife. Already in Paradise at the urging of the devil, Eve usurped the position of leadership that her husband Adam had in their marriage, and she led Adam into sin. Satan continues working on that ancient agenda. Today we are witnessing an assault on the divinely ordained male role in ecclesiastical office. Many churches have succumbed to the spirit of the age by admitting women to ecclesiastical office and giving them teaching and ruling authority over men in direct contradiction to what God himself has said in his Word.

It may be helpful to consider an apostolic teaching that helps us to see how honorable the office of a nurturing mother is. In his first letter to Timothy, the apostle Paul combines his teaching on the exclusion of women from church office with the blessing of motherhood by concluding "yet she will be saved through childbearing" (1 Tim 2: 15). To properly understand what is meant, we need to pause and first briefly consider the context in which these words occur.

The Woman's Place in Church

These remarkable words on women's salvation through childbearing immediately follow the apostolic instruction: "Let a woman learn quiet-

---

1   Form for the Solemnization of Marriage as found in *Book of Praise*, 629.

ly with full submissiveness. I do not permit a woman to teach or to exercise authority over a man; rather, she is to remain quiet. For Adam was formed first, then Eve; and Adam was not deceived, but the woman was deceived and became a transgressor" (1 Tim 2:11-14). This prohibition occurs within the apostolic instruction on aspects of public worship. 1 Timothy 2:1-7 speaks of congregational prayer, verses 8-15 speak of the place of men and women when the church convenes, and chapter 3 deals with qualifications for office bearers. A consequence of this ecclesiastical context is that although women are forbidden to teach or have authority over men in church, this prohibition does not apply outside the church. Thus we read, for example, of women teaching the way of the Lord outside the worship services (Acts 18:26; Titus 2:3-4).

The reason for the prohibition of women to teach or to have authority over a man in church is the order in which Adam and Eve were created. In other words, their roles are rooted in creation and therefore apply for all times, regardless of the local culture. This means that also today this biblical injunction is in force. The order of creation cannot be changed, and women are therefore excluded from the authoritative teaching office in the church. Furthermore, when Eve took charge and assumed leadership, she led Adam to join her in her sin when he also ate the forbidden fruit. Her leadership led to the disastrous fall. This is another reason God's Word (1 Tim 2:14) tells us why a woman should "learn quietly with all submissiveness" (1 Tim 2:11) to the teaching office bearer. In other words, women should follow the example of Mary who sat at the foot of her Savior and listened to his teaching (Luke 10:39). It is an enormous privilege to hear the gospel and to learn about what God has revealed to us. That privilege is fully accorded to both men and women. The Bible promotes the education and growth of women in the things of the Lord. They are by no means excluded or considered of secondary importance. Both male and female are children of God who fully and equally share in the blessings of salvation. There is "no male and female, for you are all one in Christ Jesus" (Gal 3:28). But there are divinely ordained distinctions that need to be maintained.

The apostle had no desire to portray women as inferior members of the congregation with his reference to Eve's sin and concluded his instruction on the place of women in the church by saying "but women will be saved through childbearing." What does that mean?

Saved Through Childbearing

We have just seen that these words come within the context of determining the correct role for women in the church. The apostle noted that Eve once fell for Satan's temptation and was deceived with all the subsequent horrible events. She had fallen into the clutches of the evil one. But the point seems to be that she can be saved from the devil if she would stick to her God-given role, duties, and obligations. That appears to be the gist of the text's meaning when the apostle, immediately after mentioning Eve's falling into sin continues with the words: "yet, she will be saved through childbearing" (1 Tim 2:15a). And lest this be interpreted to mean that women will be saved simply by sticking to their God-given role, the apostle immediately adds: "if they [i.e. women] continue in faith and love and holiness, with self-control" (1 Tim 2:15b).

To understand the biblical text here, one should realize that the term "childbearing" refers to more than simply giving birth. A woman's task in being a mother does not end with childbirth but in many ways rather begins at that point. The term "childbearing" is used here to indicate the mother's role with all that this entails in having a family, such as raising the children and managing the home.[2] Giving birth is a divinely ordained function of women and not of men. This female capability thus highlights the different roles that women are meant to have. By focussing the attention on childbearing, the apostle also underlines that being a mother is a most honorable and beautiful task. It is also an enduring task throughout all times. It is not dependent on a certain culture or time in history. It is part of God's intent at creation. Only women have been designed to be able to bear children.

When the apostle emphasized the importance of childbearing he was also speaking out against the depreciation of marriage and motherhood championed by the false teachers in his day (cf. 1 Tim 4:3).[3] The apostle's words also go against the denigration of marriage and the gift of chil-

---

2   Andreas J. Köstenberger, "Ascertaining Women's God-Ordained Roles: An Interpretation of 1 Timothy 2:15," *Bulletin for Biblical Research* 7 (1997): 141–42.

3   Also see Bruce W. Winter, "The 'New' Roman Wife and 1 Timothy 2:9–15; the Search for a *Sitz Im Leben,*" *Tyndale Bulletin* 51 (2000): 285–94.

dren rampant in our culture. While our culture undervalues motherhood, the apostle promoted it. He even basically says that if mothers stick to their God-given calling as mothers and focus on that, they will be saved from the snares of Satan into which Eve fell, provided of course "if they continue in faith and love and holiness, with self-control" (1 Tim 2:15). Obviously this does not mean or imply that women must bear children in order to be saved from Satan's deceit. Elsewhere the apostle Paul wrote in a positive way of the unmarried state (1 Cor 7:1-5). God calls women into many different callings in life which can be used in his service. The purpose in 1 Timothy 2 is not that all should be mothers, but the point is that women should honor the role that God ordained for them and to make that point, the apostle used the example of being a mother. By doing so, he underlined the blessing of motherhood.

The Blessing of Motherhood

Receiving children is a tremendous gift from the Lord. It can never be taken for granted. Indeed, to be a mother is a privileged calling which is to be embraced. Through the birth of a child, God has entrusted to the parents a new member of the covenant community whom they may with much prayer and under his blessing teach and instruct in the ways of the Lord.

To be sure, the task of being a mother can be very demanding. As a male I'm obviously no authority on the subject, but I can imagine that mothers feel challenged when they need to multi-task in arduous circumstances and remain clear-headed and focussed on the issues at hand. Being a mother can also be frustrating, and feelings of self-pity and of being tied down too much can arise. But God has also given mothers tremendous promises of being there for them in all circumstances of life. Think of those beautiful baptismal promises! Christian mothers are children of a great Father who will provide for them and who can cover all their shortcomings and sins with the blood of the Lamb.

Furthermore, mothers can be encouraged by the fact that God is also using them to increase the church in a very special way. Mothers may not have time for special evangelistic efforts, but they are doing their part according to God's plan for their role as mother. Being a Christian mother means being in a special service of love for the risen Christ who gathers his church, also by way of the cradle. It means being counter-cultural in a most meaningful and profound way.

CHAPTER 4 — The Calling of Husband and Father

In response to what had originally been written in chapter 2 when first published,[1] I received requests on doing something similar for the place of the man, more specifically that of a husband and father. I gladly complied. Christian marriage is such a beautiful gift from God that it is always profitable to reflect on aspects of it in the light of God's Word. There is much that could be said, but we need to confine ourselves to some highlights.

To begin with, let us consider how a husband and wife relate to each other in terms of headship and submission. A classic passage dealing with this issue is Ephesians 5 where the apostle Paul begins a new section at verse 22 dealing with wives and husbands.

The Husband as Head of his Wife

The apostolic instruction is clearly stated but not always properly understood. Paul wrote: "Wives, submit to your own husbands, as to the Lord. For the husband is the head of the wife even as Christ is the head of the church, his body, and is himself its Savior. Now as the church submits to Christ, so also wives should submit in everything to their husbands" (Eph 5:22–24).

To understand this passage, it is beneficial to consider for a moment what constitutes the husband's headship. To do that we need to go back to the very beginning. After the LORD God had created Adam, he said for the very first time: "it is not good." Up to now, God had always commented on his work of creation with the observation that "it was good" or

---

1   For original publication data see the appendix of this book.

something similar. But now he observed that "it is not good that the man should be alone; I will make him a helper fit for him" (Gen 2:18). Adam was the first human being, and a part of his body became the actual material from which the second human person, a woman, was made. And just as Adam had the authority to name the animals, so he also had the authority to name the woman who came from his side. Adam "called his wife's name Eve, because she was the mother of all living" (Gen 3:20).

To understand male headship in marriage one needs to keep in mind that Adam was created first and Eve in the second place. She was even made from his body. Furthermore, Adam had the authority to name the woman, Eve. These factors help us to appreciate why the male, Adam, had the position of head in the first marriage and why this pattern has applied to every God-pleasing marriage since. What happened at the dawn of history at creation continues to have relevance right up to the present time. Headship in marriage belongs to the man and not to the woman.

However, the events at creation also highlight another continuing normative element. Both Adam and Eve had an equal standing before the LORD. Both were made in God's image (Gen 1:27). A wife is not inferior to her husband. This equality also comes out in the fact that Eve was made "as a helper fit for him" (Gen 2:18). Now translating is difficult work and the term "helper" can suggest an inferior status. But that is not the meaning of the text. After all, the same term "helper" is used of God himself (e.g., Exod 18:4) and to suggest that he is inferior to human beings is out of the question! The meaning of "helper fit for him" is that God will give Adam someone like him who fits with him and corresponds to him physically and spiritually. As such she will be an equal and a suitable counterpart for him. At the same time, she as his wife is subordinate to him for he is the head as the first one created and as the one from whom she was made.

But this subordination did not make Eve unequal to her husband. Matthew Henry, a famous seventeenth century commentator, memorably commented on Eve's being made from Adam by writing that the woman was "not made out of his head to rule over him, nor out of his feet to be trampled upon by him, but out of his side to be equal with him, under his arm to be protected, and near his heart to be beloved."[2] In other words, a wife is not to rule over her husband, but she is also not to be a doormat for her husband to walk on nor his slave to be abused and treated as if she were his property.

When we keep in mind the biblical background of Adam's headship over Eve and their nevertheless being equal before God, we can understand that the apostolic call for wives to be submissive to their husbands does not suggest in any way the inferiority of the wife over against her husband. Rather, the apostle's words are a directive for Christian marriage in keeping with the divine creation of the first couple on earth. When a woman marries she voluntarily subjects herself to her husband, not only to please him, but above all to honor the Lord. "Wives, submit to your own husbands, as to the Lord... Now as the church submits to Christ, so also wives should submit in everything to their husbands" (Eph 5:22, 24). What motivates this submission? It is a deep love for her husband just as the church has a deep love for her Savior. Because of a wife's love for her husband, she is willing to enter into the marriage state and promise "to love and obey him, to assist him, and to live with him in holiness, according to the holy gospel."[3] She will live in subjection to him and love him just as the church is to be subject to the Lord and loves him. She does it without compulsion, willingly, and with great love, and so she reflects the relationship of the church to Christ.

Since a wife's loving obedience to her husband is as to the Lord himself, the onus is on the husband to fulfill his own calling towards his wife. This duty is awesome and challenging.

The Husband's Love for his Wife

While the wife reflects the submission of the church to Christ, the husband must reflect the love that the Savior has for the church and so submit to him. After all, "the husband is the head of the wife even as Christ is the head of the church, his body, and is himself its Savior" (Eph 5:23). A

---

2   Matthew Henry, *Matthew Henry's Commentary on the Whole Bible: Complete and Unabridged in One Volume* (Peabody, MA: Hendrickson, 1994), 10.

3   Form for the Solemnization of Marriage as found in *Book of Praise*, 630.

Christian husband therefore has an enormous responsibility. The apostle commands: "husbands love your wives, as Christ loved the church and gave himself up for her" (Eph 5:25). That is a difficult task and yet that is the obligation that Christ has entrusted to Christian husbands.

To love your wife as Christ loves the church! To do everything possible for her no matter what the consequences. Who is able to do that and to emulate that self-sacrificing purposeful love that the Savior showed? If anything underlines the necessity of the work of the Holy Spirit in a Christian marriage, this fact alone makes it obvious beyond any shadow of doubt that the Spirit's work is indeed necessary. To love as Christ loved means to be prepared to even give oneself up for her, that is, to die for her (Eph 5:25). Did the Savior not say: "greater love has no one than this, that someone lay down his life for his friends" (John 15:13)? How much more is this the case if it involves your wife! Indeed, the apostle points out that "husbands should love their wives as their own bodies. He who loves his wife loves himself. For no one ever hated his own flesh, but nourishes and cherishes it, just as Christ does the church" (Eph 5:28–29). As husbands would do anything for themselves so they must do every positive thing they can for their wives.

Christ himself illustrated the type of love that he expects from husbands, and indeed from us all, but now the point is that husbands are to imitate the love of Christ. How did Christ show his love to his disciples? He was as a servant to them. As their Lord and master, he became as a servant and submitted himself to them in meeting their needs. At the last supper before his betrayal, he removed his outer garment, took a towel, tied it around his waist, got water and then began to wash the feet of his disciples. After he was finished, he said: "I have given you an example that you also should do just as I have done to you" (John 13:12). In other words, as the Lord Jesus explained elsewhere: "whoever would be great among you must be your servant, and whoever would be first among you must be your slave, even as the Son of Man came not to be served but to serve, and to give his life as a ransom for many" (Matt 20:26–28). The message is clear. If a husband is to show the love of Christ, he will submit himself as a servant to his wife's needs. His Christ-like love for her will mean that he will do everything possible to make the relationship between them as one reflecting the relationship of Christ to the church. "Husbands, love your wives, as Christ loved the church and gave himself up for her" (Eph 5:25). Then the fact that both husband and wife are joint heirs will be realized in tangible ways to their mutual joy and comfort. As the apostle Peter put it: "husbands, live with your wives in an understanding way, showing honor to the woman as the weaker vessel, since they are heirs with you of the grace of life, so that your prayers may not be hindered" (1 Pet 3:7).

A husband who likes to assert his authority in a sinful way over his wife is as far removed from the love which Christ exhibited as east is from the west. A husband who does not display servant love in submission to the needs of his wife makes the task of his spouse extremely difficult. But if a husband serves his wife in love and devotion, living in submission to the Savior, and reflecting the very love of his Lord and master, then the calling of the wife to submit to her husband is made quite easy and is a joy. Who would not want to submit to such love that imitates the love of Christ himself?

The husband has a critical responsibility for making his home a happy place. As head of his wife and family he sets the tone by living in joyful submission to his head, the Lord Jesus Christ, and so reflects something of the love of the Savior who came to serve and did everything possible for those whom he loves. A Christian husband and father should do no less and so serve the family's needs to the praise of the Lord.

The Duties of a Father

As head of the family, a father has a position of enormous importance—a fact not always fully realized. The Lord holds him responsible for the well-being of the family entrusted to his care. Within the limitations of this chapter, it may be useful to summarize his task under his identity as a prophet, priest, and king in God's service. The Heidelberg Catechism rightly confesses that every Christian shares in Christ's anointing and thus has prophetic, priestly, and royal aspects to his identity (Lord's Day 12). So much more has the father this identity as head of the household.

As a prophet, the father is to enable his household to confess Christ. Although the mother also has her task in this regard, it is the father who has the first responsibility to ensure that their children are taught in the way of the Lord. As members of the new Israel of God (Gal 6:16), the words of old still retain their authority. The instructions of the Lord must be imprinted in the lives of the children. "Hear, O Israel . . . You shall teach them diligently to your children, and shall talk of them when you sit in your house, and when you walk by the way, and when you lie down, and when you rise" (Deut 6:4, 7). The teaching of the father must reach the very heart of his children (Prov 23:26).

As a priest, the father presents himself and his family as an offering of gratitude to God (cf. 1 Pet 2:5). But in order to do that he must show priestly sympathy for the weaknesses of his wife and children just as the Lord Jesus as our only high priest does toward us (Heb 4:15–16). This includes being patient and forbearing in accordance with the divine Word. "Fathers, do not provoke your children to anger, but bring them up in the discipline and instruction of the Lord" (Eph 6:4). God expects earthly fathers to be compassionate as he is. "As a father shows compassion to his children, so the LORD shows compassion to those who fear him" (Ps 103:13). Fathers are to yearn for the well-being and salvation of their children as the father in the parable of the lost son (Luke 15:11–32).

As a king, the father is to rule his family and guide it in God-fearing ways. He is to do everything possible to ensure that the family does not conform to the sinful patterns of this world (Rom 12:2). Rather he is to encourage them to focus on "whatever is true, whatever is honorable, whatever is just, whatever is pure, whatever is lovely, whatever is commendable" (Phil 4:8).

The Blessing

We live in challenging times and the family unit is under great pressure from a fast-paced secular culture that more often than not glorifies individualism and denigrates the family unit and the biblical roles of husband and wife. Yet, the family is the divinely ordained cornerstone of society and what happens within the walls of a Christian home has enormous consequences for the future spiritual well-being of the next generation and of the church.

As Christians we are blessed with knowing God's expectations for the task and place of husbands and wives. When we seek to follow God's will for our parental roles, be it with stumbling and sin, the family will, empowered by the Spirit, reflect something of the glorious relationship of Christ and his church (Eph 5:22–33)! Now that is encouraging! Such a family can experience something of the beginnings of the eternal joy. When Christian husbands and fathers do everything they can to conform to God's will and prayerfully seek the best for their spouse and family, then they can also ask with integrity that the Lord bless them as a family. When such petitions go to our heavenly Father with our mediator seated at his right hand, we receive the peace and confidence in the Spirit that we need to continue to be busy with our office and calling as husbands and fathers to God's praise and glory.

PART B

ECCLESIASTICAL OFFICES

CHAPTER 5

Calvin and the Reformation of Ecclesiastical Offices

It is difficult to overestimate the enormous influence John Calvin has had on our understanding of the offices and their function within the church. In this chapter, I would like to go through some of the highlights of the reformation of ecclesiastical offices as that took place in Geneva in the sixteenth century. It will help us to appreciate the offices we have in the church today. To that end, we will first briefly consider the situation as it was when Calvin first came to this city. Next, we will look at Calvin's views and how far he was able to implement them. Finally, we will draw some lessons for today.

Introduction

The teachings of the Reformation slowly gained acceptance in Geneva and by 1532 there were public indications of Protestantism. At this time Guillaume Farel, the famous itinerant Protestant preacher, paid his first visit to the city. He boldly attacked Roman Catholicism and urged the population to return to the teachings of Scripture. There were both political and religious factors involved in the Reformation in Geneva which we cannot discuss now.[1] Important for our purpose is to note that on May 25, 1536, a public assembly of the citizens of Geneva voted unanimously to embrace the Reformation by resolving to "live henceforth according to the law of the gospel and the word of God, and to abolish all papal abuses, images and idols."[2] The implications were enormous. This resolution meant that the city no longer recognized the authority of Rome and therefore re-

---

1   For details see, e.g., William Monter, *Calvin's Geneva* (New York: John Wiley & Sons, 1967), 29–92 and Alister E. McGrath, *A Life of John Calvin: A Study in the Shaping of Western Culture* (Oxford: Blackwell, 1990), 79–95.

2   As quoted in Carlos M. N. Eire, *War Against the Idols: The Reformation of Worship from Erasmus to Calvin* (New York: Cambridge University Press, 1986), 151.

jected the ecclesiastical hierarchy and the order and stability which it had brought to much of life in the city for centuries.

This development would have prompted many questions. With the abolition of Roman Catholicism, a key concern would have been what sort of church government would take its place? The acceptance of the Reformation had not yet meant the establishment of a Reformed church. Also, how would the government of the church relate to that of the city? After all, the two were intertwined in Roman Catholic jurisdictions.

In God's providence, a few months after the historic vote, John Calvin was hired by the city on Farel's recommendation. Although both Farel and Calvin were expelled from Geneva in 1538, Calvin was invited back in 1541. About two months after his return, on November 20, 1541, the city adopted the ecclesiastical ordinances which he had drafted.[3] These ordinances defined the organization of the church and determined the relations between the ecclesiastical and political authorities in Geneva.

Of interest to us is how Calvin defined the ecclesiastical offices and how this differed from Roman Catholic practice. Of fundamental importance for Calvin was the centrality of the Word as norm for the reformation of the church and its proclamation.

The Central Significance of the Word for the Offices

Calvin radically altered the organization of the church. He eliminated the Roman Catholic hierarchy which had the pope at its head.[4] He also removed the office of bishop due to the abuse which this office had undergone.[5] Critical for Calvin was the church's task to proclaim the Word

---

3 John Calvin, "Draft Ecclesiastical Ordinances," trans with notes and introduction J.K.S. Reid, in *Calvin: Theological Treatises*, The Library of Christian Classics (Philadelphia: Westminster, 1954), 56.

4 For a concise discussion of offices in Rome at the time of the Reformation, see Josef Freitag, "Roman Catholic Offices," in *The Oxford Encyclopedia of the Reformation*, ed. Hans J. Hillerbrand (New York: Oxford University Press, 1996), 342–45.

5 John Calvin, "The Necessity of Reforming the Church," in *On the Reformation of the Church*, vol. I of *Tracts and Treatises*, historical notes and introduction by T.F. Torrance, trans. Henry Beveridge (Grand Rapids: Eerdmans, 1958; 1st publ. 1844), 125, 140–45. Calvin was not opposed to episcopacy as such and honoured the bishops of the early church who were not subject to a pope. See John Calvin, *Institutes of the Christian Religion*, ed. John T. McNeill, trans. Ford Lewis Battles, Library of Christian Classics (Philadelphia: Westminster, 1960), 4.4.1–4, and p. 1072,

of God and to administer the sacraments. A church that administers the Word should also be governed by the Word. This was lacking in the Roman Catholic Church. As Calvin put it: "Instead of the ministry of the Word, a perverse government compounded of lies rules there, which partly extinguishes the pure light, partly chokes it."[6] Church government as ordained by God was completely overthrown by the tyranny of the papacy and the abuse of power that flowed from this despotism.[7] The church of God is founded on the Word of God and is to be ruled by this Word. "The church is Christ's kingdom and he reigns by his Word alone."[8]

The authority of the church, therefore, does not reside in the human agents, but in the Word of God. The Word of God is the Word of the Good Shepherd. He did not come to destroy and tyrannize, but to serve and to save (Matt 20:28; John 3:17). Consequently, the offices of the church are pastoral and caring—warning the flock of judgment if there is no repentance and comforting with the gospel those who seek forgiveness.[9] The offices are closely linked to the proclamation and administration of the gospel. It is this primacy of the Word both as foundation and authority of the church which informs and shapes Calvin's view of the offices of the church. Christ himself rules and guides his church through his office bearers. Of them, Calvin noted that "among the many excellent gifts with which God has adorned the human race, it is a singular privilege that he deigns to consecrate to himself the mouths and tongues of men in order that his voice may resound in them." Office bearers function as "the very mouth of God."[10]

At first Calvin spoke of two offices: pastors and deacons.[11] His views however changed. Following Martin Bucer, from whom he had

---

note 12; also see John T. McNeill, "The Ministry in the Light of the Historical Situation," *Mid-Stream* 3, no. 4 (June 1964): 41–44.

6   Calvin, *Institutes*, 4.2.2, also see 4.1.9–12.

7   *Calvin, Institutes*, 4.5.1–19; also *passim* 4.6–11.

8   Calvin, *Institutes*, 4.2.4.

9   Calvin, *Institutes*, 4.2.4. Also see the fine summary in T.H.L. Parker, *John Calvin: A Biography* (Philadelphia: Westminster, 1975), 60.

10 Calvin, *Institutes*, 4.1.5. The expression "the very mouth of God" McNeill quotes in footnote 11 on p. 1018 from a sermon of Calvin.

11 In the first edition of the *Institutes* (1536). See John Calvin, *Institution of the Christian Religion [1536]*, translated and annotated by Ford Lewis Battles (Atlanta: John Knox, 1975), chap 5, §§ 57, 66.

learned much in Strasbourg, Calvin distinguished four offices: pastor, doctor or teacher, elder, and deacon.[12] Our main sources of information on Calvin's view of the offices in the church are his *Institutes*, commentaries, and of course his Genevan church order. It is the last one, the *Ecclesiastical Ordinances*, that lays out clearly and crisply the four offices. He writes: "There are four orders of office instituted by our Lord for the government of his church. First, pastors; then doctors; next elders; and fourth deacons. Hence if we will have a Church well ordered and maintained, we ought to observe this form of government."[13] We will follow this sequence in our discussion of the offices.

Pastors

The *Ecclesiastical Ordinances* describe the office of pastors thus: "their office is to proclaim the Word of God, to instruct, admonish, exhort and censure, both in public and private, to administer the sacraments and to enjoin brotherly corrections along with the elders and colleagues."[14] Calvin stated that this office is absolutely central for the well-being of the church because without the true ministry of the Word and sacraments the church cannot stand.[15] Indeed, the government of the church is by the ministry of the Word and this is a most sacred ordinance of Christ.[16]

The importance of the office of pastor for the church was also described by Calvin as "the chief sinew by which believers are held together in one body." He mentioned this in the context of Ephesians 4:11–15: "He gave the apostles, the prophets, the evangelists, the shepherds and teachers, to equip the saints for the work of ministry, for building up the body of Christ, until we all attain to the unity of the faith and of the knowledge of the Son of God, to mature manhood, to the measure of the stature of the

---

12 François Wendel, *Calvin: The Origins and Development of His Religious Thought*, trans. from the French (London: Collins, 1963), 76 and R. E. H. Uprichard, "The Eldership in Martin Bucer and John Calvin," *Evangelical Quarterly* 61 (1989): 21–37.

13 Calvin, "Draft Ecclesiastical Ordinances," 58.

14 Calvin, "Draft Ecclesiastical Ordinances," 58.

15 Calvin, *Institutes*, 4.2.1; 4.3.4.

16 Calvin on Eph 4:11, John Calvin, *The Epistles of Paul the Apostle to the Galatians, Ephesians, Philippians and Colossians*, eds. D. W. Torrance and T. F. Torrance, trans. T. H. L. Parker, Calvin's Commentaries (Grand Rapids: Eerdmans, 1965), 178.

fullness of Christ."[17] Of the offices mentioned in Ephesians 4, Calvin considered that only the last two, shepherds or pastors and teachers, "have an ordinary office in the church." The others were temporary.[18]

Calvin considered the office of pastor to be an elder office on the basis of 1 Timothy 5:17. This passage says: "let the elders who rule well be considered worthy of double honor, especially those who labor in preaching and teaching." In his commentary on this text Calvin notes that those who labor in word and doctrine are those who preach the Word and "there were at that time two kinds of elders; for all were not ordained to teach. The words plainly mean, that there were some who 'ruled well' and honorably, but who did not hold the office of teachers."[19]

Entering the ministry is a serious enterprise and no one may take it upon oneself. One needs to be called to this office. First, there is the secret call "of which each minister is conscious before God."[20] Then there is the call from the congregation. Contrary to the practice of Roman Catholicism, Calvin involved the people in the calling of ministers of the Word. "This call is lawful according to the Word of God when those who seemed fit are elected by the consent and approval of the people."[21] Once a call was received, an examination needed to be taken to ascertain whether the one aspiring to the office of pastor had the necessary knowledge for the office.[22] Once ordained, a pastor was bound to his church and should normally restrict his activities to his flock and not meddle in another man's territory.[23] Unlike Rome, there was to be no hierarchy among the ministers. Christ is the head of the church.[24]

---

17 Calvin, *Institutes*, 4.3.1–2.

18 Calvin, *Institutes*, 4. 3.4; also see IV.3.5. For an overview of Calvin's use of Eph 4:11, as well as a historical exegetical survey, see Elsie Anne McKee, *Elders and the Plural Ministry: The Role of Exegetical History in Illuminating John Calvin's Theology*, Travaux d'Humanisme et Renaissance (Geneva: Librairie Droz, 1988), 133–70.

19 For an exegetical history of 1 Tim 5:17, including Calvin, see McKee, *Elders and the Plural Ministry*, 87–132.

20 Calvin, *Institutes*, 4.3.11.

21 Calvin, *Institutes*, 4.3.15. Also see Calvin on Acts 14:23, John Calvin, *The Acts of the Apostles, 14–28*, eds D. W. Torrance and T. F. Torrance, trans. John W. Fraser and W. J. G. McDonald, Calvin's Commentaries (Grand Rapids: Eerdmans, 1966), 19.

22 Calvin, "Draft Ecclesiastical Ordinances," 58–59.

23 Calvin, *Institutes*, 4.3.7.

24 Calvin, *Institutes*, 4.6.10. Calvin did not however condemn the position of bishops and

It is of interest to note that the duties of the pastor are similar to what Calvin had charged that the Roman Catholic bishops should have been doing, namely, to preach the Word and administer the sacraments. In other words, the office of pastor basically took the place of the Roman Catholic bishops. Calvin sees his church order as a return to the practice of the early Christian Church.[25]

Before we proceed to the office of doctor or teacher we need to pause at an important aspect of the ecclesiastical situation in Calvin's day.

Clergy and Laity

In the time of Calvin, the Roman Catholic Church distinguished sharply between the clergy and the laity. The clergy were those consecrated for special service in the church in one of the seven orders or levels of ordination: the minor orders were the porter, lector, exorcist, and acolyte; the major orders were those of subdeacon, deacon and priest. The laity on the other hand had no special standing. They were the ordinary believers. The clergy were part of the privileged spiritual estate and were considered to lead more holy lives which were more pleasing to God than the lives of the laity who belonged to the lower lay estate.[26]

Following Luther, Calvin rejected this dichotomy. All members of the church belonged to the spiritual estate. The daily work of the laity was also a holy vocation. As is clear from Scripture (1 Pet 2:5), not just the

---

archbishops in the early church saying it was rare, due to the needs of the times, and motivated by a desire to act according to God's Word. Calvin, *Institutes*, 4.4.4. See also John T. McNeill, "The Doctrine of the Ministry in Reformed Theology," *Church History* 12 (1943): 82–85.

25 Calvin noted that the New Testament usage of the terms for bishop and presbyter (elder) indicate that these terms refer to the same office, namely that of minister of the Word. See Calvin, *Institutes*, 4.3.8. For the duty of bishops to preach the Word and administer the sacraments, see Calvin, *Institutes*, 4.4.3. For the faithfulness of the early church with respect to the offices, see Calvin, *Institutes*, 4.4.1. For the importance of the early church in Calvin's thinking, see J. F. Peter, "The Ministry in the Early Church as Seen by John Calvin," *Evangelical Quarterly* 35 (1963): 68–78, 133–43.

26 On the Roman Catholic clerical orders, see Calvin, *Institutes*, 4.5.10 and 4.19.22–33. Also see Freitag, "Roman Catholic Offices," 1:342–43, Elsie Anne McKee, "Church Offices: Calvinist Offices," in *The Oxford Encyclopedia of the Reformation*, ed. Hans J. Hillerbrand (New York: Oxford University Press, 1996), 1:337, and Lorna Jane Abray, "Laity," in *The Oxford Encyclopedia of the Reformation*, ed. Hans J. Hillerbrand (New York: Oxford University Press, 1996), 2:384.

clergy but also the laity were a holy priesthood called to serve the Lord.[27] One implication was that regular church members with the necessary gifts could be ordained into ecclesiastical office. This was a radical break from the past. Thus the office of doctor, elder, and deacon have been described as lay ministries in the church.[28] The linking of gifts with these offices was done on the basis of Romans 12:6–8 and 1 Corinthians 12:28. Some of the gifts were temporary, such as the gift of healing, but others are permanent and equip for office.[29] We now turn to these so-called lay ministries of the church; first, the office of doctor.

Doctors

According to the *Ecclesiastical Ordinances*, the task of a doctor is "the instruction of the faithful in true doctrine, in order that the purity of the Gospel be not corrupted."[30] Since this duty is very close to that of the minister, Calvin took pains to separate the two. In his commentary on Ephesians 4:11 he acknowledged that some would say that the two offices of pastor and teacher are one office, but then he wrote: "Pastors, to my mind, are those to whom is committed the charge of a particular flock. I have no objection to their receiving the name of doctors, if we realize that there is another kind of doctor, who superintends both the education of pastors and the instruction of the whole church. Sometimes he can be a pastor who is also a doctor, but the duties (*facultates*) are different."[31]

Calvin considered the office of doctor or teacher as corresponding to the ancient prophets.[32] The duties of the doctor or teacher were quite different from those of a pastor. While the pastor had a congregation and preached the Word and administered the sacraments, the doctor was fo-

---

27 Calvin, *Institutes*, 4.19.25; also I.11.7.

28 McKee, *Elders and the Plural Ministry*, 216–17, 222; Allan F. Farris, "Calvin and the Laity," *Canadian Journal of Theology* 11 (1965): 58.

29 Calvin, *Institutes*, 4.3.8–9. For a detailed discussion on how Rom 12:6–8 and 1 Cor 12:28 have been explained and applied by Calvin and others as biblical bases for offices, see McKee, *Elders and the Plural Ministry*, 171–209.

30 Calvin, "Draft Ecclesiastical Ordinances," 62.

31 Calvin, *Galatians, Ephesians*, 179.

32 Calvin, *Institutes*, 4.3.5. For a discussion of the teacher as prophet, see Robert W. Henderson, *The Teaching Office in the Reformed Tradition* (Philadelphia: Westminster Press, 1962), 24–31.

cussed on teaching in all branches of knowledge, especially the biblical subjects. The education of the citizens was a very high priority for Calvin, and he was instrumental in reorganizing Geneva's educational system. In 1559 the civil government founded the Geneva Academy and subsequently maintained it. The pastors of Geneva nominated teachers to the civil authorities for their appointment. The two key objectives of the school were to make sure that properly trained persons might be equipped for the ministry of the church and the functioning of the civil government. This school attracted an international student body and was of great importance for spreading the Reformed faith.[33]

Calvin seems to have been somewhat ambivalent about the teacher being an ecclesiastical office. His *Institutes* of 1543 specifically mention only three offices by treating pastors and teachers as one office. This mention of only three offices was maintained right up to the last edition of 1559.[34] However, at the same time and in the same 1559 edition, he elsewhere speaks of the separate office of teacher.[35] Furthermore, once appointed, a teacher appears to have become part of the Company of Pastors.[36] Perhaps this fluidity or inconsistency is due to the fact that given the complex situation in Geneva of religious and civil relationships the title teacher or doctor was more a term descriptive of the work he did than an indication of an ecclesiastical office. On the one hand, these teachers were in the employ of the church which had a vital interest in the education of the citizens of Geneva. On the other hand, the teachers were in the employ of the city which funded the school. Ultimately, it seems, Calvin was more concerned with the educational work that had to be done than to sort out in a consistent manner the problem of the position of pastor and teacher. In any case, by the seventeenth century few Calvinists considered the teacher or doctor to hold an ecclesiastical office.[37]

---

33 Calvin, "Draft Ecclesiastical Ordinances," 62–63; Henderson, *The Teaching Office*, 60–71; Farris, "Calvin and the Laity," 58–59. For the Academy, also see Jeannine E. Olson, "Geneva Academy," in *Oxford Encyclopedia of the Reformation*, ed. Hans J. Hillerbrand (Oxford: Oxford University Press, 1996), 2:163–64; for Geneva's importance for training missionaries and generally spreading the Reformed faith, Philip Edgcumbe Hughes, ed. and trans., *The Register of the Company of Pastors of Geneva in the Time of Calvin* (Grand Rapids: Eerdmans, 1966), 25–30.

34 Calvin, *Institutes*, 4.4.1; Wendel, *Calvin*, 303.

35 Calvin, *Institutes*, 4.3.5.

36 Henderson, *The Teaching Office*, 67.

37 See W. F. Dankbaar, "Het doctorenambt bij Calvijn," *Nederlands theologisch Tijdschrift* 19

Elders

With respect to the office of elder, according to the *Ecclesiastical Ordinances*, "their office is to have oversight of the life of everyone, to admonish amicably those whom they see to be erring or to be living a disordered life, and where it is required, to enjoin fraternal corrections themselves and along with others."[38] It is clear from this description that the focus of their office was the discipline of morals. A church needed this. As Calvin noted: "as no city or township can function without magistrate and polity, so the church of God . . . needs a spiritual polity."[39]

However, to ascribe this kind of authority to an ecclesiastical office was very controversial in Calvin's day. After all, Christian princes and magistrates were expected to maintain both moral as well as civil order. Why should the church encroach on their territory and claim to have jurisdiction in maintaining moral order? While Calvin would accord the civil authorities their duty to uphold Christian morals, he rightly insisted that the church had its own responsibilities in this regard. Furthermore, there was a difference between the civil and ecclesiastical rule. Civil authorities could use coercion to establish justice, while the church could only use God's Word to bring sinners to repentance.[40]

In any case, it was especially in this area that Calvin ran into heavy resistance from the civil authorities in Geneva and they insisted on considerable control. After describing the basic task of the elders, the *Ecclesiastical Ordinances* therefore continue by stating that two elders would be elected from the Little Council, four from the Council of Sixty, and six from the Council of the Two Hundred. The Little Council would present to the Council of Two Hundred for their approval nominations for the eldership after conferring with the ministers. They would then be sworn into office. These twelve elders should come from different parts of the city to

---

(1964): 135–65; McKee, "Church Offices: Calvinist Offices," 1:336–37.

38   Calvin, "Draft Ecclesiastical Ordinances," 63.

39   Calvin, *Institutes*, 4.11.1. Also see P. Coertzen, "Presbyterian Church Government: Ius Divinum, Ius Ecclesiasticum or Ius Humanum?" in *Calvin: Erbe und Auftrag: Fesetschrift Für Wilhelm Heinrich Neuser Zum 65. Geburtstag*, ed. Willem van't Spijker (Kampen: Kok, 1991), 329–42.

40   Calvin, *Institutes*, 4.12.1; 4.11.1–5. Also see McKee, *Elders and the Plural Ministry*, 15, 30, 195–97.

make it possible "to keep an eye on everybody." Their election to office had to be renewed every year by the civil authorities.[41] This procedure as set down in the church order adopted in Geneva differs from Calvin's desire to have elders elected by the congregation.[42] As a result of the insistence of the civil authorities, "the elders, instead of being officials of the Church, really were in consequence officials of the state."[43]

Not only did the civil authorities have considerable influence in determining who would be the elders, they also refused to give the church the right of excommunication. It was not until about fourteen years after the adoption of the *Ecclesiastical Ordinances* that the civil authorities acknowledged excommunication as a right of the church.[44] By excluding unrepentant sinners, "the church claims for itself nothing unreasonable but practices the jurisdiction conferred upon it by the Lord."[45]

With respect to the task of safeguarding morals and the holiness of the church, Calvin stressed that this duty could not be done by only the elders, but that the entire congregation had to be involved as well.[46]

It is noteworthy that Calvin made a clear distinction between the offices of pastor and elder. They had different tasks, namely teaching and moral supervision respectively. But Calvin also distinguished them by saying that pastors be ordained with the laying on of hands, but not the elders.[47] However, the *Ecclesiastical Ordinances* as they were finally adopted did not even make any mention of the laying on of hands with the ordination of a pastor "since the ceremonies of time past have been perverted into much superstition" and "because of the weakness of the times.[48]

---

41 Calvin, "Draft Ecclesiastical Ordinances," 63–64.
42 In Calvin, *Institutes*, 4.3.8, Calvin mentions "elders chosen from the people." In the light of his insistence that pastors be chosen by the congregation (*Institutes*, 4.4.10), one can assume that the lay elders be chosen likewise. Also see Wendel, *Calvin*, 304 and Farris, "Calvin and the Laity," 59.
43 Farris, "Calvin and the Laity," 60.
44 Wendel, *Calvin*, 74, 77–78. Cf. Calvin, "Draft Ecclesiastical Ordinances," 70–71, including the notes.
45 Calvin, *Institutes*, 4.12.4.
46 Calvin, *Institutes*, 4.6.4; 4.12.7. McKee, *Elders and the Plural Ministry*, 28–30.
47 Calvin, *Institutes*, 4.3.16; McKee, *Elders and the Plural Ministry*, 29.
48   . Calvin, "Draft Ecclesiastical Ordinances," 59 note 11.

Deacons

With respect to the office of deacon the *Ecclesiastical Ordinances* note that there were two kinds of deacons in the early church, "the one deputed to receive, dispense and hold goods for the poor, not only daily alms, but also possessions, rents and pensions; the other to tend and care for the sick and administer allowances to the poor."[49] Calvin justified this distinction on the basis of Romans 12:8 "he that gives, let him do it with simplicity . . . he that shows mercy with cheerfulness." The first refers to deacons for the poor, the second for the sick.[50] The office of deacon as such he based on Acts 6, which recounts how the apostles prayed and laid their hands on those chosen to take care of the poor, as well as on 1 Timothy 3:8–13.[51]

According to the *Ecclesiastical Ordinances*, the election of the deacons was to follow the pattern set for the elders. In other words, the civil authorities retained considerable control. The two diaconal offices translated into procurators and hospitallers. The procurators handled the funds and made sure they were well used by supervising the hospital for the poor and sick and the hospitallers cared for the sick and poor. Begging was strictly forbidden.[52] Men were ordained to the diaconal office and women "were accorded a subordinate, non-ordained diaconal task of nursing the sick and giving personal care to the poor."[53]

The Reformation's understanding of the diaconal office was radical for its day. According to Roman Catholicism, the deacon was a liturgical assistant of the priest or bishop, a position which was basically a stepping-stone to the priesthood. Protestants, however, understood the deacon to

49 Calvin, "Draft Ecclesiastical Ordinances," 64.
50 Calvin, *Institutes*, 4.3.9. For a full discussion of this exegesis, see Elsie Anne McKee, *John Calvin on the Diaconate and Liturgical Almsgiving*, Travaux d'Humanisme et Renaissance (Geneva: Librairie Droz, 1984), 185–204.
51 Acts 6 is referenced in Calvin, *Institutes*, 4.3.9. For a full discussion of this exegesis, see McKee, *John Calvin on the Diaconate*, 139–58. Calvin deals with 1 Tim 3 in his commentary on this passage.
52 Calvin, "Draft Ecclesiastical Ordinances," 65–66. For the argument that Calvin had a double diaconate because he saw it operate successfully in Geneva and then found biblical warrant for it, see Robert M. Kingdon, "Calvin's Ideas About the Diaconate: Social or Theological in Origin?" in *Piety, Politics, and Ethics: Reformation Studies in Honor of George Wolfgang Forell*, Ed Carter Lindberg (Kirksville, MO: Sixteenth Century Journal Publishers, 1984), 167–80.
53 McKee, "Church Offices: Calvinist Offices," 1:338.

be a separate ecclesiastical office charged with the care for the poor. New Testament references to the deacon were understood in the light of Acts 6:1–6.[54]

This understanding of Scripture had enormous practical impact, both in liturgy as well as in the actual care of the poor. Giving money for the poor had dropped out of the Roman Catholic liturgy, although the indigent were not forgotten. Charity was still associated with the place of worship with the practice of begging in the church. Furthermore, although excluded from the liturgy of the Latin mass, collections for the poor were taken in the more relaxed unofficial vernacular preaching service called the Prône. Such collections were authorized for the support of beggars, hospitals, and orphans.[55] Calvin, however, brought the offerings for the poor back into the official worship service. He declared that "no meeting of the church should take place without the Word, prayers, partaking of the Supper, and almsgiving."[56] This became a defining feature of the great majority of Reformed churches.[57]

The recognition of an official ecclesiastical diaconal office for the poor also had major repercussions in the way practical help was given. Since Geneva had chosen for the Reformation prior to Calvin's coming, several hundred priests, sisters, friars, monks, and nuns had left, leaving a vacuum, among others, in the care for the poor. New institutions had to be created. The General Hospital became important as the city welfare center. It cared not only for the sick, but also for the orphans, the crippled, the elderly and any who could not take care of themselves. Because of the many religious refugees, voluntary refugee organizations with close ties to the church were also established. These could be seen as a "'disestablished'" form of Calvin's diaconate. In any case, both the hospital and the refugee organizations can be considered diaconal ministries. "Both diaconates

---

54 For more detail see McKee, *John Calvin on the Diaconate*, 168–71.

55 McKee, *John Calvin on the Diaconate*, 21, 28–30.

56 Calvin, *Institutes*, 4.17.44. Also see Calvin's essay on the Lord's Supper and the place of alms in worship in some editions of his *La forme des prieres*. McKee, *John Calvin on the Diaconate*, 50.

57 McKee, *John Calvin on the Diaconate*, 30–65. It is noteworthy that Geneva apparently did not have an alms collection until after Calvin's death. This was "a practical concession, not a theological position" because it was assumed that the city's charitable needs could be met by the redirected ecclesiastical properties. McKee, *John Calvin on the Diaconate*, 64.

were considered ecclesiastical offices, and together they stand as clear witness to Calvin's concern for the role in the social sphere of the Church as Church."[58] The church's concern for the needy can be considered to have been a success. As it has been stated: "in the sixteenth century the little nation of Geneva was organized like a large family the heads of which did not abandon any of its members, small or great, sick or healthy, young or old. All were objects of a touching solicitude."[59]

In Conclusion

Now that we have considered Calvin's view of the offices, allow me some concluding comments to highlight some important elements.

For the reformation of the church, Calvin went back to the Word of God. It alone is authoritative. He thereby rejected the place of tradition which had such a great influence in Roman Catholicism and simply went back to the Scriptures.

In the second place, by going back to the Word, Calvin uncovered once again God's gift of office bearers: ministers, elders, and deacons. Calvin was somewhat ambivalent about the office of teacher or doctor and it is no longer considered an ecclesiastical office today. But we have the treasures of the pastorate, eldership, and diaconate, thanks to God's work through his servant John Calvin. We have the privilege of knowing that the Good Shepherd rules his church through these offices. Let us not underestimate this great treasure of the offices, but safeguard and honor it! Connected with this rediscovery of the offices was also the renewed appreciation of the honorable and responsible place of the regular members of the church as "a royal priesthood, a holy nation" (1 Pet 2:9). Their daily work is also to be in God's service.

In the third place, it is clear that the reformation of the church is never an easy enterprise. Calvin did not get everything he wanted. The situation is never ideal in this world and the sixteenth century reformers had

---

58 The quotes are from McKee, *John Calvin on the Diaconate*, 112, 113 and the general discussion runs from pp.106–13.

59 Henri Heyer and Johannot as quoted by Farris, "Calvin and the Laity," 62.

to settle for less than the ideal. That can also be the case today. But we must do our best given the circumstances in which God has placed us.

And finally, in the fourth place, Calvin correctly saw the great importance of Christian education both for the ministry as well as the general population. It was so important for him that he, at times, considered the teacher to hold ecclesiastical office. Today, too, the education for the ministry and the training of our children in the fear of the Lord remains critical for the future well-being of the church. These are areas which we, too, must always work at.

6 Some Aspects of the Office of Minister of the Word

What is a minister of the Word? What is specific to his identity? What is an ecclesiastical office? To answer these and similar questions, we will consider important aspects of the office of minister of the Word which provide indirect continuity with those who served in the special Old Testament offices of elder, prophet, priest, and even king. We will also consider some implications of the ministerial identity with respect to the dignity and authority of his office for the egalitarian times in which we live.

The Office of Minister is a Calling

To understand properly the office of a minister of the gospel, we need to be clear about what is meant when we speak about the offices in the church. The ecclesiastical offices need to be distinguished from the general office of all believers which all those who share in Christ's anointing have; namely, to be prophets in confessing Christ's name, priests in giving themselves as living sacrifices of thankfulness to the Lord, and kings in fighting and conquering sin and Satan.[1] Obviously, this description of what it means to be a believer is fundamental to one's identity as a Christian. Its importance cannot be exaggerated.

Our focus now, however, is about the special ecclesiastical office of minister of the gospel. For our purpose, an ecclesiastical office can be defined as a special service for the edification of the congregation to which Christ calls an individual whom he has endowed with the necessary gifts. Some implications of such a definition include the fact that one needs to be called, in this case, to the office of minister of the Word. The special office of minister is a gift of the risen Savior through whom Christ works to equip

---

1 See Heidelberg Catechism, Q.A. 32.

the saints for building up the body of believers (Eph 4:11–12).[2] The minister is accountable to his Sender and he is in his work not to be an overlord, but to be a servant (Matt 20:25–28).

A vitally important aspect of the identity of a minister of the gospel is the element of calling. Although God does not now usually call in some dramatic way as he called some of the Old Testament prophets (e.g., Jer 1:4–10), also today God is the one who calls individuals to the ministry. The Holy Spirit works in the heart and conscience of some of his children the desire to be in God's special service to proclaim his Word. Indeed, God's Word says: "If anyone aspires to the office of overseer, he desires a noble task" (1 Tim 3:1). "Overseer" here is literally "bishop" and can refer to the teaching elder or minister of the Word.[3] An aspiration for the office must be characterized, as Calvin reminds us, "not with ambition or avarice, not with any other selfish desire, but with a sincere fear of God and desire to build up the church." He notes that this is a "secret call, of which each minister is conscious before God, and which does not have the church as witness."[4] However, this secret call and desire for the office is confirmed when a student finishes his studies for the ministry and a congregation recognizes his God-given gifts and calls him to be their minister (cf. Rom 12:6–8; Eph 4:11–12). Being a minister is a calling, not a career. It is not an occupation, as that is generally understood, but a vocation. The office of minister means being called, ultimately by God himself. This calling is true of all office bearers. As the apostle reminded the elders of Ephesus: "the Holy Spirit has made you overseers, to care for the church of God, which he obtained with his own blood" (Acts 20:28).

The classic Reformed ordination form highlights this aspect of being called. The first question asks the one to be ordained in the ministerial office whether he feels in his heart that God himself, through his congregation, has called him to this holy ministry. God needs to call a person to

---

2   See the discussion in William Hendriksen, *Exposition of Ephesians*, New Testament Commentary (Grand Rapids: Baker, 1967), 197–99.

3   Cf. the gift of being "able to teach" mentioned in this context (1 Tim 3:2); Cornelis Van Dam, *The Elder: Today's Ministry Rooted in All of Scripture* (Phillipsburg, NJ: P&R, 2009), 115.

4   Calvin, *Institutes*, 4.3.11. Also see Edmund P. Clowney, *Called to the Ministry* (Chicago: InterVarsity Press, 1964); Craig Tucker, "Calvin and the Call to Ministry," *The Reformed Theological Review* 76 (2017): 101–20.

the office of minister, and he does so through the agency of a congregation that recognizes the God-given gifts for that office in an individual so he can preach the gospel and shepherd the flock. What was true of the office of the high priest in Israel, is also true of the office of minister of the Word today. "No one takes this honor for himself, but only when called by God, just as Aaron was" (Heb 5:4).[5] Thus, to be a minister of the gospel cannot simply be described as a job given to him by the congregation. It is a calling from God himself.[6] In other words, one ordained into the ministry has been sent by the Lord to that particular congregation with the awesome responsibility to declare the whole counsel of God, to administer the sacraments, to lead the congregation in worship and, together with the elders, to shepherd the flock.[7] It means that the minister is responsible to God in the first place for the execution of his office.

God has through the ages called individuals to this special office to serve his people for their edification. It may be profitable for a greater appreciation of this office to consider some of the larger biblical context of the office of minister of the Word as we have it today. This office has continuities with the offices of the elder, prophet, and priest of Old Testament times and even to some extent to the office of king as God had desired for Israel. Recognizing connections with the past will help us to appreciate something of the glory of the ministerial office and its significance for the church today.

The Minister as Elder

When considering the office of minister and its biblical context, we need to remember that although it is a distinct office, it is an elder office, and the office of elder goes back a long way into ancient Israel.[8] Not sur-

---

5   See also Simon J. Kistemaker, *Exposition of Hebrews*, New Testament Commentary (Grand Rapids, MI: Baker, 1984), 133–34.

6   See, e.g., in this context John Piper, *Brothers, We Are not Professionals: A Plea for Radical Ministry* (Nashville, TN: Broadman & Holman, 2002), 1–5.

7   For the Form for the Ordination of Ministers of the Word, see *Book of Praise*, 618–21. It is a fair question whether these elements of being called by the congregation and being sent by God are not in jeopardy when a congregation advertises and solicits for a minister to apply to fill their vacancy.

8   For a discussion of the elder office as it functioned in Old Testament times, see Van Dam, *The Elder*, 41–95.

prisingly, after the outpouring of the Holy Spirit, elders were soon found in every church. That was indeed to be expected. After all, the first Christians were Jews and their synagogues had always included elders. That was part of their ecclesiastical heritage going back to ancient times. Why should they not have elders now that the Messiah had come? Indeed, the first Christian congregation at Jerusalem was called a synagogue (thus literally in James 2:2) and the apostles saw to it that every church had elders (Acts 14:23; Titus 1:5).

Now it is important to realize that the term "elder" was also used of other offices.[9] That was already the case before Christ's coming. For example, although the Jewish Sanhedrin included both the chief priests and teachers of the law (Luke 22:66; cf. Acts 5:21), the Sanhedrin was known as the Council of the Elders. The word elder was therefore considered to encompass the chief priests and teachers of the law, although these offices remained distinct from the eldership as such. Another example of this broad use of the term elder is the apostle Peter identifying himself as a fellow-elder when addressing the elders in the congregations to whom he is writing (1 Pet 5:1). The apostle John also identified himself as an elder (2 John 1, 3 John 1). So an apostle was also an elder but there remained a clear distinction between the office of apostle and that of an elder in a congregation. The latter was not an apostle.[10]

That the term elder could encompass more than one office in the church is also clear from the fact that the eldership can refer to both the preaching-teaching elder and the elders whose main task is to rule. We read in 1 Timothy 5:17, "Let the elders who rule well be considered worthy of double honor, especially those who labor in preaching and teaching." This passage has generally and correctly been interpreted as indicating that there are two distinct elder offices: the ruling elder and the preaching-teaching elder; or, as we usually identify them, the elder and the min-

---

9   See Günther Bornkamm, *"presbus,"* in *Theological Dictionary of the New Testament,* eds Gerhard Kittel and Gerhard Friedrich, trans. and ed. Geoffrey Bromiley (Grand Rapids: Eerdmans, 1964–76), 6:658–61.

10   See also Simon J. Kistemaker, *Exposition of James, Epistles of John, Peter, and Jude,* New Testament Commentary (Grand Rapids: Baker, 2002), 188 (in 1 Peter commentary).

ister.[11] There is however an underlying unity between these two offices. In the New Testament church they are bound together in the eldership. In a sense, the minister is a specialized elder.

An important implication of this commonality between the ruling and teaching elder is that although the teaching and ruling elders are distinct offices, the common element underlying both offices undercuts any idea of clericalism or ecclesiastical hierarchy in the church. Also, the ruling elder is a shepherd of the flock with all that this entails. There is to be no domineering of the one elder office over the other. It is striking how the apostle Peter did not, as an apostle, set himself up above the elders when he wrote to the Christians in northern Asia Minor: "I exhort the elders among you, as a fellow elder" (1 Pet 5:1). Calvin in his commentary noted that "if Peter had the right of primacy he would have claimed it; and this would have been most suitable on the present occasion. But though he was an Apostle, he knew that authority was by no means delegated to him over his colleagues, but that, on the contrary, he was joined with the rest in the participation of the same office."[12] John Murray put it well: "There is not the slightest evidence in the New Testament that among the elders there is any hierarchy."[13] Indeed, the only "boss" in the church is the Lord Jesus Christ who rules the church as the head the body (Eph 1:20–22). The relationship of both elder offices to each other as well as towards the congregation is one of serving (cf. 1 Pet 5:3, 5). Both offices are to reflect the self-giving love and servant attitude displayed by their Sender, the Lord Jesus when he was on earth (cf. Matt 20:26–28; Luke 22:27).

Yet, the distinction between the two elder offices must never be forgotten. Their distinctive tasks go back to Old Testament times, namely the distinction between the tasks of ruling and preaching and teaching. The ministerial office of preaching and teaching has continuities with the Old Testament offices of prophet and priest, but not as much with that of the elder. The prophets were busy with proclaiming the word of God as the

---

11 See, e.g., the Reformed form for ordination of ministers of the Word in *Book of Praise*, 618–19.

12 John Calvin, *The Catholic Epistles*, trans. John Owen (Edinburgh, UK: Calvin Translation Society, 1855), 143–44.

13 John Murray, "The Form of Government," in *Collected Writings of John Murray*, vol. 2 (Edinburgh: Banner of Truth, 1977), 2:346.

LORD inspired them and the priests were occupied, along with their other duties, with teaching the people the will of the LORD. On the other hand, the elders, although obligated to teach the way of the LORD as occasion warranted (Deut 32:7), did not have this as their primary task.

Let us now consider the continuities of the office of minister of the Word with the Old Testament offices of prophet, priest, and king, beginning with the office of prophet.

The Minister as Prophet

There are of course considerable differences between an Old Testament prophet and a contemporary minister of the Word of God. A minister of the gospel is not a prophet in the Old Testament sense of the word. Yet, there are important continuities. At the very basis of the office of a prophet was his identity as a servant of the LORD who was called to proclaim his Word. That identity also lies at the heart of the character of the ministerial task. The contemporary minister is a servant of the One who sent him to preach and is called to proclaim the Word. Let us consider each element in turn.

Called to Serve

God raised up prophets to serve him (Deut 18:15; Amos 2:11), a service that required close communication between God and his prophet. The relationship between God and his prophet was such that he could be known as a "man of God" (1 Kings 13:11, 18), a designation applied to Moses (Deut 33:1), Samuel (1 Sam 9:6), Shemaiah (2 Kings 12:22), Elijah (1 Kings 17:18), Elisha (2 Kings 4:7), and others (e.g., 2 Kings 23:17).

To engage men in his service, God called them and when he called, those addressed had little choice but to heed the call and obey. And so, for example, when God called Amos, the shepherd, he left his flock and became a prophet (Amos 1:1; 7:14–15). Indeed, the Hebrew word for "prophet" literally means "one who is called" or "one who has been called."[14] We

---

14 This meaning is evident from its association with a similar ancient Near Eastern word, the Akkadian *nabû*. Ludwig Koehler, Walter Baumgartner, and Johann Jakob Stamm, *The Hebrew and Aramaic Lexicon of the Old Testament*, trans. and ed. M. E. J. Richardson (Leiden: Brill,

have already seen at the beginning of this chapter how vitally important it is to recognize that today as well God calls to the special office, also that of minister of the Word.

Those whom God calls, he also equips. Moses and Jeremiah both protested that they were not able or suitable, but God who had called them also equipped them (Exod 4:13–16; Jer 1:6–10). It is a calling to service. Prophets were known as servants of the LORD. God repeatedly character-ized prophets through the mouth of Jeremiah and others as "my servants the prophets."[15] As servants they were obliged to be meticulous in doing their Master's bidding. They were completely subservient to his will. Their most important task was to be God's voice (cf. Exod 7:1–2) and to speak in his name (Dan 9:6). Because God called them, he also equipped them for their task.

Proclaimers of the gospel are also servants of God, as were Paul and Apollos (1 Cor 3:5). The Lord also equips his contemporary servants whom God calls into the ministry of the gospel today. God uses the spe-cial gifts and talents he has given to those whom he has called, but he also engages their responsibility to equip themselves for the task with prayerful dedication and a proper seminary education. Indeed, churches have the responsibility to set the bar at an appropriate level.[16] As the prophets of old, a minister of the gospel can also be called a "man of God" due to his close relationship to his Sender (1 Tim 6:11).[17] And like those spokesmen for God of Old Testament times, the minister of the Word today can count on the power of the Spirit to enable him in his task to work for the glory of God's name, and to be a blessing to those who listen. As a "man of God," a

---

2001), 661–62; H.-P. Müller, "*nābî'*," in *Theological Dictionary of the Old Testament*, ed. G. Johannes Botterweck, Helmer Ringgren, and Heinz-Josef Fabry, trans. David E. et al Green (Grand Rapids, MI: Eerdmans, 1998), 9:133.

15 Jer 7:25; 25:4; 26:5; 29:19; 35:15; 44:4; also, e.g., 1 Kings 14:18; 2 Kings 9:36; 10:10; 14:25; Isa 20:3; Ezek 38:17; Dan 9:6.

16 For this responsibility see Cornelis Van Dam, "Why a Federational Seminary?" in *Your Word is Our Light: Celebrating Fifty Years of the Canadian Reformed Theological Seminary*, ed. Cornelis Van Dam and Jason Van Vliet (Hamilton, ON: Lucerna, 2019), 14–35.

17 However, since all Christians have received the anointing of the Spirit and are "in Christ", that designation can also be applied to members of the congregation although Timothy's office remains distinct as "man of God" (cf. 1 Tim 6:11; 2 Tim 3:17); William Hendriksen, *Exposition of the Pastoral Epistles*, New Testament Commentary (Grand Rapids: Baker, 1957), 202.

minister especially needs to cultivate a close relationship with his Sender and spend time in prayer with him and so be confirmed in his calling and equipped for it. As a sinful human being, a minister cannot be an effective instrument to proclaim the gospel without the power of the Spirit from on high. As Harry Goodykoontz commented: "Unless the minister grows steadily in his own relationship to God, he will become in the end a pathetically shallow preacher and an inept pastor in times of deepest need."[18]

Proclaimer of the Word

A prophet was, above all, someone who proclaimed and heralded the word of God. For that reason, a hallmark of the prophetic message was: "thus says the LORD!" This formula introduced the authoritative divine Word. It could be for all sorts of circumstances. These words were used by Moses telling Pharaoh to let Israel go (Exod 5:1); by an unidentified prophet pronouncing judgement on the house of Eli (1 Sam 2:27–36); by Nathan informing David of God's promises for an everlasting throne and kingdom (2 Sam 7:5–17); by Isaiah encouraging Israel with God's promise of victory over Assyria (Isa 10:24–25); by Jeremiah calling Israel to repentance (Jer 4:3–4); and by Zechariah with the comforting message of hope and salvation (Zec 1:14–17). Many more examples could be given. The point is that the prophets functioned in a wide variety of situations and their messages varied, but it was always God's word, not their own, that had to be proclaimed (Deut 18:15–20; Jer 1:9). It was the word of God that gave their proclamation authority. Consequently, when the prophet's message was rejected, divine wrath followed (cf. Deut 28:15).

This duty to pass on the divine message was an awesome responsibility. The prophets had to proclaim exactly what God wanted. Not a word was to be left out of what the LORD instructed the prophet to say (cf. Jer 26:2). The message which a prophet had to give was sometimes difficult to deliver, especially, as for example in the case of Jeremiah, the message was one of judgment on God's people for their sins. Then someone like Jeremiah may have wished to keep God's Word to himself, but he could not. "There is in my heart as it were a burning fire shut up in my bones, and I am

---

18 Harry G. Goodykoontz, *The Minister in the Reformed Tradition* (Richmond, VA: John Knox Press, 1963), 141.

weary with holding it in, and I cannot" (Jer 20:9). Also bad news needed to be proclaimed as the word of the LORD (also, e.g., 2 Kings 24:2).

Ministers of the gospel are also called to proclaim and herald God's Word. That is the primary way that they are as shepherds to take care of the sheep entrusted to them by Christ.[19] However, unlike the prophets of old, the Lord God does not give preachers today new divinely inspired messages to pass on to his people. God's revelation in his Word is now complete and it is the task of ministers of the gospel to "preach the word" (2 Tim 4:2), that is the gospel (1 Tim 1:15).[20] To preach is to publicly declare the good news. As a prophet was under compulsion to pass on the divine message, so preachers today must do the same. God's Word and not their own must ring forth! A minister must be able to proclaim with conviction: "this is what the Bible says and, therefore, thus says the Lord!"

After the apostle Paul urged Timothy to preach the word, he added "be ready in season and out of season; reprove, rebuke, and exhort, with complete patience and teaching" (2 Tim 4:2). Like the prophets of old, the preacher is God's mouthpiece. The message has to go out whether people are receptive or not ("in season and out of season"); sin has to be confronted and sinners convicted ("reprove, rebuke, and exhort"). Courage is needed to proclaim and apply the Word and to confront the sins, the decadent culture, and the false gods and idols of today. The prophetic preaching task is not easy. But those called and charged to this responsibility have no choice. As the apostle Paul said: "Woe to me if I do not preach the gospel!" (1 Cor 9:16). That gospel also includes proclaiming the comfort of the forgiveness of sins through the one sacrifice of Christ (Luke 24:47; 1 Tim 1:15) and the Lord's sustaining care through all the challenges of life (cf. Rom 8). In this way the minister as a shepherd in the service of the great Shepherd feeds the flock and helps to equip it for its task in this world.

In our current image-orientated and sound-bite culture, the sense of having a sermon as the medium in which to convey the gospel has come

---

19 See the Form for the Ordination of Ministers in *Book of Praise*, 618.
20 1 Tim 1:15 literally reads: "The word is trustworthy and deserving of full acceptance, that Christ Jesus came into the world to save sinners, of whom I am the foremost." The "word of God" is divine revelation (2 Tim 2:9; Titus 1:3; 2:5).

under scrutiny and ridicule. However, Scripture underlines the importance of faithful preaching. The apostle Paul asked: "how are they to believe in him of whom they have never heard? And how are they to hear without someone preaching? . . . How beautiful are the feet of those who preach the good news! . . . So faith comes from hearing, and hearing through the word of Christ" (Rom 10:14–15, 17). As the Heidelberg Catechism puts it, faith comes "from the Holy Spirit who works it in our hearts by the preaching of the gospel" (QA 65). Every congregation member may have a personal copy of the Bible, but the proclamation of Scripture is still necessary. Although the unbelieving world may consider the gospel nonsense, the apostle Paul declared that: "It pleased God through the folly of what we preach to save those who believe . . . The foolishness of God is wiser than men" (1 Cor 1:21, 25). Faithful preaching is a key of the kingdom of heaven which opens the door to the treasures of the great King (Heidelberg Catechism, QA 83–84).

Conclusion

The Old Testament prophet and the contemporary minister of the gospel have a number of characteristics in common. Each is a man of God called to serve his sender by proclaiming his Word, in season and out of season. The task can be very difficult, but God who calls to the ministry of the Word also equips his servants. Today's preacher can take comfort in the fact that if he faithfully proclaims the gospel, the Holy Spirit will use that proclamation to work faith in human hearts of his choosing and open wide the gates to the heavenly treasures of forgiveness and reconciliation with God.

The Minister as Priest

Although the prophetic office is often considered the origin of the proclamation task of the minister of the gospel, one must not forget the continuities of the preacher's task with that of a priest of Old Testament times. These continuities are significant and should not be underestimated. To both the priest of Old Testament times and the current minister God entrusted the duty to present and teach the gospel to his people. In ancient Israel teaching was primarily done by the priests (Lev 10:11; Deut 33:10;

Mal 2:4–9), although the elders also had teaching responsibilities (Deut 31:9–12; 32:7). But it was up to the priests and the tribe of Levi in the first place to expound the gospel and to pass it on to the people (Deut 33:10; cf. 18:1–8). It was not for nothing that the Levitical cities were spread over the entire country (Num 35:1–8; Josh 21:1–42). God scattered them throughout the land because the people needed teachers of the gospel to educate them in the ways of the LORD. As the prophet Malachi put it, the priest "is the messenger of the LORD of hosts" (Mal 2:7; cf. Neh 8:1–3, 13).

Now if the Old Testament had a teaching office in the priest, then one would expect that in the new Israel of God, the church (Gal 6:16), there would also be an office with similar responsibilities. Indeed, as we have seen, the apostle Paul identified elders "who labor in preaching and teaching" (1 Tim 5:17). These elders, the ministers of today, have inherited this task from the priests. There is thus a direct continuity between the teaching task of the priest and the office of the minister of the Word.

To prevent possible misunderstanding, one point needs to be made very clearly. The minister of the gospel is not a priest. Discussing the ministerial task as a priestly one does not mean starting on a road that leads to Rome and the reintroduction of a priesthood. Scripture never calls a minister of the gospel a priest. However, the New Testament does indicate that there are priestly aspects to the ministerial task. There are certain continuities in the responsibilities of the priests and pastors today and it is beneficial to consider these. It helps us appreciate the richness of the ministerial office.

Although more could be said, there are especially two passages that we will consider. First there is Romans 15:16 and then 2 Corinthians 5:18–20. After looking at these passages, we will also consider some implications.

Romans 15:16

In Romans 15 the apostle Paul described himself as "a minister of Christ Jesus to the Gentiles." He continued by saying that this identity means that he is in "the priestly service of the gospel of God, so that the offering of the Gentiles may be acceptable, sanctified by the Holy Spirit" (Rom 15:16).

Notice that the preaching of the gospel is here understood as a priestly task. One can also translate the phrase "the priestly service of the gospel" by "ministering as a priest the gospel of God" (NASB). It is in preaching the gospel that Paul and any subsequent preacher acted as a priest.

Given the Old Testament background, such a description of the office of minister is not unexpected. The preaching task of the Levitical priests has been taken over by the New Testament office of the proclamation of the gospel. Now the purpose of Paul's preaching was that "the Gentiles might become an offering acceptable to God sanctified by the Spirit" (Rom 15:16 NIV). In an analogous way, the modern preacher as Christ's servant proclaims the gospel in the expectation that God may receive the Spirit-sanctified offering of a congregation eager and willing to serve him, as is their spiritual service (Rom 12:1–2; 1 Pet 2:5). All of this is a far cry from the Roman Catholic position that the priest offers up Christ again and again in the mass. No, when a minister of the Word acts as a priest he is preaching the gospel so that people—old and young—may be an offering acceptable to God because they have been brought to the obedience of the gospel. The purpose in view for a preacher is, to use Calvin's expression, "the offering to God of souls purified by faith."[21]

When speaking of the present day minister taking over the proclamation task of the priest, we should also take note of a prophecy in the Old Testament. When Isaiah predicted the inclusion of the Gentiles into the church, he included the promise that the Lord would select some of them to be priests and Levites (Isa 66:21). Since the Old Testament worship has been abrogated, these priests and Levites can only mean the ministers of the gospel. They are the priests and Levites of today.[22]

We now turn to a second passage, 2 Corinthians 5:18–20.

---

21 John Calvin, *The Epistles of Paul the Apostle to the Romans and to the Thessalonians*, trans. Ross MacKenzie, Calvin's Commentaries (Grand Rapids: Eerdmans, 1960), 310–11.

22 John Calvin, *Commentary on the Book of the Prophet Isaiah*, trans. William Pringle (Grand Rapids: Baker, 1984), 4:436–37; Edward J. Young, *The Book of Isaiah*, New International Commentary of the Old Testament (Grand Rapids: Eerdmans, 1965–72), 3:535; similarly "The Form of Presbyterial Church Government"(1645) in *The Directory for the Publick Worship of God Agreed Upon by the Assembly of Divines at Westminster* (Philadelphia: B Franklin, 1745), 51.

2 Corinthians 5:18–20

The preaching of the gospel as a priestly task can also be seen in 2 Corinthians 5:18–20. In Old Testament times, a priest administered the reconciliation between God and his people. He did this by way of offering sacrifices, teaching the law, and giving the priestly blessing. It was this ministry of reconciliation which God gave to his apostles and their co-workers. The apostle Paul writes that God:

> gave us the ministry of reconciliation; that is, in Christ God was reconciling the world to himself, not counting their trespasses against them, and entrusting to us the message of reconciliation. Therefore, we are ambassadors for Christ, God making his appeal through us. We implore you on behalf of Christ, be reconciled to God. (2 Cor 5: 18–20)

Within the context of our present discussion, three inferences can be drawn from this passage.

First, as in the Old Testament, there is also in the New Testament church a special service or ministry (*diakonia*), "the ministry of reconciliation." This ministry restores peace between God and human beings, a peace that had been lost because of sin (cf. Rom 5:1, 10; 16:20; Col 1:19–20).

Second, this ministry of reconciliation, which had been entrusted to the priests in the Old Testament, has been committed in the New Testament church to Christ's ambassadors, such as Paul and his co-workers. Being in a priestly service of reconciliation also meant that the apostolic calling included praying for those under their care (e.g. Rom 1:9–10; 2 Cor 13:7; Eph 1:16). Likewise, a minister of the gospel remembers his congregation in his prayers. God's people are on his heart and always before him as the names of the tribes of Israel were on the Old Testament high priestly breastpiece when he entered God's presence (Exod 28:21, 29). Also, as the high priest went into God's presence with prayer for the people, symbolized with the cloud of incense (Lev 16:12–13; cf. Rev 8:3–4), so a minister of the gospel can also be expected to do.[23]

---

23 On the ministry and public prayer, J. Smith, *Prayers of the Saints*, The Reformed Guardian (Armadale, Western Australia: Reformed Guardian, 2010).

Third, as the priests in ancient Israel not only acted on God's instructions, but also spoke for him when teaching and explaining his Word
to the people,[24] so the ambassadors in the New Testament church speak for
God with the authority given by Christ. Such ambassadors speak not only
on behalf of God, but also in his place ("God making his appeal through
us"). The enduring ambassadorial office in the church is that of minister or
teaching elder. Those holding this office are charged to proclaim the Word
of God, as a herald (Rom 10:14–15; 2 Tim 4:2; cf. 1 Tim 4:13–14). This
proclamation is central for the ministry of reconciliation. The message is:
"We implore you on behalf of Christ, be reconciled to God" (2 Cor 5:20).

And so the office of preaching and teaching the gospel essentially
replaces the Old Testament priest in the official ministry of reconciliation
and it is little wonder that the preaching and teaching task is mentioned
as a separate office. We see this, for example, in Ephesians 4:11 where besides apostles, prophets, and evangelists, also "shepherds and teachers" are
mentioned as Christ's gift to his church. The reference to "shepherds and
teachers" can best be considered to refer to the same office, namely that of
the teaching elder.[25] The ruling elder is not mentioned. Teachers are also
mentioned as being present, along with prophets, in the church at Antioch
(Acts 13:1). Furthermore, the apostle Paul mentions the office of teacher
after apostles and prophets in 1 Corinthians 12:28. This clear differenti-
ation of the teaching office, with its own special responsibilities and ac-
countability, sets it apart from the ruling elder.

Now the qualifications for the elder or overseer are listed in well-
known places such as 1 Timothy 3:1–7 and Titus 1:5–9. These qualifications
count for both the teaching and the ruling elder. No distinction is made in
these passages. This seems to imply that beyond these basic qualifications,
the teaching elder must have a special gift for teaching and exhortation.
That seems to be the point of the apostle Paul when he combines different
gifts with different people in Romans 12 where he writes: "We have different gifts, according to the grace given us. If a man's gift is prophesying,

---

24 See earlier in this chapter and Lev 10:11; Deut 17:10–11; 33:10; Hos 4:1, 6; Mal 2:6–7.
25 Hendriksen, *Exposition of Ephesians*, 197; L. Floor, *Efeziërs: Één in Christus*, Commentaar Op
    Het Nieuwe Testament. Derde Serie (Kampen: Kok, 1995), 153.

let him use it in proportion to his faith. If it is serving, let him serve; if it is teaching, let him teach; if it is exhorting, let him exhort" (Rom 12:6–8). The one with the gift of teaching should use it as a teacher and the one with a gift of exhortation, as an exhorter. These last two gifts are vital for the office of a teaching elder or minister. It stands to reason that a priest in ancient Israel would have been specially trained for his task in the ministry of reconciliation. Also in the New Testament church only the best preparation possible is sufficient to honor the responsibilities that the risen Christ gives to his ambassadors and messengers. In light of the special demands and expectations for the teaching elder, beyond that of a ruling elder, it is understandable that a distinction was made between the teaching and ruling elder as two separate offices. It is in this light that we must read 1 Timothy 5:17 which speaks of the elders who direct the affairs of the church, or rule, and the elders who preach and teach.

Some Consequences of the Distinctions

Earlier we saw that a minister of the gospel is a teaching elder. He holds an elder office along with the ruling elder. Perhaps especially when we reflect on the priestly aspects of the office of minister, we realize how important it is to distinguish between the two elder offices. It is not just an academic exercise. It has some very real ramifications. I would like to mention two implications, first, for their specific tasks and second for their support.

First, with respect to their task, in Old Testament times, only the priests were ordained and designated by the LORD to function in the official service of reconciliation, be it by sacrificing, teaching, and blessing the people. Anyone else who attempted to do their specific task had to be put to death.[26]

Ministers of the gospel, the teaching elders, may function in the ministry of reconciliation as spokesmen for God (cf. 2 Cor 5:18–20). In this sense they are heirs of this aspect of the Old Testament office of priest.

---

26 For the anointing of the priests for holy service see: Exod 28:41; 30:30; Lev 8:30); for the exclusive privilege of the priests and the penalty of death for others, see Num 3:5–10, 38; 16:40; cf. Lev 22:10.

As the priests of old, they teach, exhort, and bless the congregation before God. The force of the analogy would seem to indicate that normally only the teaching elders may administer the Word officially as spokesman for God in the public worship services. Reformed churches therefore have the practice that when no ordained minister is present, the officiating elder reads a sermon prepared by a minister. Also, in giving the blessing, an officiating elder simply reads the words of Scripture (e.g. Num 6:24–26; 2 Cor 13:14), but he does not raise his hands in blessing. That has always been the prerogative of the priest. Following the pattern of Aaron, after the priest had brought the sacrifices for atonement, he would give the blessing (Lev 9:22). In this way the priest symbolically and officially administered the gospel of reconciliation on the people. With the giving of the blessing, the priest was God's instrument to place his name on his people (Num 6:27) thereby symbolizing how God claimed those blessed for himself.[27] Also beyond Old Testament times, this practice was the norm. Synagogue services normally ended with the priestly blessing given by a priest with uplifted hands (Num 6:22–27). If there was no priest, no blessing with upraised hands was given; instead, the words of benediction were simply recited.[28] It therefore stands to reason that today lifting the hands in blessing should be the sole privilege of an ordained minister of the Word who has the authority to officially administer the gospel of reconciliation. They are the ones who after all have received "the ministry of reconciliation" (2 Cor 5:18; cf. Heb 5:4) as the Reformed form for the ordination of ministers of the gospel reminds us.[29]

---

27 For the priestly prerogative to bless, Deut 21:5; Num 6:22–27; Deut 10:8; 1 Chron 23:13; cf. Lev 9:22. By way of exception, theocratic kings, David and Solomon, also blessed the people as a whole. David did so when the ark was brought into Jerusalem (2 Sam 6:18; 1 Chron 16:2) and Solomon at the dedication of the temple (1 Kings 8:55; 2 Chron 6:3). On the significance of the priestly blessing, also see Van Dam, *Worship Matters*, 95–106.

28 See Emil Schürer, *The History of the Jewish People in the Age of Jesus Christ (175 B.C. - A.D. 135)*, vol. 2, ed & revised by Geza Vermes, et al. (Edinburgh: T. & T. Clark, 1979), 453–54.

29 See further Ryan M. McGraw, "The Benediction in Corporate Worship," *The Confessional Presbyterian* 7 (2011): 116–20; A. N. Hendriks, *Om de bediening van de geest: bijdragen over het ambt, de prediking en het pastoraat* (Kampen: Van den Berg, 1983), 83–93; Hughes Oliphant Old, *The Patristic Roots of Reformed Worship*, Zürcher Beiträge Zur Reformationsgeschichte (Zürich: Theologischer Verlag, 1975), 332–34; Hughes Oliphant Old, *Leading in Prayer: A Workbook for Ministers* (Grand Rapids, MI: Eerdmans, 1995), 350–51.The duty of the minister of the gospel "to bless the people from God" is specifically mentioned in *The Form of Presbyterial Church Government " in The Directory for the Publick Worship*, 52.

A second implication of the distinction between the ruling and teaching elder (or minister) relates to their support. Because the priests and Levites were employed full time in the ministry of reconciliation, the LORD guaranteed the livelihood of the tribe of Levi by granting them the tithe as their inheritance (Num 18:21–24). Ministers of the gospel are likewise to receive their livelihood from the gospel (1 Cor 9:9–14). As in Old Testament times, there is no general mandate for God's people today to support financially the ruling elder. We do read in 1 Timothy 5 that:

Let the elders who rule well be considered worthy of double honor, especially those who labor in preaching and teaching. For the Scripture says, "You shall not muzzle an ox when it treads out the grain," and "The laborer deserves his wages." (1 Tim 5:17–18)

This would seem to indicate that those laboring in preaching and teaching, namely the minister of the Word, should especially be honored and such honor should include wages. The ruling elder should also be honored and financial support is not necessarily excluded in showing that honor, but this support especially applies to the minister of the gospel.[30]

Conclusion

There are continuities between the Old Testament office of priest and the teaching elder or minister of the gospel. This background of the office of minister of the Word is evident from the way the apostle described the proclamation of the gospel as a priestly service (Rom 15:16) and as an administration of reconciliation between God and his people (2 Cor 5:18–20)— a duty formerly characterizing the Levitical priesthood (e.g., Lev 1:4; 4:20; 5:16). Furthermore, this continuity with the office of the Old Testament priest also underlines the difference between the ruling elder and the teaching elder, who is ordained into the ministry of the Word.

The Minister as King

This heading may be a surprise. When we think of a king, we generally think of someone ruling authoritatively with all the good and bad con-

---

30 Herman Ridderbos, *De pastorale brieven*, Commentaar op het Nieuwe Testament (Kampen: Kok, 1967), 138–39; Hendriksen, *The Pastoral Epistles*, 180–81.

notations such a concept may bring to mind. A minister of the Word does not rule in that sense. He is above all a servant (cf. Matt 20:26–28; John 13:12–17).[31] There is however a very important element in biblical kingship as God ordained it for Israel that is relevant for the ministerial task.

The King as Shepherd

An important Old Testament image for the office of king is that of the shepherd. At David's anointing to be ruler over God's people, the Israelites recalled that the LORD had said to David: "You shall be shepherd of my people Israel, and you shall be prince [*nāgîd*] over Israel" (2 Sam 5:2). David was anointed as leader (*nāgîd*), that is, to be God's representative on earth. He is of course elsewhere called King David, but it is significant that his anointing was as a leader, as God's representative.[32] As such David and the kings who succeeded him were to function as under-shepherds of the LORD, who is the chief shepherd of his people (e.g., Gen 49:24; Ps 80:1; 95:6–7). God led his people "like a flock by the hand of Moses and Aaron" (Ps 77:20), leading them "like sheep" through the wilderness (Ps 78:52). Since the LORD used human shepherds to guide his flock, he held his kings responsible to shepherd his people with the loving care which he expected of them, and he denounced those who did not do so (Jer 23:1–2; 50:6; Ezek 34:1–24; Zec 11:17).

Implications for the Office of Minister

There are at least two profound implications of this shepherd-king aspect for the ministerial task. The first is the matter of caring for and feeding the flock with biblical nurture. This responsibility comes into focus when we consider how the LORD as Shepherd cares for his sheep as confessed in Psalm 23. He accompanies them through all of life and in all circumstances; he comforts and guides them into the green pastures. The Shepherd's loving care is also described by Isaiah: "He will tend his flock

---

31 It is also noteworthy that the apostles identified themselves as servants of God and of the people. Phil 1:1; James 1:1; 2 Pet 1:1; Jude 1:1; also Goodykoontz, *The Minister in the Reformed Tradition*, 28.

32 On the meaning and significance of *nāgîd*, see Cornelis Van Dam, "The Office of David: A Preliminary Look at David as *nagid*," *Koinōnia* 1, no. 1 (1978): 5–19 and Cornelis Van Dam, "The Messianic Office of David as Son of God" (forthcoming).

like a shepherd; he will gather the lambs in his arms; he will carry them in his bosom and gently lead those that are with young" (Isa 40:10–11). Not surprisingly, when the Son of God came into this world, he revealed the Father by being the Good Shepherd (John 10:11; cf. 14:9). He truly cared for the people. "He had compassion for them, because they were harassed and helpless, like sheep without a shepherd" (Matt 9:36). The sheep recognized the voice of the Good Shepherd and followed him (John 10:14, 16, 27). Christ's love for the sheep is such that he even laid down his life for them (John 10:15).

It is the love and care for the flock of this Shepherd that ministers of the Word are to emulate today. Indeed, the New Testament Greek word translated "pastor" is literally "shepherd" (*poimēn*; Eph 4:11). As with the Israelite kings, shepherding involves having authority and ruling. Indeed, the Greek verb "to shepherd" (*poimainō*) can be translated "to rule" (Rev 2:27; 19:15). Ministers are shepherds of the flock entrusted to them by the great Shepherd, Jesus Christ who called them to this task. Pastors, like the elders, therefore, are to shepherd the sheep entrusted to them (1 Pet 5:1–3). The Lord Jesus said to Peter and so to ministers as well: Feed my lambs; tend my sheep; feed my sheep (John 21:15–17). Those who are straying and wandering need special attention. A conscientious shepherd will look for them and minister to them in such a way that they hear the voice of the Good Shepherd (Matt 18:12–13; John 10:27–28).

The second closely related implication for a minister of the gospel as a shepherd-king is his duty to lead the flock and protect it from the evil one. The holy obligation to safeguard the sheep from danger is one that the apostles highlighted. Paul counselled the Ephesian elders to pay careful attention to themselves and to the flock of which the Holy Spirit had made them overseers. He then continued: "I know that after my departure fierce wolves will come in among you, not sparing the flock; and from among your own selves will arise men speaking twisted things, to draw away the disciples after them. Therefore be alert" (Acts 20:29–31). The sheep need to be protected so that they are not "carried about by every wind of doctrine, by human cunning, by craftiness in deceitful schemes" (Eph 4:14). A preacher of the gospel like Timothy needed to fight the good fight (1 Tim 1:18) and to be "a good soldier of Christ Jesus" (1 Tim 2:2) in the war against the evil one. Safeguarding the sheep is a huge responsibility since Satan will never miss a chance to attack and malign the gospel and attempt to lure the sheep away from their Shepherd Jesus Christ. In today's digitally interconnected world the devil's potential avenues of infiltration into the minds and hearts of believers are many. It is, therefore, also very important that the authority of the minister to lead the flock is recognized.

Ministerial Authority

The biblical injunction remains important: "Obey your leaders and submit to them, for they are keeping watch over your souls, as those who will have to give an account" (Heb 13:17). Indeed, the responsibility of ministers of the Word for the well-being of the sheep is awesome. As those who are to bring the pure word of God to the people, they are to lead the flock into the nurturing rich pastures of God's Word and so equip them as children of God with the glorious gospel to live holy meaningful lives in Christ, in a sinful world. If a minister sees a danger threatening the congregation, he needs to be like the watchmen on the city walls and warn of the coming threat to their well-being. Their responsibility is so weighty that God told the prophet Ezekiel that if he, as a watchman for the house of Israel, did not warn the people of danger which he saw coming, and souls entrusted to him perished as a result of his negligence, their blood would be required from him (Ezek 33:1–9). Ministers are accountable to God for the safety of the flock. For that reason, the sheep must obey their shepherd and submit to him when he faithfully ministers the Word to them. If he does not proclaim the true gospel, he has no authority.

It is the Word that a minister proclaims and applies to the lives of his sheep that gives him the authority that demands obedience from the flock. The pastor is not to be obeyed because of any imagined higher status as a minister or his personality. His person as such does not give him authority. The authority is found in the Word of God. And therefore, his office as spokesman for God is the critical element. He is to be obeyed as one called by the Lord to proclaim the gospel and shepherd the flock safely to the great destination.[33] Simply put, when the sheep hear the voice of the

---

33   See further Calvin, *Institutes*, 4.8.2.

Good Shepherd through the mouth of his servant on earth, they have no option but to obey (John 10:3–4). Not to do so could endanger their eternal well-being. It is the authority of Christ himself that needs to be recognized in his human representative. That is why those who are to be obeyed (Heb 13:17) are characterized as leaders "who spoke to you the word of God" (Heb 13:7). They are to be known as "rightly handling the word of truth" (2 Tim 2:15). Their task is "to make the word of God fully known" (Col 1:25). The apostolic request to the Thessalonian Christians is therefore appropriate: "We ask you, brothers, to respect those who labor among you and are over you in the Lord and admonish you, and to esteem them very highly because of their work" (1 Thess 5:12–13). And their work, their office, is to pass on and proclaim the word of the Good Shepherd.

God's Word is powerful beyond our imagination. As the LORD said through his prophet Isaiah: "my word . . . that goes out from my mouth; it shall not return to me empty, but it shall accomplish that which I purpose, and shall succeed in the thing for which I sent it" (Isa 55:11). "All Scripture is breathed out by God and profitable for teaching, for reproof, for correction, and for training in righteousness" (2 Tim 3:16). Indeed, "the word of God is living and active, sharper than any two-edged sword, piercing to the division of soul and of spirit, of joints and of marrow, and discerning the thoughts and intentions of the heart" (Heb 4:12). The minister, as servant shepherd-king under his Sender, the King of glory (Ps 24:8), wields this powerful sword when he proclaims God's Word. Indeed, the preaching of the gospel is a key that opens and shuts the door to the riches of the kingdom of heaven (Heidelberg Catechism, QA 84).

And so when Christians heed the voice of the Good Shepherd, they realize with a true faith the promises of the gospel such as the forgiveness of sins and fellowship with God. Then the reality of which Psalm 23 speaks is experienced. Believers will lack nothing. Their souls will be restored as the Shepherd leads them in righteous paths. Even though the valleys of life will be dark and even deadly, there is no need to fear evil since the Lord gives true comfort. The Good Shepherd will ensure that those who heed his voice will dwell in the house of the LORD forever.

But, if there is unbelief, the same proclamation of the gospel closes the door to these riches of the kingdom of heaven for they are told that "the

95

wrath of God and eternal condemnation rest on them as long as they do not repent" (Heidelberg Catechism, QA 84).

To be a spokesman of the chief Shepherd is the glorious task of the minister of the gospel as he lovingly shepherds and leads his flock while constantly on the lookout for their welfare and safety. In Christ's name he is opening the door to his kingdom. But the minister's task also includes shutting the door to the kingdom for those who do not believe. The authority to proclaim this gospel as Christ's herald is no small matter! A minister is an instrument of God for opening and shutting the door to the kingdom. It is no small thing to hold such an office with God-given royal authority on behalf of "the King of kings and Lord of lords" (1 Tim 6:15; Rev 19:16).

To shepherd the sheep is an awesome task given to the ruling and teaching elders. It requires knowing the sheep. Ben Arbour put it well when he noted that "pastoral leadership *requires* relationship." Therefore, "delegating this responsibility to Sunday school teachers or small group coordinators, important as those roles may be, amounts to an abdication of leadership, especially when we consider the type of authority required for biblical shepherding."[34] As we saw, it needs the authority of a shepherd-king, exercised according to the example of the Good Shepherd who knows his sheep (John 10:14).

Conclusion

Since the Old Testament kings were the LORD's shepherds in his service to take care of his flock, the people of Israel, we can see that the office of minister of the Word has a royal aspect to it. He is God's instrument to shepherd the flock, his people. His duty therefore includes caring for and feeding the sheep in his charge and leading them into the nurture of God's Word so that they can be kept safe from the adversary, Satan. The pastor must alert the flock to any danger that threatens. And they are to obey the authoritative Word which the minister proclaims. After all, faithful preaching means that the voice of the Good Shepherd is heard, and that voice must always be obeyed.

---

34 Ben Arbour, "Shepherding like the Good Shepherd," *Modern Reformation* 22, no. 2 (2013): 15–16, italics are original.

The Seriousness and Dignity of the Office of Minister

Ministers of the gospel are men called by the Lord to be his spokesmen for the proclamation of the gospel and the edification of the church. These servants of God who have this high calling are of themselves not notable or imposing. They are mere vessels of clay (2 Cor 4:7). But as Calvin observed, the office has prestige and dignity. It is a high honor. "How beautiful . . . are the feet of those who bring good news, who proclaim peace, who bring good tidings, who proclaim salvation" (Isa 52:7). "This office could not be more splendidly adorned than when he said: 'He who hears you hears me, and he who rejects you rejects me'" (Luke 10:16). Indeed, the ministry is a glorious ministry that "brings righteousness!" (2 Cor 3:9).[35]

Not surprisingly, such a ministry that speaks with divine authority when proclaiming God's Word requires a level of dignity or gravity (in Greek: *semnos* and *semnotēs*). This is specifically required for leaders in the church (1 Tim 3:4, 8; Titus 2:7) and is understood to be included with other characteristics such as being sober-minded and respectable (1 Tim 3:2). The dignity which office bearers are to exhibit, is, as Howard Marshall put it, to be "reflecting seriousness of purpose and solemnity which are visible in one's conduct and speech." This is a dignity that commands respect.[36] Such dignity on the part of ministers is in danger of being lost in our egalitarian culture.

The Challenge of Current Culture

This erosion of dignity can sometimes be seen in the central ministerial task of preaching the Word which has continuities with the prophetic, priestly, and shepherd-king offices. Reformed preaching is sometimes in danger of being pressured and influenced by evangelical preaching as seen on the electronic media. Such preaching can be larded with personal illustrations, stories, and even jokes. But the focus should be on the Word.

---

35 Calvin, *Institutes*, 4.3.3.

36 I. Howard Marshall, *A Critical and Exegetical Commentary on the Pastoral Epistles*, in collaboration with Philip H. Towner, The International Critical Commentary (Edinburgh: T&T Clark, 1999), 188; also see Philip H. Towner, *The Letters to Timothy and Titus*, New International Commentary on the New Testament (Grand Rapids / Cambridge, UK: Eerdmans, 2006), 262, note 8.

That is what needs to be proclaimed (2 Tim 4:2). To preach Christ crucified (1 Cor 2:2) is to proclaim the man of sorrows who "descended into hell" for us. With all the joy of redemption, the awesome sacrifice required to make that happen should in no way be trivialized. Proclamation is passing on the very Word of God. That includes confronting sinners with the demands of God's law. Jon Payne noted that "a troubling trend in contemporary preaching is the emphasis upon the indicatives of Scripture to the neglect of the imperatives." In other words, only emphasizing the function of the law as a mirror to expose our sins and need for salvation is to focus on the indicative. However, the preacher also needs to stress the imperative; namely, that each of these commands needs to be obeyed. Payne acknowledged that "some may be secretly worried that preaching God's commands will potentially undermine the gospel" and "lead to new forms of legalism or even weaken the believer's assurance." But he also noted that "the faithful preaching of biblical imperatives (that which is built on gospel indicatives) in no way compromises the good news. The very structure of Paul's Epistles underscores this point."[37]

The minister of the Word also needs to project the dignity of his office in his demeanor and appearance. Now one may object and say: "But we live in a culture that frowns on dignity. It's now okay, for example, to come on the pulpit in casual dress or visit members of the congregation in clothes you would wear when working in the garden. People do not like too much formality." The difficulty with such objections is that they forget that there are biblical norms which one should not forget. These norms transcend and counter the current culture. We have rightly gotten rid of pompous clerical vestments, but we should still retain the dignity of the office by wearing clothes as a minister that reflect something of the high calling of being in God's service in the ministry of reconciliation.[38] Jon Payne put it well: "The preacher is called to be a royal ambassador of the crucified, risen, and exalted Lord Jesus Christ (2 Cor. 5:20). The preacher's message and appearance, therefore, should reflect the seriousness and dignity of his office

---

37 Jon D. Payne, "Hipster or Herald?" *Modern Reformation* 22, no. 4 (2013): 12; David P. Murray, "Serious Preaching in a Comedy Culture," *Puritan Reformed Journal* 3, no. 1 (2011): 328–38; see also John Carrick, *The Imperative of Preaching* (Carlisle, PA: Banner of Truth Trust, 2002).

38 See also Van Dam, *Worship Matters*, 231–45.

and divine calling." Furthermore, "dignity in preaching is severely impaired when pastors refuse to dress suitably for the occasion, or even appropriately for their age. There are reasons why presidents and prime ministers dress formally. They hold a dignified office, and they want people to take them, and what they say, seriously."[39]

Christian Dignity

Actually, what especially applies to the minister of the gospel does apply to all Christians as well. It is not right to expect only from a minister a dignity that should characterize all Christians. Do they not all share in Christ's anointing as prophets, priests, and kings? The office of Christians is also awesome. In their talk and walk they are to show themselves as sharing in Christ's anointing. Christians are to pursue whatever is dignified, that is, honorable or "worthy of respect" (Phil 4:8 NET). Christians are to pray that they may lead lives that are "godly and dignified in every way" (1 Tim 2:2). Titus is told that both old and young are to be dignified along with being sober-minded and self-controlled (Titus 2:2, 6–7). The word that translates into "dignified" (Greek: *semnos* and *semnotēs*) does not mean that Christians are to put on a pretentious air of gravity or act as if they are far above others.[40] Rather, the original term indicates that Christians are to project themselves in their interaction with others as sincerely morally upright and noble. Marshall puts it well. "A Christian's behaviour should be such as to win respect from other people because they take life seriously and devoutly and do not trifle."[41]

If this is true of Christians, how much more is it of ministers of the Word.

Conclusion

The office of minister of the Word of God is a high calling and a great gift of God. Through the means of this office, Almighty God is

---

39   Payne, "Hipster or Herald?" 13.
40   Dangers noted when discussing these issues by Wilhelmus à Brakel, *The Christian's Reasonable Service*, ed. Joel R. Beeke, trans. Bartel Elshout (Grand Rapids, MI: Reformation Heritage Books, 1992–95), 2:133.
41   I. Howard Marshall, *The Pastoral Epistles*, 189; also see Towner, *Timothy and Titus*, 175.

pleased to have his Word proclaimed to his people. It is an office which brings together so much of the Old Testament offices which functioned in anticipation of the coming Messiah. Although we cannot equate the office of minister with any of these Old Testament offices, we have seen that the office of a minister of the Word does have continuities and aspects of the Old Testament offices of prophet, priest, and king. We need to maintain the high view of this office as Scripture presents it and treasure it as coming from God's hands.

There are many challenges to this office in our egalitarian culture which wants to erase all distinctions and has little respect for any authority, including that of our triune God. But as Calvin reminds us: "God often commended the dignity of the ministry by all possible marks of approval in order that it might be held among us in highest honor and esteem, even as the most excellent of all things. God testifies that, in raising up teachers for them, he bestows a singular benefit upon men when he bids the prophet exclaim, 'Beautiful are the feet and blessed the coming of those who announce peace [Is 52:7].'"[42] Elsewhere Calvin notes that "the fact that the Church is ruled by the preaching of the Word, is not a human invention, but the appointment of Christ." Indeed, through the preaching of the gospel "the Lord wishes to govern his Church, that it may remain safe in this world, and ultimately obtain its complete perfection."[43]

Let us continue to treasure and love this office and accord it the authority and dignity it entails.

---

42 Calvin, *Institutes*, 4.3.3.
43 Calvin, *Galatians, Ephesians*, 178.

7

The Preacher as Teacher: The Importance of Catechetical Proclamation

An important duty of a minister of the gospel is to teach the congregation the biblical truths in an organized way, that is, to instruct them in the doctrine of the Word of God. That doctrine has been summarized in the Reformed confessions. The Heidelberg Catechism was specifically designed to be a teaching tool. It is therefore used to teach the youth in the Catechism classes during the week. This same confession is also used to instruct the congregation in the second service on the Lord's Day.

Questions have been raised about the practice of confessional preaching, that is, using a human document such as the Catechism as an aid to preach the Word of God. It is, therefore, good to take a closer look at this practice. In this chapter we will consider some historical background to confessional preaching, objections to catechetical preaching, the decrease of such preaching, and the blessing of catechetical preaching.

Historical Background

A quick overview of the history of catechetical preaching is helpful in underlining how important this type of preaching has always been considered to be. Confessional or catechetical preaching can be defined as instructing God's people in the basic truths of the Christian faith. Many of these truths are systematically expounded in the Catechism by a discussion of the Apostles' Creed (LD 7–22), the sacraments (LD 25–30), the Ten Commandments (LD 34–44), and the Lord's Prayer (LD 45–52), for a total of 37 of the 52 Lord's Days. Now it is precisely these doctrines that were prominent in being systematically expounded for God's people from the very beginning of the early Christian Church. This fact is evident from the sermons of Cyril of Jerusalem (313–386), John Chrysostom (347–407),

Theodore of Mopsuestia (350–428), and Augustine of Hippo (354–430).[1] So catechetical preaching is nothing new. It was there from the beginning.

Although doctrinal teaching was neglected during the Middle Ages, its importance nevertheless continued to be recognized. In 789, bishops had to see to it that priests preserved the true faith by preaching on the Lord's Prayer, and in 852 every priest was told to study the Lord's Prayer and the Apostles' Creed and preach sermons on them. In 1281, the Synod of Lambeth in England told the priests to deliver sermons on the Ten Commandments, the Apostles' Creed, and the sacraments, along with other subjects. Similarly, in 1294, priests in the Netherlands were charged to preach on the Lord's Prayer and the Apostles' Creed, and three times a year they were expected to preach on the Ten Commandments and the sacraments. In 1498, a book was published in Germany extolling the virtues of preaching the contents of the Apostles' Creed and the Ten Commandments. So, from this brief overview one can see that regular systematic preaching on key elements of doctrine as found in our Catechism was known from the very beginning of the Christian church.

It was, however, especially the sixteenth century Reformation that revived catechetical preaching. Luther, Zwingli, and Calvin promoted it. This preaching was enormously stimulated by the publication of the Heidelberg Catechism. It was designed for preaching. Elector Frederick III, the ruler of the German province, the Palatinate, had commissioned the writing of the Heidelberg Catechism. In the preface of the first edition, published in 1563, he exhorted preachers to instill the contents of this Catechism into the minds of the common people by preaching from it. Indeed, in the same year, he included instructions for the use of the Heidelberg Catechism in the Church Order of the Palatinate. The Catechism was divided into 52 sections called Lord's Days. In addition to preaching from each Lord's Day over the course of a year, the minister was also to read

---

1   For the preceding and what follows, see Joel R. Beeke, "Catechism Preaching," *Puritan Reformed Journal* 7 (2015): 217–18, Nicolaas H. Gootjes, "Catechism Preaching," in *Teaching and Preaching the Word: Studies in Dogmatics and Homiletics*, ed. and comp. Cornelis Van Dam (Winnipeg, MB: Premier, 2010), 389–92, and A. N. Hendriks, "Preaching from the Catechism," *Diakonia* 1, no. 3 (1988): 2–8; Daniel R. Hyde, "The Principle and Practice of Preaching in the Heidelberg Catechism," *Puritan Reformed Journal* 1 (2009): 114.

from the Heidelberg Catechism each Lord's Day so that within 9 weeks the entire Catechism was heard. Furthermore, during the service the minister would ask the questions and the catechumens would answer them in the presence of the entire congregation.[2]

By 1566 preaching from the Heidelberg Catechism also spread to the Netherlands. In 1586, the Synod of The Hague required all ministers to preach from the Heidelberg Catechism during the second service on Sunday. Very important and telling is that the famous Synod of Dort (1618-1619) reaffirmed this decision of 1586 by approving Article 68 of the Dort Church Order which reads: "Ministers shall on each Lord's Day, ordinarily in the afternoon sermons, briefly explain the sum of Christian doctrine contained in the catechism which at present is accepted in the Netherlands Churches in such a way that it may be completed annually, following the division of the catechism itself made for that purpose."[3] This directive is reflected in the second half of Article 52 of the Canadian Reformed Church Order: "The consistory shall ensure that, as a rule, once every Sunday the doctrine of God's Word as summarized in the Heidelberg Catechism is proclaimed." The United Reformed Churches in North America also practice confessional preaching. Article 40 of their Church Order (2018) reads: "At one of the services each Lord's Day, the minister shall ordinarily preach the Word as summarized in the Three Forms of Unity, with special attention given to the Heidelberg Catechism by treating its Lord's Days in sequence."

Over against objections to the 1586 decision mandating catechetical preaching, the Synod of Dort (1618-1619) responded by stating, among other things, the following, here presented in summary form:[4]

---

2   Peter Y. De Jong, "Comments on Catechetical Preaching (1)," *Mid-America Journal of Theology* 1, no. 2 (1985): 173–75; Beeke, "Catechism Preaching," 219.

3   For this translation, see Richard DeRidder, trans & comp, *The Church Orders of the Sixteenth Century Reformed Churches of the Netherlands: Together with Their Social, Political, and Ecclesiastical Context*, with the assistance of Peter H. Jonker and Leonard Verduin (Grand Rapid, MI: Calvin Theological Seminary, 1987), 555, for the Dutch decisions see F. L. Bos, *De orde der kerk toegelicht met kerkelijke besluiten uit vier eeuwen* ('S-Gravenhage: Uitgeverij Guido de Bres, 1950), 245–48.

4   See the digest in Idzerd Van Dellen and Martin Monsma, *The Church Order Commentary* (Grand Rapids: Zondervan, 1941), 279; for the original decision made on November 27, 1618, see *Acta, of Handelingen der Nationale Synode: In de Naam Van Onze Heere Jezus Christus: Gehouden Door Autoriteit der Hoogmogende Heren Staten-Generaal der Verenigde Nederlanden Te Dordrecht*

1. Ministers who fail to preach Catechism sermons would be censured. These sermons should be brief and understandable to the common people.

2. Even if the attendance in the second service is small and only his family is present, the minister should still preach a Catechism sermon and so set a good example for the flock.

3. Every church should if at all possible have its own minister. If one minister serves two or more congregations, the Catechism sermon should be held at least every other Sunday afternoon.

4. Church visitors had to carefully note that Catechism sermons are held. Negligent and unwilling ministers were to be reported to Classis for censure and communicant members who refused to attend the Catechism sermons also had to be censured.

These responses show how critically important the Synod of Dort considered preaching from the Heidelberg Catechism.

It should be noted that the foreign delegates from Great Britain, from different parts of Germany, and from Switzerland who attended the Synod of Dort were in strong agreement with the necessity of catechetical preaching and thus supported Article 68 of the Church Order. In other words, the whole Reformed world understood and supported the necessity of sound doctrinal preaching.[5]

In sum, there is a very strong tradition for confessional preaching extending all the way back to the early church that we need to be aware of.

---

in de Jaren 1618 en 1619: Hier Zijn Ook Bij Opgenomen de Volledige Beoordelingen Van de Vijf Artikelen en de Post-Acta of Nahandelingen, reprint of the original Dutch edition of J.H. Donner and S.A. van den Hoorn (Houten: Den Hertog, 1987), 24–25 (the 14th session of the synod).

5   For the sentiments of the foreign delegates, see *Acta Dordrecht 1618–19*, 25–35 (the 15th session of the synod); also see Gootjes, "Catechism Preaching," 396–99; for the Catechism in the Netherlands, see Ronald Cammenga, "The Homiletical Use of the Heidelberg Catechism: An Examination of the Practice of Systematic Preaching of the Heidelberg Catechism in the Dutch Reformed Tradition," *Protestant Reformed Theological Journal* 41 (2007): 2–10; for an excellent overview of the second (catechetical) service, see Donald Sinnema, "The Second Sunday Service in the Early Dutch Reformed Tradition," *Calvin Theological Journal* 32 (1997): 298–333.

Objections to Catechism Preaching

There were, however, some strong objections to Catechism preaching: the Catechism is made equal to the Word of God; abstract doctrine is preached; it is too repetitive; and the Catechism is out of date. Let us consider each of these objections. In the process, we will also begin to see the true nature and blessing of such preaching.

The Catechism is Made Equal to the Word of God

Catechism preaching faced some hurdles in the Netherlands of the sixteenth century. Especially the Arminians objected. They objected that such preaching gave too much honor to a human document. Indeed, they wanted the Synod of Dort to treat the Heidelberg Catechism like it treated the Apocrypha and thus place a preface before the Catechism with a warning that this was a human document. Now the Arminians, of course, disagreed with Reformed teaching, but in order to make clear that the Catechism was based on Scripture, provincial synods prior to the Synod of Dort had already prescribed the reading of the main biblical texts on which a particular Lord's Day was based before the sermon was given. Every effort was made to make clear that Scripture and the Heidelberg Catechism were not on the same level.[6] Indeed, preaching from the Catechism was not preaching the Catechism, but preaching the Word of God on which the Catechism was based.

This fact is also obvious from the Catechism itself. When the Heidelberg Catechism deals with the Ten Commandments (LD 34–44) and the Lord's Prayer (LD 45–52), it is basically explaining Scripture (Exod 20:1–17; Matt 6:9–13). Even when the connection is not that obvious, the proof texts given with each Lord's Day show that not the Catechism, but the Scriptures, are to be the basis of the sermon. The minister therefore has to make clear that what we confess is indeed thoroughly rooted in God's Word.

Not surprisingly then, it has become customary for a minister to introduce his text by saying that he will preach God's Word as summarized in the Heidelberg Catechism, Lord's Day such and such. After all, the

---

6   Hendriks, "Preaching from the Catechism," 4–6.

doctrines found in the Heidelberg Catechism are not man-made but are doctrines which are found in Scripture. The Heidelberg Catechism simply brings together the teachings of Scripture on particular subjects and explains them. In this way, the Heidelberg Catechism attempts to bring forward the main elements of the whole counsel of God. And this is precisely what the apostles did in the early church (Acts 20:28). It is God's Word that is proclaimed and not the Heidelberg Catechism as such.[7] And yet, even today, the erroneous idea that catechetical preaching is simply expounding a human document exists. It is then argued that by preaching on a human document you confuse the people "by blurring the distinction between what is normative revelation and what is to be judged by that revelation."[8] Office bearers need to be vigilant that no wrong impressions are created. Catechetical preaching must always be preaching God's Word.

Abstract Doctrine

Another objection that has been made is that "confessions and catechisms present doctrine abstracted from its existential context—the life-situation of Scripture—and thus obscure its practical relevance or tempt us not to apply it at all."[9] In other words, catechetical preaching is not practical.

It has rightly been pointed out that the problem of preaching not connecting to real life is a problem common to all preaching.[10] One can also preach abstractly on a biblical passage and not connect it to the life of those listening. Furthermore, the Heidelberg Catechism is so intensely practical! If there is one creedal formulation that is deeply personal and realistic, it is surely the Heidelberg Catechism. The famous first question and answer sets the tone: "What is your only comfort in life and death?" That personal concern runs right through the entire Heidelberg Catechism.

---

7   For a discussion countering the view that the Catechism is more than Scripture because it pulls doctrinal elements together, see Gootjes, "Catechism Preaching," 400–404.

8   Donald Macleod, "Preaching and Systematic Theology," in *The Preacher and Preaching: Reviving the Art in the Twentieth Century*, ed. Samuel T. Logan (Phillipsburg NJ: Presbyterian and Reformed, 1986), 269. For other examples, see Cammenga, "The Homiletical Use of the Heidelberg Catechism," 17–19.

9   Macleod, "Preaching and Systematic Theology," 269.

10 Gootjes, "Catechism Preaching," 404–5.

Take, for example, Lord's Day 8, which treats a very difficult dogmatic concept, the trinity. But the Heidelberg Catechism makes it personal! It speaks of God the Father and *our* creation; God the Son and *our* redemption; God the Holy Spirit and *our* sanctification. We are very blessed to have such a personal confession of faith in the Heidelberg Catechism. It is the task and challenge for ministers to convey that personally relevant aspect also in their sermons and not preach in such a way that the doctrine goes above the heads of the congregation and does not touch their lives.

Too Repetitive

It is said that to hear catechetical preaching year after year is sterile and deadening. That of course, in part, depends on how a minister does his catechetical preaching. If he, year after year, just analyzes and parses the different questions and answers, that indeed can be deadening. But if he approaches the Catechism year after year with a different emphasis and focuses on preaching on other Scripture passages that inform the Heidelberg Catechism, then any deadening repetition will be a thing of the past.[11] It has been rightly said that "wise mothers soon learn the art of serving healthful food in ways which whet the appetite; preachers called to break the bread of life ought to do no less."[12]

Having made this point, it should also be stressed that repetition is actually a very good thing, The key doctrines of salvation, as outlined in the Heidelberg Catechism, are critical for a believer to hold on to and to be reminded of. How often does the LORD God in the Old Testament not urge his people to remember his great and mighty deeds of salvation? Think, for example, of Psalm 105:5–6: "Remember the wondrous works that he has done, his miracles, and the judgments he uttered, O offspring of Abraham, his servant, children of Jacob, his chosen ones!" (cf. 1 Chron 16:12). An old adage is that "repetition is the mother of learning." That is so true, and this truth certainly applies to our life before God. Remembering him is key to living a life of holiness with the comfort of the gospel.[13] So the fact that the

---

11 Some suggestions of different approaches can be found in Beeke, "Catechism Preaching," 235–39.
12 Peter Y. De Jong, "Comments on Catechetical Preaching (3)," *Mid-America Journal of Theology* 3, no. 1 (1987): 89.
13 . So God urged Israel to remember their past in Egypt and his deliverance to stimulate them to

doctrines are heard over and over again is a plus. The apostle Paul wrote to the Philippians: "to write the same things to you is no trouble to me and is safe for you" (Phil 3:1). Although the Philippians knew Paul's teaching, he repeated it so that they would not forget and disown the faith as happened to some (cf. Phil 3:18). "Catechism preaching is an important means to keep fresh the basic knowledge of the mighty works of God."[14] It also prevents possible one-sidedness which would happen if a preacher only preached on texts he likes. Going through the Catechism prevents this and helps the congregation to remain obedient "to the standard of teaching to which you were committed" (Rom 6:17).[15]

Catechism is Outdated

The objection is raised that we should not spend time on dealing with theological issues of the sixteenth century. Why, for example, have several Lord's Days on the Lord's Supper and the Roman Catholic Mass? However, when you reflect on this you start to realize that these doctrines are just as crucial for us to understand today as they were in the sixteenth century. We live in a time when differences between Rome and the Reformation are being minimized. There are numerous efforts to bridge the theological gap without directly addressing the differences forthrightly or blurring them.[16] The Catechism is also most relevant with respect to the time it spends on Baptism and especially infant baptism. The attraction of believer baptism and visiting their worship services is present in Reformed churches. The Heidelberg Catechism gives a biblical antidote. If there is an area which in view of the current challenges a minister thinks is not covered as well in the Heidelberg Catechism as he would like—for example, there is just a single Lord's Day on the Holy Spirit—he can still preach on

---

a life pleasing to him. See, e.g., Deut 5:15; 8:2; 16:12 etc. See Leslie C. Allen, "*zkr* Remember," in *New international dictionary of Old Testament theology and exegesis*, ed. Willem VanGemeren (Grand Rapids: Zondervan, 1997), 1:1102.

14 Gootjes, "Catechism Preaching," 408.

15 Gootjes, "Catechism Preaching," 409.

16 For example, evangelical Charles Colson and Roman Catholic Richard John Neuhaus spearheaded the effort to produce the ecumenical statement *Evangelicals and Catholics Together*. Charles Colson and Richard John Neuhaus, eds., *Evangelicals and Catholics Together: Toward a Common Mission* (Dallas, TX: Word, 1995), ix-xiv. Differences between Rome and the Reformation, also with respect to the Lord's Supper, are duly observed, but the impression of having a common task tends to minimize the importance of the differences noted.

that topic from Scripture in the morning service. But as it stands, the Heidelberg Catechism is a wonderful summary of biblical doctrine which we need as much today as it was needed hundreds of years ago. Scripture does not change, and its teachings as summarized in the Heidelberg Catechism are just as relevant now.

Objections against the Catechism have been around for a long time. But Reformed churches have always defended it. What is however new at the present time is that Catechism preaching in Reformed churches has declined. And there appears to be less and less zeal to defend the practice. Why is that?

Why is Catechetical Preaching Diminishing?

First some historical background.[17] In 1860, the Reformed Church of the Netherlands (NHK), the state church, decided that Catechism sermons were no longer compulsory and so its usage has declined in that church. The Reformed Churches in the Netherlands (GKN) retained catechism preaching until the mid-twentieth century. It has also declined in the Christian Reformed Church,[18] but remained strong in the more conservative Reformed churches.

Why is catechetical preaching falling out of favor? At present there are more factors than those objections that have been raised earlier. As noted, some of those objections have been around for hundreds of years, but the Reformed churches have always maintained the practice. However, now, fairly recently in the history of the church, catechetical preaching is actually declining within churches that call themselves Reformed. Why is that? I think that an underlying reason is postmodernism which is the reigning philosophical mindset of today. People may not realize that they are influenced by it, but the impact of postmodernism is felt everywhere. It is part of our civic culture.

---

17 For more detail on the history of the decline see Arie Baars, "'The Simple Heidelberg Catechism...': A Brief History of the Catechism Sermon in the Netherlands," in *Power of Faith: 450 Years of the Heidelberg Catechism*, ed. Karla Apperloo-Boersma and Herman J. Selderhuis (Göttingen: Vandenhoeck & Ruprecht, 2013), 161–67 and Beeke, "Catechism Preaching," 225–26.

18 See the comments of James Daane, "After 400 Years: Still the Sweetest!" *Reformed Journal* 13, no. 3 (1963): 4.

What is characteristic of postmodernism that is relevant for this discussion? Postmodernism is suspicious of any claim to absolute truths, challenges the notion that there are norms that must apply to everyone, and distrusts a single explanatory worldview framework, such as the Christian one. There are no absolutes, and nothing is really sure. Anyone who disagrees is considered intolerant. When it comes to the Bible, one has to make one's own decisions regarding the meaning of biblical texts.[19]

This sort of thinking also impacts churches. One indication of the influence of postmodernism within the Christian church in the Western world is a marked shift that has taken place "away from the dogmatic propositional preaching of past generations towards a more seeker-friendly approach" which is often little more than moralism. Our "society is in danger of becoming driven by image and devoid of content." The same danger faces God's people.[20]

This danger becomes clearer when one realizes that a central thought behind postmodernism is that objective truth is not as important as one's subjective experience. The desire for theological truth, stated in clear formulations, is not as important as the pursuit of "personal truth" and what is true and important for me. Subjectivism and individualism are the order of the day. To say that something is absolutely true is simply not acceptable in our current culture.[21] Such a mind-set is of course contrary to biblical claims that what Scripture says about God and the way of salvation is absolutely true. The postmodern person does not like to be told that what the Catechism summarizes as biblical fact is unquestionably true. The typical postmodern person simply does not want to accept what Scrip-

---

19 See, e.g., Richard N. Soulen and R. Kendall Soulen, *Handbook of Biblical Criticism*, edition no. 3, revised and expanded (Louisville, Kentucky: Westminster John Knox, 2001), 140–41.

20 James Paton, "Preaching Christian Doctrine in a Post-Christian Society," D.Min dissertation (Ashbury Theological Seminary, 2005), 61. It is remarkable that in Pope Francis's *Amoris Laetitia (The Joy of Love)*, he stated that Roman Catholics "should look to their own consciences more than Vatican rules to negotiate the complexities of sex, marriage and family life, demanding that the church shift its emphasis from doctrine to mercy in confronting some of the thorniest issues facing the faithful." Associated Press, "Look to Your Conscience, Pope Says." found in https://nationalpost.com/news/religion/look-to-your-conscience-pope-says-in-major-new-document-on-sex-marriage-and-family-life April 8, 2016.

21 For the above see Stephen Dray, "Postmodernism and the Renewal of the Reformed Faith," *Evangel* 20, no. 2 (2002): 33.

ture clearly teaches as absolutely true. According to postmodern thinking, Scripture needs to be reinterpreted for our time and situation. It does not matter what the biblical writers meant or even what they obviously said. Words have no intrinsic meaning. So, if the Bible clearly says that a homosexual lifestyle is abhorrent to God, churches, even Reformed churches, are now saying that is not so. This is just an illustration of how people today don't like to be told that what the Bible states as true facts and divine norms should be accepted as such. Scripture is reinterpreted to suit one's agenda. It reminds us of the question Satan asked in paradise. "Did God really say?" (Gen 3:1).[22] Indeed, for consistent postmodernists, absolute truth does not even exist.[23]

Catechism preaching and teaching thus faces enormous challenges today. The media, the sciences, and our entire culture promote the notion that there is no absolute propositional truth. Truth is what works for you. Don't impose your ideas on me. God's Word, the demands of the gospel, and the clear doctrinal formulations of the confessions (this is how it is) are contrary to the spirit of the times we live in. Being aware of the challenges can help us to meet them in the strength of the Lord. But our cultural context illustrates how badly we need systematic proclamation of the truth as summarized in the Heidelberg Catechism. Catechetical preaching of the doctrines of God's Word is now more important than ever! This is precisely not the time to let go of it. It is exactly confessional preaching that is re-

---

22   For an illustration, see Bob Wenz, "'Truth' on Two Hills," *Christianity Today* 48, no. 7 (July 2004): 46–48. "Postmodern biblical interpretation contends that the meaning of a text is not 'in' the text waiting to be recovered through the use of neutral, generally applicable criteria. Rather textual meaning is constructed through the interplay of a text's semantic and rhetorical aspects and the reader's own life-world. In effect the reader constructs the meaning of a text by creative use of the language, nuances, and conventions in which the reader is immersed. Thus postmodern biblical interpretation shifts the focus of attention from the historical origins of a text ('the world behind the text') and even from the text itself ('the world of the text') to the reader's use of a text within a given community of interpretation ('the world in front of the text')." Soulen and Soulen, *Handbook of Biblical Criticism*, 141. Also see, e.g., A. K. M. Adam, "Postmodern Biblical Interpretation," in *The New Interpreter's Dictionary of the Bible*, ed. Katharine Doob Sakenfeld (Nashville, TN: Abingdon, 2006–9), 4:572.

23   See also the treatment of postmodernism in Gene Edward Veith, *Postmodern Times: A Christian Guide to Contemporary Thought and Culture*, Turning Point Christian Worldview Series (Wheaton, Ill.: Crossway Books, 1994), 209–23; Frederika Oosterhoff, *Ideas Have a History: Perspectives on the Western Search for Truth* (Lanham, Maryland: University Press of America, 2001), 261.

quired today. We need to be counter-cultural and, over against the denial of absolute truth, affirm boldly also on the Lord's Day the clear truth of Scripture. And let the Word of God, the sword of the Spirit, do the rest. The good news is that the catechetical proclamation using the Heidelberg Catechism, if properly done, is ideally suited for the task of proclamation in this postmodern age. And over against the lack of objective truth and subjective certainty, the Heidelberg Catechism rightly defines faith as a "sure knowledge" and a "firm confidence" (LD 7)—precisely what our postmodern times needs.[24]

And, let's face it, is it not a great privilege to have the Confessions and to have confessional preaching? It is extremely important. First, if you love someone, don't you want to know as much as possible about him or her before committing to a life together? Well, the Confessions, and in particular the Catechism, are ideal as road maps through the Bible to teach us who God is and how we can be right with him. Furthermore, in the second place, living as we do in a crooked and sinful world, the Catechism helps us to know how to live with him according to his will so that the joy and freedom he intended for his creation can be ours in Christ. We'll also better understand why sin grieves our heavenly Father so much. Thirdly, if we know God, the Father, the Son, and the Holy Spirit, we will better understand the world we live in, as well as God's plan for this world. Fourthly, if we know the key contents of our faith and have it reinforced weekly, we will be able to give a good account to our neighbor if they ask for the reason of the hope we have in Christ. Does the apostle Peter not say: "Be prepared to make a defense to anyone who asks for a reason for the hope that is in you" (1 Pet 3:15)?

These considerations take us to consider more fully the blessings of catechetical preaching.

The Blessings of Catechetical Preaching

The following blessings underline the importance of catechetical preaching.

---

24 It is interesting to note that maintaining the church's confession as the appropriate response to postmodernism is also the view of Veith, *Postmodern Times*, 220.

1. The Whole Counsel of God is Preached

It can be fairly easy for a preacher to zero in on his favorite passages and in the process give the congregation a somewhat one-sided proclamation of God's Word. Catechetical preaching ensures that all of Scripture's key teachings are systematically covered and given due attention. This provides balance and comprehensiveness in the congregation's growth in Christian knowledge and maturity.

By covering all the doctrines of Scripture, ministers of the Word follow the good example of the apostle Paul. When he said farewell to the elders of the church at Ephesus, he declared: "I am innocent of the blood of all, for I did not shrink from declaring to you the whole counsel of God" (Acts 20:26–27). The counsel of God can be identified with "the gospel of the grace of God" and "proclaiming the kingdom" (Acts 20:24–25). The word for "counsel" also means "plan, intention." God has worked through history according to his plan. The apostle emphasized that he left nothing out. All of God's work of salvation was proclaimed by him.[25] And this is also what ministers should do today and the Heidelberg Catechism is an ideal tool for proclaiming all the key biblical truths in an orderly and timely way so that the congregation is fed a balanced and nutritious diet of the living Word of God from the pulpit.

And let us make no mistake about it. Doctrine and preaching the doctrine is extremely important. Paul exhorted Timothy to "preach what is in accord with sound doctrine" (Titus 2:1). The congregation must therefore know this doctrine.

A key result from such preaching is that we offer our hearts and lives as a sacrifice of thankfulness to the worship and praise of God.[26]

2. The Catechism is Eminently Suitable for Teaching

Reformed churches are blessed with having catechetical instruction for their youth. The question and answer format of the Catechism

---

25 See on this Gootjes, "Catechism Preaching," 403–4.
26 Catechetical preaching has rightly been called doxological. See De Jong, "Comments on Catechetical Preaching (1)," 186 and De Jong, "Comments on Catechetical Preaching (3)," 102.

is a method of teaching that goes back to great antiquity and is of proven worth. How wonderful to see this teaching in the classroom during the week reinforced on Sunday afternoon with a catechetical sermon.

There are ministers who, for the sake of variety, preach from the Belgic Confession or Canons of Dort. There are some advantages to such confessional preaching. With rampant Arminianism around us, proclamation using the Canons of Dort can, for example, be justified. However, the Heidelberg Catechism is ideally suited for teaching and was indeed written for that purpose. It is therefore also specifically mentioned in the Church Order. The Heidelberg Catechism should remain preeminent in confessional preaching. Indeed, the Catechism was also meant to be used on the pulpit.[27]

After all, the afternoon sermon has a didactic, teaching, purpose, to more fully explain the biblical teaching in an organized way.[28] This follows the biblical example. Our Savior taught in the synagogues (Matt 4:23; 9:35) and after the resurrection the disciples were charged to teach everything he had commanded them (Matt 28:20) which they subsequently did (Acts 4:2; 5:28; 2 Tim 4:1–2). For teaching, the Heidelberg Catechism is an excellent tool for the afternoon service.

Another blessing of the Catechism sermon is that it equips the congregation against heresies.

3. This Preaching Equips the Congregation against Heresies

According to the Form for the Ordination for Ministers of the Word, part of preaching the whole counsel of God is to "expose all errors and heresies as unfruitful works of darkness and to walk as children of light."[29] The Heidelberg Catechism is well suited for that. Virtually every current challenge to the faith can be answered from the Heidelberg Catechism. And so doctrinal instruction through the catechetical sermon equips the congregation to fulfill its calling to be a light in a world of dark-

---

27 According to Frederick III's preface to the Heidelberg Catechism. Hyde, "The Principle and Practice of Preaching," 115.
28 For what follows, see Hendriks, "Preaching from the Catechism," 6–7.
29 *Book of Praise*, 619.

ness (Matt 5:11) and "a pillar and buttress of the truth" (1 Tim 3:15). Scripture exhorts and warns us, in 1 John 4:1 "Beloved, do not believe every spirit, but test the spirits to see whether they are from God, for many false prophets have gone out into the world." Rather we are, in the words of Jude, "to contend for the faith that was once for all delivered to the saints" (Jude 1:3). "The faith" is the summary, the doctrine, the full gospel entrusted to the church. Preserving that doctrine is ultimately a matter of life and death. As Timothy was exhorted by the apostle Paul: "Keep a close watch on yourself and on the teaching (the doctrine). Persist in them for by so doing you will save both yourself and your hearers" (1 Tim 4:16).

Because the Heidelberg Catechism provides such a beautiful summary of core biblical teaching, it is admirably suited to address contemporary thinking or practice that is contrary to Scripture. In this way the congregation is equipped "so that", as the apostle put it, "we may no longer be children, tossed to and fro by the waves and carried about by every wind of doctrine, by human cunning, by craftiness in deceitful schemes (Eph 4:14). As the apostle Peter put it (2 Pet 3:17-18): "You therefore, beloved . . . take care that you are not carried away with the error of lawless people and lose your own stability. But grow in the grace and knowledge of our Lord and Savior Jesus Christ."

It has been rightly said that "confessional Reformed churches call for confessing people who know what they believe and are eager to articulate this in word as well as deed."[30]

4. This Preaching is Pastoral

Another great blessing of preaching with the use of the Heidelberg Catechism is that such preaching is very pastoral. After all, the Catechism speaks to the individual. The first Lord's Day sets the tone. It begins by asking about "your comfort" and answers it in the first person. This personal and pastoral characteristic is evident throughout. All the way through the emphasis is on the benefit of the biblical doctrine and the comfort God gives to his children who believe the Bible's teaching. The teaching found in

---

30 Peter Y. De Jong, "Comments on Catechetical Preaching (2)," *Mid-America Journal of Theology* 2, no. 2 (1986): 167.

the Heidelberg Catechism is absolutely not abstract or separated from real life. It gives God's children all they need to go through life in communion with the living God. This means that the Heidelberg Catechism and its preaching are also very practical. Abstract doctrinal catechetical sermons do a grave injustice to both the nature and contents of the Catechism. Catechetical sermons must remain proclamation of the gospel that instructs, encourages, and comforts God's people en route to eternity.[31]

It is interesting to note that Dr. James I. McCord, President of Princeton Seminary, once said that on a preaching mission in Hungary, when it was still under Communist rule and behind the Iron Curtain, "he had been told that one of the reasons for the large number of young people in the churches, in spite of Communist pressure, was the fact that each minister used the Heidelberg Catechism to instruct his young people every Sunday afternoon."[32] The Heidelberg Catechism is pastoral and encourages believers. It also gives God's people the doctrinal basis to fight false ideologies.

5. This Preaching Promotes the Unity of the Church

The confessions of the church give the congregation and the church federation as a whole a common doctrinal basis. The fact that this doctrine is regularly proclaimed promotes this harmony and unity, for people realize it is these truths that bind us together. This is what we agree on. In this way, the brothers and sisters can also support each other against error and realize their unity with the church that has preceded them. These doctrines are ecumenical doctrines, doctrines agreed upon by former generations as well. They are also doctrines that bind Reformed churches the world over. It is a tremendous thing to visit Reformed churches in other countries and hear the same doctrines proclaimed.[33]

Conclusion

Reformed people may not always appreciate catechetical preaching

---

31 See on this theme also,e.g., De Jong, "Comments on Catechetical Preaching (1)," 173–84.
32 Quoted in Daane, "After 400 Years," 4.
33 One of the original purposes of the Heidelberg Catechism was ecumenical. De Jong, "Comments on Catechetical Preaching (1)," 176–77.

because they are so used to it, but the Heidelberg Catechism is a treasure! Someone in a missionary situation taught those interested, and when he thought they might be ready for some more meat, introduced the Heidelberg Catechism. The reaction on the part of those being evangelized was unbelievably positive. One person said, you should have started with this! This Catechism is precisely what we need! Well, the Heidelberg Catechism was written well over 450 years ago and it has stood the test of time. As a matter of fact, as late as the beginning of the twentieth century it "was the most widely translated and circulated piece of Christian writing, surpassed only by Thomas á Kempis' *Imitation of Christ* and Bunyan's *Pilgrim's Progress*"[34] It has rightly been called "the book of comfort." It stands in a class all by itself when it comes to the confessional formulations of the sixteenth century. Its comprehensiveness, directness, and personal concern make it a classic that we would neglect to our hurt. It was designed to help the preacher be a teacher. This treasure, therefore, needs to be acknowledged on the pulpit as an excellent aid to expounding biblical truth in a relevant, practical and pastoral way. May such proclamation continue from generation to generation!

---

34   Daane, "After 400 Years," 5.

8 **Elders, a Treasure to Cherish: A Reformation Day Reflection**

On Reformation Day, October 31, we may celebrate God's goodness in unwrapping once more the glories of the gospel rediscovered through his servants such as Luther and Calvin. The Word was proclaimed again in its fullness and the good news of being justified by faith alone resounded from the pulpits. Another, perhaps less known fruit of going back to the authoritative Word of God, was the rediscovery of the office of elder. It is easy for us to take this office for granted, but we would do so at our peril. This office is a gracious gift of God, established for the well-being of the church.

Some Background

Right from the very beginning, the early Christian church had elders. This is not surprising given the fact that the first Christians were Jews and the elder had always played a vital role in giving leadership and direction to Israel and the Jewish people. As the new Israel (cf. Gal 6:16), the Christian church simply continued using this office. It was a matter of course. Indeed, as we saw in chapter 6, the first churches were called synagogues (thus literally James 2:2). And what is a synagogue without an elder? Because of this continuity with the Old Testament, Luke can mention Christian elders for the first time in Acts 11:30 without needing to give any explanation. All Jewish Christians were familiar with this office, and it became standard throughout the entire church, including the congregations originating from Gentile believers (See, for example, Acts 14:23).

When the apostle Paul writes Timothy, he speaks of elders "who direct the affairs of the church well," but he also mentions those elders "whose work is preaching and teaching" (1 Tim 5:17). This passage has been correctly understood to mean that there are two elder offices: the ruling elder and the teaching elder, or, as we are more accustomed to say: elders and ministers. These two elder offices were charged to shepherd the flock entrusted to their care. This shepherding meant especially that the Word was administered to the sheep in the public worship services as well as in the privacy of their homes (cf. Acts 20:20).

In the grand scheme of history, this beautiful setup of shepherding elders visiting the families and administering the Word to them did not last long.

The Corruption of the Elder Offices and their Recovery

The early Christian church initially followed the apostolic example. The elders saw believers in their homes and ministered to them. But over time that changed. Elders became known as priests.[1] This is a great tragedy in the history of the church. With this change of identity, the focus of their work shifted from the congregation to the sacraments. Indeed, this change happened in part because the Lord's Supper celebration came to be regarded as a sacrificial meal which needed priests to administer. And instead of family visitation where Christ's under-shepherds visited the homes, the priest expected the people to come to him for the sacrament of penance. The church kept watch over the souls entrusted to them by making the church members visit the priest to do confession.[2]

It was not until the Reformation during the sixteenth century that the important place of the elder was recognized again and teaching elders and ruling elders functioned once more in the church according to the biblical pattern. Our main concern here is the ruling elder. It is noteworthy that Luther was willing to settle for what he considered a purified form of penance and so he never really gave the office of elder its full due. Calvin, however, broke radically with the sacrament of penance and restored the prerogative of the eldership to its proper place in shepherding the flock. Shepherding by the teaching and ruling elders is a great gift from God that he gave back to the church during the time of the Reformation.

---

1   See further Van Dam, *The Elder*, 116.
2   Van Dam, *The Elder*, 163.

We may be grateful heirs of this legacy. It is therefore fitting to remember this treasure on Reformation Day, for history teaches that this office cannot be taken for granted. When it is simply assumed and not valued, it tends to disappear or become an empty formality. One very good way to make sure this does not happen is to have a renewed appreciation for this office and to cherish it.

A Treasure to Cherish

Blessed is the congregation whose elders diligently do their work! They watch over the well-being of the church and apply the gospel to the lives of those in their charge. They are not distant from the people or wait for the people to come to them, but they are shepherds who minister to those in their care. They do it humbly, seeking to serve rather than to domineer as is fitting for those in Christ's service for Christ himself came to serve and not to be served (Matt 20:28). In this way elders also stimulate the congregation to their duty to build each other up in the faith. Furthermore, ruling elders are to safeguard the pulpit and ensure that the preaching is sound. And they do all this and more as servants of Christ who have been called for this special task.

When one considers the duties of an elder, it is obvious that it is not easy to be one. While the office is a great privilege for those who have been called to it, it is also an enormous responsibility. The Chief Shepherd will hold the under-shepherds accountable for the safety of Zion and for the souls of those whom they have not warned or shepherded (Ezek 33:1–20; Acts 20:28–31). Also, the elders will constantly need to cultivate their gifts and use every opportunity to increase their knowledge of the Word of God. After all, that is the Word of their Sender and the Holy Spirit uses the Word to also equip the office bearers for their weighty task. Furthermore, through the Word, office bearers also grow in the Lord. The Good Shepherd uses his Word and Spirit to give office bearers the confidence they need to do their task.

The upshot of all of this is that congregations must cherish their office bearers as Christ's gift to them. Practically speaking this means that church members should regularly remember the office bearers and their labors in prayer during family devotions. Furthermore, they will honor and obey their leaders. That's not a popular thing to do in our secular egalitarian culture which has little respect for authority. But that's what God's Word says. "Obey your leaders and submit to them, for they are keeping watch over your souls, as those who will have to give an account. Let them do this with joy and not with groaning, for that would be of no advantage to you" (Heb 13:17). Elsewhere Christians are exhorted: "We ask you, brothers, to respect those who labor among you and are over you in the Lord and who admonish you, and to esteem them highly in love because of their work" (1 Thess 5:12–13). And who would not gladly do that? These under-shepherds are Christ's gift to his church!

Celebrating Reformation Day means celebrating the treasures Christ has entrusted to his people. Elders are an integral part of that treasure. After all, they are his instruments to guide the congregation to the greatest treasure of all—the gospel of being right with God by faith alone in Christ alone.

CHAPTER 9

Aspiring, Preparing, and Equipping for the Office of Elder: Is Special Training Required?

The apostle Paul wrote in his first letter to Timothy: "Here is a trustworthy saying: if anyone aspires to the office of overseer, he desires a noble task" (1 Tim 3:1). In this way the apostle commends the office as a fine work and so encourages the desire to serve as an overseer, be it as a ruling or teaching elder. The task of the overseer certainly has its challenges. It is quite a responsibility to hold office in the church which is "a pillar and buttress of the truth" (1 Tim 3:15). But the weighty obligations do not deter the apostle from stressing that one can set one's heart on it and have godly aspirations for it.

Our Responsibility

The fact that seeking the eldership is commendable indicates that although God is the one who calls men to the office of elder, yet God's call does not exclude human responsibility. And indeed, after issuing the encouragement to aspire for the office, the apostle set out the basic requirements. This is where the emphasis falls. The point, therefore, is that it is good to aim at being an elder, but realize what is necessary, and prepare for it by seeking to fulfill the basic requirements.

The preparations for the office begin with a godly life, that is being "above reproach, the husband of one wife, sober-minded, self-controlled, respectable, hospitable, able to teach, not a drunkard, not violent but gentle, not quarrelsome, not a lover of money. He must manage his own household well, with all dignity keeping his children submissive" (1 Tim 3:2–4). Furthermore, "he must not be a recent convert, or he may become puffed up with conceit and fall into the condemnation of the devil. Moreover, he must be well thought of by outsiders, so that he may not fall into disgrace, into a snare of the devil" (1 Tim 3:6–7).

It needs to be stressed that *the* preparation for the office indeed begins with a life close to the Lord and in his ways in all aspects of life. The qualifications stressed by the apostle are requirements, not ideals to be realized sometime in the future. The prospective elder must be exemplary in his relationship with his wife and children, and with others. The apostle also mentions that one must be able to teach (2 Tim 3:2). This means that one aspiring to the office must be knowledgeable in Scripture and its teachings and how to apply them to real life situations. This entails much reading and studying of the Word of God as a member of the congregation, both personally and with others in Bible study groups. It means taking whatever opportunity arises to become familiar with the riches of salvation, including the reading of good Reformed books and participating in conferences as the opportunity arises.

It is good to remember that in Israel and in the early church elders were chosen for their exemplary walk of life and for their being endowed with gifts in the area of giving leadership and teaching. In the churches of the Reformation, such gifts are also determinative for being considered for the office. Traditionally, in the Reformed churches, the younger, inexperienced elders would continue to grow by learning from their older and more seasoned colleagues while doing the task of shepherding the flock entrusted to them. No special training was assumed. This point needs to be noted. In our day and age, more education is sometimes confused with more wisdom. This is unfortunate for more education does not necessarily mean more gifts in terms of leadership, shepherding, and watching over the flock.

Yet, the question whether those who aspire to the office of elder require special preparation needs to be faced. It is often those who are called to serve in the office themselves who ask for such special training. And indeed, the demands of the office are very high. Would some type of special training not help to prepare for the office? Let us consider the case for no special training with an example coming from a Dutch Reformed background, and then look at the argument for specialized training prior to ordination coming from an American Presbyterian environment.

No Special Preparatory Training

It may be instructive to recall some of the history of this issue in the Reformed churches in the Netherlands for this matter is not new.[1] Already in the seventeenth century, a certain Jacob Koeleman argued for a special training so that the churches would receive competent and knowledgeable elders. He based his contention on 1 Timothy 3:10 which informs us that those to be considered for the office should first be tested. In 1839 the Rev. Dr. A. C. van Raalte gave lessons to those who were already elders and deacons in order to meet the need for further training. Underlining the necessity of knowing the Scriptures was a long-standing nineteenth century custom of Classis Apeldoorn to inquire about the Bible knowledge of elders and deacons. In 1913 the issue of pre-ordination training came up again when Prof. L. Lindeboom of the Theological College in Kampen defended the necessity of a separate education for the elders. His reason was basically that the many duties required of the office of elder demanded a special training.

There was however opposition to a special pre-ordination training for elders. Dr. H. Bouwman, the well-known Reformed church polity expert, was one of those who opposed this both in principle and for practical reasons. His arguments were as follows.[2] Firstly, the Reformed character of the office of elder would be threatened. It was precisely to avoid hierarchy that Calvin had considered it necessary that men be chosen from the congregation so that they could exercise supervision and discipline over the congregation together with the minister of the Word. Unlike ministers, elders are not called *to* the congregation but *out of* the congregation. A special training for elders would result in future elders forming a new type of clergy. Secondly, if elders are only chosen from people who have been specially trained for the office, then a large portion of those who have undergone the training will not be chosen. They will feel bypassed and slighted. Thirdly, the gifts for the office of elder must not be acquired by an academic or specialized instruction but should be cultivated by the schooling received in the catechism class, the Bible study societies, and in their own study of the Scriptures. What is necessary for an elder is not, in the first place, book knowledge but practical wisdom, insight in the true doctrine,

---

1   For the historical data that follows I am dependent on H. Bouwman, *Gereformeerd kerkrecht* (Kampen: Kok, 1928), 1:538.

2   For what follows see Bouwman, *Gereformeerd kerkrecht*, 1:538–39.

an understanding of life and people, tact in dealing with people, and the ability to give good leadership. Fourthly, the most qualified would probably not participate in such training for reasons of modesty while those who are less modest in evaluating their capabilities would sign up for such a course. The latter, however, may be the less qualified than those who decline to participate. Fifthly, not all churches would support such an institution of training and it would thus be doomed to failure. Sixthly, it would promote lifelong elders which is contrary to Reformed church polity. Seventh, the admonition of Paul in 1 Timothy 3:10 that the deacons be tested first so that they be proven to be blameless refers to practical life experience not to an academic exam. The apostle Paul was probably thinking of an investigation of such a person's walk of life, doctrinal purity and suitability for the office. When it is evident that God endows someone with the gifts of faith, wisdom, and love for the service of God, then such a person can be considered for office.

Dr. Bouwman's warnings against the possibility of a new hierarchy and elitism are well taken. He was also justified in reminding us that elders are chosen from the congregation on account of the gifts they exhibit and which they have developed over time by their careful walk with the Lord and by using the opportunities available to them. Academic training as such will not endow one with those gifts. And so, whatever steps may be initiated at a local or broader level for the training of elders or elders-to-be, one should be sensitive to the concerns which Bouwman raised. Having said that, however, one also needs to add that experience has taught many a Reformed pastor that first-time elders often feel very insecure and ask about training possibilities to help prepare them for the successful execution of their office. This cry for help cannot be ignored. If formal training of elders is not desirable for the reasons given, then the following approaches should be considered. These suggestions can be used even if there is formal training for the elder prior to ordination.

The first line of action in heeding this plea for assistance should be that pastors of local churches make a point of emphasizing in their catechetical training the tremendous privilege the catechumens have of preparing themselves for Christian service, be it as believers fulfilling their calling as prophet, priest, and king in the fullness of life or as a special office bearer in the church. Ministers teaching the youth of the church are in an ideal position to stimulate interest in and a longing for participating in a special service to God, including the office of elder. Such stimulation also serves as an encouragement for young people to take advantage of the educational opportunities to learn and grow in Christ. Then they will be ready for service wherever God in his providence leads their lives. The young women will be preparing themselves for their calling in all of life, including the likely possibility that the Lord calls them to be wives and mothers, with a key role in nurturing little ones for God. The young men will be equipping themselves for their future occupation and leadership roles, be it within the home as husbands and fathers, or in serving the Lord outside the home in church as an office bearer, or in a special service in society at large. If catechetical training is taken seriously and maximized, then young people will not only be equipped as well as possible for their planned future roles but also those men who may eventually be called to the special office of elder would have had a solid basic training in the knowledge of Scripture, the Reformed confessions, and church polity. The importance of this early training and stimulation for a desire to serve can never be overestimated. It is of great consequence for the health of the church.

This early education should be continued by way of special congregational meetings or adult education classes dealing with all kinds of topics of interest to the church, including the study and discussion of the special offices in the church. There would be no direct linkage to seeking the office by attending such classes since they would be open for the entire congregation. Let us not forget how important it is for all members of the church to know the basic principles governing the task of those who serve in the special office. More meaningful prayers can be offered for those laboring among them as elders and the spouses of the elders can be of even greater support if they understand more fully the privileges and burdens of the office.

Furthermore, consistories or sessions should make it a regular point on the agenda of their meetings to take the time for further educating and equipping themselves for the demands of their office. In the process, the younger elders can learn much from their older and more experienced fellow workers in the duties assigned to them. Taking the time to work through a book and discuss a chapter at a time is a wonderful way to build each other up and continue to equip for the office.[3] Making use of a periodical geared to the needs of the office bearers and discussing articles is another good way to become more equipped.[4] Furthermore, the inexperienced can be teamed up with the experienced when visiting and shepherding the flock. Learning from example "on the job" remains an effective way to gain experience and increase in knowledge (cf. Phil 3:17; 4:9). Also, the pastor may be able to prepare a manual, geared to the local situation, which can give many valuable tips to the beginning elder in terms of what is expected of him and where he can go to get biblical information on some of the more dominant practical issues of the day. Furthermore, local churches can get together and organize conferences for elders and interested church members to deal with topics of mutual concern. Again, this would provide an avenue for equipping oneself for the office.

There appears, to my knowledge, to be little in the way of a systematic or institutionalized eldership training in Reformed churches. Probably this is so because of some of the concerns vocalized by Bouwman. Presbyterian churches on the other hand seem to be more open to specialized training, perhaps because once chosen an elder, one is expected to serve for life. However, here too such formal training is not found in all Presbyterian churches. The Free Church of Scotland, for example, has available a handbook that can be used as "the basis for occasional training days, perhaps arranged on a presbytery basis." This church has no required formal training for becoming an elder.[5] On the other hand, a pre-ordination training for elders-to-be is as a rule compulsory, for instance, in the Orthodox Presbyterian Church. It will be good to consider their approach as an example of a more formal training and to try to understand the reasons for it.

---

3   For suitable material for study, Van Dam, *The Elder*, 253–55. This book can also be used since it has questions for discussion for each chapter. A resource subsequently available is William Boekestein and Steven Swets, eds., *Faithful and Fruitful: Essays for Elders and Deacons*, foreword by Michael Brown (N.p.: Reformed Fellowship Inc., 2019).

4   One can mention here the excellent work done by *Diakonia: A Magazine for Office Bearers* since 1987 (available at https://www.brooksidepublishing.ca) and *Ordained Servant: A Journal for Church Officers* since 1992 (available at https://opc.org/os.html).

5   Free Church of Scotland Board of Ministry, *Elders and Deacons in the Free Church: A Study Guide for Office Bearers*, 2; Charles Anderson, Clerk to Board of Ministry, in an email to myself on Feb 23, 2021.

Special Preparatory Training

Concerning the electing, ordaining, and installing of ruling elders and deacons, the Form of Government of the Orthodox Presbyterian Church specifies the following:

> In order that these sacred offices not be committed to weak or unworthy men, and that the congregations shall have an opportunity to form a better judgment respecting the gifts of those by whom they are to be governed and served, no one shall normally be eligible for election to office until he has been a communicant member in good standing for at least one year, shall have received appropriate training under the direction of or with the approval of the session, and shall have served the church in functions requiring responsible leadership. Men of ability and piety in the congregation shall be encouraged by the session to prepare themselves for the offices of ruling elder or deacon so that their study and opportunities for service may be provided for in a systematic and orderly way.[6]

Two important points can be noted from this Form of Government that are applicable even if there would be no formal preparatory training of the elders. First, the congregation has a very important place in the process of elders being called to office. The membership needs to be involved and they need to be able to form a considered judgment concerning the qualifications of those who are to be elders. Second, a new member of the congregation should not be made an office bearer too soon. Let him first prove himself with a godly walk and a demonstration of his gifts, be it of leadership or otherwise.

When it comes to receiving "appropriate training", this shall be done "under the direction of or with the approval of the session." Moreover, potential candidates for the office of elder are to be encouraged to prepare themselves "so that their study and opportunities for service may be provided for in a systematic and orderly way." To appreciate the possible rationale for this formalized training, it is appropriate to listen to Rev. Law-

---

6   The Form of Government, Chapter 25.3 in *The Book of Church Order of the Orthodox Presbyterian Church* (Willow Grove, PA: The Committee on Christian Education of the Orthodox Presbyterian Church, 2011), 67–68.

rence R. Eyres, who ministered in the Orthodox Presbyterian Church and who addressed this topic in his writing.[7]

Eyres noted that the twelve disciples only became twelve apostles after three years of training by Christ. Also, Saul of Tarsus spent about three years preparing before the Holy Spirit sent him out in the Lord's service (Gal 1:14–17; Acts 11:25–26; 13:1–3). If these infallibly called men needed such preparation, how much more when the choice of men rests upon fallible human judgment. Although teaching elders receive adequate training, this is not so with the ruling elder. They are often ordained shortly after being elected without any kind of examination. Eyres does not think this is right since this procedure presupposes that the office of ruling elder is essentially different from that of the minister of the Word.

It is good that Eyres raised this issue as forcefully as he did for the matter of having properly qualified office bearers is critical for the health of the congregation. Without taking anything away from the value of a well-educated eldership (see further below), it does need to be noted that his basic premise for a formalized education for ruling elders prior to their ordination needs further examination. It is true that there is an essential unity between the office of teaching elder and ruling elder. Both are elders. At the same time, their offices are distinct and should not be confused. The people of God have always had a teaching office alongside that of the ruling elder. The minister of the gospel, the New Testament teaching elder, has taken over the teaching task of the Old Testament priest and Levite, and the ruling elder has inherited the task of the Old Testament elder. Furthermore, as shown elsewhere in this book, the minister's task has continuities with the offices of prophet and king as well. Although there is a very important underlying unity between the teaching and ruling office of the present day elder, a unity which shows their essential equality, still one must not confuse the different tasks each office has.

---

7   What follows is dependent on Lawrence R. Eyres, *The Elders of the Church* (Phillipsburg, NJ: Presbyterian and Reformed, 1975), 54–57. It is evident from these pages that Rev. Eyres wrote at a time when there was no formal training requirement for ruling elders in the Orthodox Presbyterian Church. It is not clear what the official reasons were for mandating appropriate training for prospective elders in the Orthodox Presbyterian Church. This change seems to have come about when the Orthodox Presbyterian Church adopted a revised Form of Government in 1979. (Private correspondence from G. I. Williamson, Dec 8, 2003).

Equality of office does not mean that the tasks and expectations of these offices are the same. For example, when it comes to safeguarding the church against false doctrine, the teaching elder or minister has the greater responsibility. Another example, not the ruling elder, but the teaching elder has the duty of bringing God's Word by means of a sermon he prepared to the congregation each Lord's Day. Both of these examples suggest that a teaching elder needs a more academic preparation than does the ruling elder, just as the apostles of old (to use Eyre's example) needed more preparation than the ruling elder in the church. This is not to slight the office of ruling elder, but simply to recognize the different responsibilities. With the responsibilities, especially in the area of teaching and preaching, also come the need for formal specialized training prior to ordination. The church has recognized this by insisting on well-educated ministers or teaching elders.

On the other hand, one can hardly object to an education program for ruling elders-to-be which seeks to prepare them for the office in a biblical manner. Indeed, one can welcome and rejoice in possibilities of this kind. If all communicant males of the congregation are invited to attend such a program, then some of the concerns and potential pitfalls that Bouwman mentioned can be addressed. Such a training course can be especially important in a Presbyterian context where ordination to office means ordination for life. It does seem the better part of wisdom to have a more elaborate education and screening process when the ordination has a permanent quality to it.[8] The matter is less pressing in a Reformed church with a specified term for office. An elder who turns out not to have the necessary gifts can simply not be proposed for office the next time around. However, as noted above, the more the entire congregation is educated in the nature and task of the offices, the better it is for the church.

---

8   For an example of a training program see John R. Hilbelink, "A Training Course for Elders and Deacons," *Ordained Servant* 2 (1993): 3–15, 27–37. This course covers 5 weeks of Westminster Confession of Faith (and reading the Catechisms), 4 weeks of Church Government (and reading the Book of Discipline and Directory of Worship), and 4 weeks on the work of the elder and deacon. Another example is found in Gregory Reynolds and William Shishko, "A Training Program for Elders," *Ordained Servant* 10 (2001): 55–58. It spends 13 weeks on the Westminster Confession and 5 weeks on the eldership. See also on training elders, Eyres, *The Elders of the Church*, 53–58.

Summary

Aspiring for the office is a good thing, but with such aspirations come responsibilities. One must seek to equip oneself. Ultimately, the preparation of godly young men for the office starts in the home where they are raised in a Christian manner. This preparation is continued in the catechetical instruction and in Christian schools. Much of the type of material that could be included in a pre-ordination eldership training program is material that could have been learned, at least in part, in the normal process of growing up in a Christian environment. This learning and development is however not just academic, or even in the first place so, but it consists largely in the forming of a Christian character. A godly young man shows his Christian commitment in the way he relates to those around him, such as, his wife, children, and others, and in exhibiting behavior which is temperate, loving, gentle, self-controlled, not quarrelsome, holy in life and action, hospitable, and of good reputation. He is also able to pass on to others the love of God by applying the Word within the context of real life and so comfort and encourage with the gospel. Those who deny the truths of Christianity he can oppose. Indeed, the type of qualifications required of elders in 1 Timothy 3:1–7 and in Titus 1:5–9 emphasize precisely character traits such as these.

A formalized pre-ordination training program for the ruling elder will not necessarily solve potential problems of inadequacy, lack of preparedness for the office, or the like. Academic training is often overrated in our day. Book knowledge can never replace the kinds of qualifications that Scripture demands to be present in a candidate for the eldership, both ruling and teaching. And yet these qualifications need to be present. Furthermore, a major disadvantage of a special training program for elders-to-be is that a somewhat artificial separation is made in the congregation between those who sign up and those who for various reasons do not. The impression is easily aroused that a new "elite" is being created which strikes at the very core of the character of an elder as one chosen from the congregation and not from a list of those who passed a course. Also, those who for various and good reasons did not or could not sign up can feel bypassed and unjustly slighted in not being considered for the office.

On the other hand, an important advantage of a special program is that something of the awesome responsibility of the office of elder is recognized. The danger is not unimaginable that one can enter the office too easily and not be adequately prepared for the enormous challenges that are to be expected. Also, a special pre-ordination course is undoubtedly of great help to those aspiring to the office and does much good. Especially those who are relatively new to the faith can be greatly helped should they be called to serve as a ruling elder. These are factors in favor of pre-ordination training. It is certainly understandable that in Presbyterian polity the issue of such training is a very important one. When being ordained to the office of ruling elder means the beginning of a lifetime tenure, then all precautions should be used to make sure that justice is done to the office.

No matter which approach is followed, with or without a special pre-ordination program, the church and its leadership should be sensitive to any ongoing training that may be needed so they can be adequately prepared to meet current and new challenges. The local minister has a responsibility to either head or stimulate such a training and to encourage the reading of good literature and the attendance of appropriate conferences. Furthermore, if no special pre-ordination course is in place, private encouragement and counsel can be given to those who have the gifts for the office so that they can prepare themselves more effectively for such a time as the Lord may call them to his special service.

In conclusion, it needs to be borne in mind that one of the greatest gifts an elder could wish for is wisdom, wisdom to deal with the flock in a God glorifying way. Wisdom is not picked up in a special seminar or in reading a book. It is attained gradually through a life that is lived in the fear of the Lord and that is sensitive to the demands of the great Shepherd Jesus Christ. It is gifts of the Spirit such as wisdom, godly leadership, and a love for the sheep that are absolutely essential. However, to say this is not to underestimate the great help that an elder can receive in special training and supportive activities that are available to him. To be in the Lord's service is a privilege for which one is never well enough equipped. The equipping for office is actually a process that never ends.

CHAPTER 10 — Congregational Involvement in Electing to Office

In Reformed and Presbyterian churches, the process of becoming an elder or deacon typically involves the communicant members of the congregation participating in an election and casting their votes for their preferred candidates for the office. The question has been raised whether the female members of the church should take part in the election alongside the male members. Both the Reformed Churches (Liberated) in the Netherlands and the Canadian Reformed Churches have dealt with this issue at some point in their relatively recent history. Both federations ultimately decided that the sisters of the congregation can join the brothers in the Lord in participating in the election of office bearers.

These decisions have however not put an end to the discussion about this issue. A major concern for some is whether allowing the communicant female members to vote does not in a sense empower them, give them some sort of governing authority, and open the road to their assuming the office of elder themselves. If you allow the women to vote, why not let them become office bearers? So the thinking goes. This slippery slope argument has considerable appeal, especially because this sequence of events happened in the Netherlands. Women were allowed to vote in the Reformed Churches in the Netherlands (Liberated) in 1993 and by 2017 all the ecclesiastical offices were opened to them![1]

---

1 For a summary of the decision by Synod Ommen 1993 (*Acta van de Generale Synode van de Gereformeerde Kerken in Nederland Ommen 1993* [Barneveld, NL: De Vuurbaak, 1993], Art. 24) to allow voting by women, F.H. Folkerts, "Women's Voting Right in the Church," *Lux Mundi* 14, no. 2 (1995): 2–7; for the decisions by Synod Meppel 2017 (*Acta Generale Synode Meppel 2017*, Found online at http://kerkrecht.nl/sites/default/files/Acta%20GS%20Meppel%202017.pdf, Art 18) to open all offices to women, J. De Gelder, et al., *Report Subcommittee Relations with Churches in the Netherlands for Synod Edmonton 2019*, Https://canrc.org/documents/8717, appendix H; for Canadian Reformed Churches allowing voting by women, *Acts of General Synod 2010 of the Canadian Reformed Churches Held at Burlington, Ontario from May 11–26, 2010* (Winnipeg, MB: Premier Printing, 2010), Art. 176.

However, does this slippery slope argument hold water? To address this issue, we first need to consider whether the involvement of the congregation in the process of ordaining men into ecclesiastical office is biblically justified. The answer to that question is yes. Next we will consider whether women are to be included in this process, as well as the nature of the involvement of the congregation.

The Biblical Basis for Congregational Involvement

A foundational principle in Scripture is that God's people are involved in determining who their leaders are to be, but the final appointment is made by the ordained leadership. This fundamental rule was already evident in Old Testament times. When Moses needed help to relieve his burdens of leading Israel, he instructed "all Israel" to "choose for your tribes wise, understanding, and experienced men, and I will appoint them as your heads" (Deut 1:1, 13; cf. Exod 18:21).[2] Israel had to do the choosing, but Moses would do the appointing.

The same principle is evident in the New Testament. The congregation was involved, but the responsibility and authority for ordaining new office bearers fell on the shoulders of those already ordained. They took the initiative, for example, in starting the process that led to choosing the seven to serve at tables and help with the daily distribution of food to the needy (Acts 6:2–3). Other examples can be given. Paul and Barnabas "appointed elders" (Acts 14:23). Titus as the apostle Paul's "partner and fellow worker" (2 Cor 8:23) was charged to "appoint [kathistēmi] elders in every town" (Titus 1:5). The office bearer, Timothy (1 Tim 4:14), was able to ordain elders since Paul counselled him: "Do not be hasty in the laying on of hands" (1 Tim 5:22).

From these instances, it is clear that the authority to appoint or ordain office bearers does not come from the congregation, but from office bearers who are in the service of Christ, the head of the church. At the same time, Scripture indicates that the congregation is not to be excluded from the process of choosing men for ecclesiastical office.

---

2   See further Van Dam, *The Elder*, 68–69.

In Acts 6, the congregation was summoned and involved in find-ing men to be ordained to serve tables (Acts 6:2, 6). But they could not just choose anyone. The apostles were in charge and gave clear criteria. Biblical norms had to be followed; in this case, "men of good repute, full of the Spirit and of wisdom" (Acts 6:3). When Paul and Barnabas "appointed" elders "in every city" (Acts 14:23), more is going on than initially meets the eye. The original Greek translated "appointed" [cheirotoneō] can also be rendered to read that Paul and Barnabas "had elders elected."[3] The term in question literally means "elect by show of hands." In other words, the con-gregation was probably involved in selecting someone for the office, but it was done under the guidance of the apostles who were charged to oversee the proceedings and, as the text indicates, made the actual appointment.[4] In all these cases, the qualifications that Christ the head of the church de-sired in his office bearers had to be followed (1 Tim 3:1–13; Titus 1:5–9). We also read of congregations appointing (cheirotoneō) someone for col-lecting funds for the church at Jerusalem (2 Cor 8:19).

Consistent with the above testimonies of congregational involve-ment was the practice of the early Christian church as reflected in the Di-dache or Teaching of the Twelve Apostles, as it is also called, which may have been written as early as 70–80 AD. Concerning the election of office bearers it says: "Select [cheirotoneō], then, for yourselves bishops and dea-cons worthy of the Lord" (15.1). The command is addressed to the entire church community which is told to choose their own bishops (or over-seers) and deacons from among themselves.[5]

Not surprisingly, in light of the above, John Calvin was insistent on the congregational right to have a say in choosing its office bearers. He said this in the historical context of the Roman Catholic hierarchy not giving

---

3   NIV footnote.
4   R. C. H. Lenski, *The Interpretation of the Acts of the Apostles* (Minneapolis, MN: Augsburg Publishing House, 1961), 585–86; Simon J. Kistemaker, *Exposition of the Acts of the Apostles*, New Testament Commentary (Grand Rapids: Baker, 1990), 525.
5   See further K. Niederwimmer and H. W. Attridge, *The Didache: A Commentary*, Hermeneia (Minneapolis: Fortress Press, 1998), 200; for the Greek text, Michael W. Holmes, *The Apostolic Fathers: Greek Texts and English Translations* (Grand Rapids, MI: Baker, 1999), 267. Elders (*presbuteroi*) and overseers or bishops (*episkopoi*) refer to the same people. Compare, e.g., Acts 20:17 and 28; Titus 1:5 and 7.

the congregation any voice in such matters. The "clergy" was self-perpetuating. Using the example of Paul and Barnabas having the elders elected (Acts 14:23), Calvin wrote: "these two apostles 'created' them [the elders], but the whole group, as was the custom of the Greeks in elections, declared whom it wished to have by raising hands."[6] The church has to be involved. We therefore confess in the Belgic Confession: "We believe that ministers of God's Word, elders, and deacons ought to be chosen to their offices by lawful election of the church" (Art 31).

Should Women be Voting?

If the congregation is to be involved in the process to ordination, the question arises whether women are entitled to vote since they are part of the congregation. Are the female members of the church part of the congregational involvement in choosing office bearers? Indications are that they were not included before Pentecost, but they were included after the outpouring of the Holy Spirit and therefore should be included today.

After the ascension of the Lord Jesus to heaven, but before Pentecost, the eleven disciples wanted a replacement for Judas Iscariot so that their number would again be twelve. "In those days, Peter stood up among the brothers (the company of persons was in all about 120)" (Acts 1:15) and then proposed finding a replacement for Judas. This process seems to have involved only the men, although the matter remains debatable.[7] In favor of the selection being done by men only are the following considerations. It is noteworthy that on this occasion, with the beginning of a new section in the narrative, only the men and not the women are mentioned as being present, although the sisters were specifically noted to be part of the body of believers earlier (Acts 1:14). Also, the number 120 is significant and could allude to 120 men. According to Jewish tradition that number of adult males was able to constitute a local Sanhedrin or council which

---

6   Calvin, *Institutes*, 4.3.15; cf. 4.5.2.
7   For a discussion which includes the possibility that women were included, see, e.g., Darrell L. Bock, *Acts*, Baker Exegetical Commentary on the New Testament (Grand Rapids: Baker Academic, 2007), 81; D.A. Carson, *The Inclusive Language Debate: A Plea for Realism* (Grand Rapids, Michigan: Baker, 1998), 124–25.

would then have authority over those who belonged to the faith.[8] Another indication that only men may have participated in choosing another apostle is that Peter addressed those assembled as "brothers" (ESV), using the compound expression: "men brothers." Such an address is normally used when referring to men.[9] In light of these considerations we get the impression that only males participated in the process of choosing a successor for Judas which culminated with the drawing of lots. If this analysis is correct, then there are two important differences with the election of office bearers in the church before and after Pentecost. After the outpouring of the Holy Spirit, there is no mention that the lot was ever used and females probably participated in the process.

Before looking at the female involvement in election for office bearers, a general comment is in order. When the term "brothers" is used as an address in the book of Acts and elsewhere in the New Testament, this manner of speaking can include women. Indeed, this has resulted in modern Bible translations like the NIV (2011) to simply translate "brothers and sisters" when the original only has the term "brothers," if the context warrants it. The ESV often includes this rendering in a footnote.[10] This usage of the term "brothers" is already seen when the Lord Jesus spoke of believers as "brothers," clearly intending to include sisters (e.g. Matt 25:40). In short, the masculine has historically been the default gender when referring to both male and female, also in the ancient world.[11] Perhaps an analogous modern expression is "you guys" or "hey guys" which is still being used for a group composed of both men and women.[12] In any case, when the apostles

---

8   Eduard Lohse, "*sunedrion*," in *Theological Dictionary of the New Testament*, eds Gerhard Kittel, et al. (Grand Rapids: Eerdmans, 1964–76), 7:866, 871. Such local councils or sanhedrins are also mentioned in Mark 13:9 (ESV translates "councils"). See also Schürer, *The History of the Jewish People*, 185.

9   F.W. Danker, rev & ed, *A Greek-English Lexicon of the New Testament and Other Early Christian Literature*, 3rd ed. (Chicago: University of Chicago Press, 2000), 79.

10 So, e.g., in Acts 6:3; 11:29; 12:17; 16:40; 18:18, 27; 21:7, 17; 28:14, 15. With the exception of Acts 16:40, the footnote in the ESV on all these verses include "sisters." It is beyond the scope and need of this chapter to go into the many issues that arise with gender and translations. See, e.g., Vern Poythress and Wayne Grudem, *The Gender-Neutral Bible Controversy* (Nashville, Tennessee: Broadman & Holman, 2000) and Howard I. Marshall, "Brothers Embracing Sisters?" *Technical Papers for The Bible Translator* 55, no. 3 (2004): 303–10.

11 See the references in Danker, *A Greek-English Lexicon of the New Testament*, 18.

12 Although that expression is becoming suspect in our politically correct culture since it is not

directed their letters to the "brothers", they undoubtedly did not exclude but included the women of the congregations addressed as well.[13] Other passages also show that the term "brothers" can include women.[14] We need to keep this general well-attested usage in mind when we consider biblical passages describing congregational involvement in the ordination process.

After the day of Pentecost when the Holy Spirit was poured out on the believers, the apostles were looking to ordain seven men to serve tables to prevent further neglect of the Hellenist widows. "The twelve summoned the full number of the disciples" and they said to them "therefore, brothers, pick out from among you seven men of good repute" (Acts 6:2–3). There is an emphasis on inclusiveness since the "full number of disciples" were summoned. Women must therefore have been included in those addressed as "brothers." Indeed, the ESV rightly states this in their less literal translation in the footnote to this passage. We can therefore assume that the women participated in the process of selecting the seven men of good repute. The apostles recognized that since the Spirit was also poured out on the women, they too were equipped, as well as the men, with the gifts of the Spirit including the gift of discernment (cf. Acts 2:17).

Another example of congregational involvement is in a meeting that took place in Jerusalem to decide how to deal with Gentile believers with respect to keeping Old Testament laws. As a result of this meeting, "it seemed good to the apostles and the elders, with the whole church, to choose men from among them and send them to Antioch with Paul and Barnabas" (Acts 15:22). So it appears that both male and female ("the whole church") took part in the choosing. We are not told how, but the entire congregation was clearly involved. But it appears that the apostles and elders did the actual appointing. This authority was reflected in the fact that the letter was sent in the name of "the brothers, both the apostles and the elders" (Acts 15:23).

---

gender inclusive enough. See, e.g., Joe Pinsker, "The Problem with 'Hey Guys," *The Atlantic*, 23 August 2018 available at www.theatlantic.com.

13 E.g., Rom 1:13; 1 Cor 1:10; 2 Pet 1:10; 1 John 3:13. In all these instances, ESV includes females in a footnote. For a detailed justification of "brothers" including the entire congregation in the addressees to these letters, see Howard I. Marshall, "Brothers Embracing Sisters?" 307–8.

14 E.g., Eph 6:23; Rev 12:10 where ESV includes "sisters" in a footnote.

To summarize our findings so far, we note that the entire congregation or the total number of people present participated in choosing men to serve tables. "The full number of disciples" was involved (Acts 6:2–3). Also, "the whole church" participated in selecting a delegation to go to Antioch (Acts 15:22). In both these instances, the female members of the church were undoubtedly present and probably took part in the process of selecting the needed men.

Such involvement should not be surprising but expected. As already noted, these events took place after the outpouring of the Holy Spirit. All believers, both male and female are in Christ conformed into his image (Rom 8:29) and "have put on the new self . . . after the image of its creator" (Col 3:10). And so, of God's children of both genders, it can be said, "Children . . . you have been anointed by the Holy One, and you all have knowledge" (1 John 2:18, 20). Enlightened by the Word and Spirit, both male and female have the necessary insight to judge a person's suitability for office. As those sharing in Christ's anointing and being renewed in God's image, all believers have the office of prophet, priest, and king with all the responsibilities and rights connected with that identity (Heidelberg Catechism, QA 32).

As a further consideration, it should be noted that the difference between male and female is not abolished when the privilege of voting is granted to the sisters of the congregation, just as the distinction between parents and children is not abolished when communicant children participate in elections for office bearers along with their parents. Other factors can also be mentioned. Scripture emphasizes the importance of the family unit. But if women are not allowed to participate in selecting office bearers, some households such as those headed by a widow or those of unmarried women living on their own, are marginalized in church life and have no voice in important events such as helping to determine who their office bearers will be.

Furthermore, we need to avoid inconsistencies with respect to the church acknowledging the responsibilities of communicant women. If they can participate in nominating candidates whom they consider suitable and also be part of the process of approbation, that is, to bring in biblically-based objections to those proposed for ordination if necessary, they should also be allowed to use their gift of discernment when the electing from a slate of candidates put forth by the office bearers takes place. Not to do so is inconsistent with their right to be part of the process of nomination and approbation.

However, with all the similarities of male and female in God's church, there are differences that need to be maintained. Within the context of voting, the issue of authority needs to be noted. The renewal in Christ has not abolished the subordinate position of the women in God's order of creation. They are to be submissive and not to exercise authority over men in church worship services (1 Cor 14:12, 34–35; 1 Tim 2:11–12) and they are therefore not qualified to hold ecclesiastical office (1 Tim 3:1–13; Titus 1:5–9). But if this is so, what about voting? Is that not a wielding of authority? It certainly is in our democratic society. Voters determine much.

Is Voting Exercising Governing Authority?

Is voting by the congregation an exercising of authority? To put the issue differently: is a church a democracy or is the vote only advisory, simply stating a preference and leaving the final decision to the office bearers? What actually is involved in the selecting of an office bearer by the congregation?

The Church is not a Democracy

A church of Jesus Christ is not a democracy. It is Christ's church. He has supreme authority. He sets the norms for the offices, and he ultimately is the one who calls men to the ecclesiastical offices. The whole notion of democracy and the power of ruling by means of voting has no place in the church. Christ rules the church by his Word and Spirit through his office bearers. The apostolic admonition to the Ephesian elders makes that clear. "Pay careful attention to yourselves and to all the flock, in which the Holy Spirit has made you overseers, to care for the church of God" (Acts 20:28). The Holy Spirit, the Spirit of Christ (Gal 4:6), the head of the church (Col 1:18), he set the elders or overseers over the church. They are therefore responsible to Christ in the first place and not to the people. This point is also made in Ephesians 4:11–12. The Lord Jesus is the One who "gave the apostles, the prophets, the evangelists, the shepherds and teachers, to equip the saints." Consequently, they are accountable to the Lord in the first place and not to the congregation.

We need to lay aside democratic notions when discussing election for office bearers. The elders rule the church as Christ's representatives. Voting for church office bearers is not exercising governing authority. With their vote, the congregation simply indicates their preference for whom they would like to see ordained. If the congregation had governing authority, there would be another governing body in church government besides that of the consistory or session. Such a setup is foreign to Scripture and thus to Reformed and Presbyterian church polity.

It is important to note that the biblical examples of congregational participation underline the important authority of the office bearers over believers when it comes to selecting office bearers. Those ordained as representatives of Christ, such as apostles and elders, set the norms that had to be fulfilled in order for a selection to be valid (Acts 1:21–23; 6:3). In the case of Matthias, they left the final decision up to God by way of casting lots (Acts 1:26), thus recognizing that the ultimate authority for making a selection came from heaven. On other occasions, office bearers, as those in ordained leadership positions, made the final choice (Acts 14:23; 15:23–26). Through them the Lord calls people to office.

In sum, Scripture affirms the right of the congregation to be involved in the process of selecting future office bearers, but at the same time God's Word underlines the special place of office bearers who have been set over the congregation, who determined the criteria for selection, who did the appointing to office, and where this is mentioned, who also did the ordination (Acts 6:6). Scripture gives no basis for the notion that a congregation has governing authority. To the contrary, there are many exhortations for the congregation to obey and submit to the leadership of the church (1 Cor 16:16; 1 Thess 5:12–13; Heb 13:17; cf. Acts 20:28). When voting for office bearers, the congregation is simply making known to the leadership of the church their preference from the slate of candidates presented by the church leadership based on how they evaluate the gifts Christ has given to the various candidates for the office. The congregational vote is part of the process of calling and should be seen in light of the form for ordination when the new elders and deacons give an affirmative answer to the questions: "Do you feel in your hearts that God himself, through his congregation, has called you to these offices?"[15]

If the congregation has no governing authority, all arguments about women not being given the right to vote because it would mean exercising authority over the men (cf. 1 Tim 2:12) fall by the wayside and are irrelevant. A. N. Hendriks and K. Deddens said it well with respect to women voting when they described the election process. "This election guided by the consistory is a communal act of both the consistory and the congregation, in which members of the congregation do not participate in the ruling of the church, but in which the consistory involves the congregation who, by virtue of her maturity reached at Pentecost, continually looks for the gifts necessary for the office."[16] In a similar vein, W.W.J. Van Oene asserted that the notion

> that taking part in elections is a act of governing is definitely incorrect. The consistory gives the congregation the opportunity to advise the consistory by means of an election, but ultimately the consistory is not bound by this advice, although it must have good and compelling reasons to deviate from it. It is the congregation that elects; it is the consistory with the deacons that appoints and calls [in the case of a minister]. Advising is still not the same as governing.[17]

Past and Current Testimony

The notion of giving the communicant sisters of a congregation the opportunity to participate in the election of office bearers is not a new idea. Stalwart Reformed men have defended the voting rights of women within the church. Already in the seventeenth century, the orthodox Scottish Presbyterian, Samuel Rutherford, defended the right of the entire congregation, including women, to elect office bearers. When the objection was

---

15 Form for the Ordination of Elders and Deacons as found in *Book of Praise*, 626 (my emphasis).

16 A. N. Hendriks, "The Place and Significance of the Offices in the Congregation of Christ," *Diakonia* 4, no. 2 (1990): 37–38 (emphasis is in the original).

17 W. W. J. Van Oene, *With Common Consent: A Practical Guide to the Use of the Church Order of the Canadian Reformed Churches* (Winnipeg: Premier, 1990), 19.

made that if you can elect them, you can ordain them, Rutherford answered that you have to distinguish between election and ordination. Ordination is more than election and thus the two are distinguished in Acts 6:3 and 6.[18] Moving to more recent church history in the Dutch Reformed tradition, notable faithful Reformed men have defended the right for communicant women to take part in the election of office bearers. They include such luminaries as Lucas Lindeboom, professor of New Testament in Kampen,[19] the well-known dogmatician Herman Bavinck,[20] and a prominent minister, J. C. Sikkel.[21]

It is also noteworthy that women in faithful churches elsewhere have been enjoying this right. In the case of Scotland, the female vote for office bearers was a general practice in the Secession Church since 1820 and in the Free Church since 1843.[22] Female communicant members may also vote in other conservative churches such as: the Evangelical Presbyterian Church of Ireland, Reformed Presbyterian Church of Ireland, Presbyterian Church of Eastern Australia, Églises Réformées Évangéliques Indépendantes in France, Greek Evangelical Church, Église Réformée Confessante au Zaire, African Evangelical Presbyterian Church of East-Africa (Kenya), Reformed Church of East Africa (Kenya),23 the Canadian Reformed Churches and the United Reformed Churches in North America.

Conclusion

It is clear from Scripture that the congregation participated in the

---

18 Samuel Rutherford, *The Due Right of Presbyteries for the Government of the Church of Scotland* (London: Whittaker & Crook, 1644), 198–202, 476–77, 493–94; Travis Fentiman, *An Analysis of Rutherford and M'Crie on Whether Ladies Have the Right to Vote in the Election of Church Officers* (2015), Available at https://reformedbooksonline.com/.

19 His grandson, who was also in favor of women voting, noted that in 1918 Prof. Lindeboom stated that for forty years he had seen the refusal of the voting right to women as a misjudgment; quoted in A.M. Lindeboom, *Een recht van eeuwen her: de zusters der gemeente bij de verkiezing van ambtsdragers, en de opbouw van het tempelhuis* (Amsterdam: S.J.P. Bakker, 1941), 89.

20 H. Bavinck, *De vrouw in de hedendaagsche maatschappij* (Kampen: J.H. Kok, 1918), 149–52. He also mentioned that Abraham Kuyper defended the women's right to vote in church.

21 J.C. Sikkel, *De grote toekomst en de vrouw* (Rotterdam: Libertas, 1920), 37–39.

22 L.O. Macdonald, "Women in Presbyterian Churches," in *Dictionary of Scottish Church History and Theology*, ed. Nigel M. de S. Cameron (Downers Grove, Ill: InterVarsity, 1993), 885–86.

23 This list is derived from the *Commissierapport inzake het vrouwenstemrecht* found in *Acta GKv 1993*, 299.

process leading up to the ordination of office bearers. According to biblical church polity, the authority in the church is the Lord Jesus Christ who is represented by his office bearers. They are the ones who have governing authority in the church. The congregation does not have this authority. The sheep are under the ordained shepherds. The congregation can make its wishes known, but a meeting of the office bearers decides which biblically qualified candidates are presented to the congregation for consideration. After ascertaining the congregation's preferences by way of the elections, the church leadership appoints men to the respective offices and after congregational approbation ordains them.

In this chapter, I have tried to show that if the congregation votes for office bearers, women as part of the congregation should participate in the election as well. In my view, Scripture supports this position. However, the issue remains controversial among some. Since the purpose of Scripture is not to give us a ready-made church order, the Bible does not give a specific and unambiguous answer to the question of female congregational voting. Since Scripture does not directly address this issue, one can assume that it is a matter about which different views can be held without fracturing the fellowship of believers. The local church is free to make its rules for the election of office bearers. If a consistory or session makes a decision with which one is not satisfied, whether the decision be for or against allowing the women to vote, one should acquiesce in the decision made and not stir up needless trouble. In the grand scheme of things this is a relatively minor matter. It should not be blown out of proportion and made into a divisive issue. If women are denied the vote, they are still involved in proposing candidates and in the approbation phase of the election process. Furthermore, there are still many other contributions that the sisters in the congregation can make for the upbuilding of the church as can be seen elsewhere in this book.

There is one argument that should not be part of this discussion, namely, that granting women the right to vote indicates a slippery slope that will lead to female ordination. These two issues are in completely different categories. On the matter of female ordination Scripture is very clear and there should be no question about the illegitimacy of female ordination into ecclesiastical office. See further chapters 12 and 13 in this book.

Furthermore, the history of the Scottish churches shows that giving communicant females the right to vote need not lead to female ordination. The Free Church of Scotland has had female voting for many generations and it does not allow the ordination of women into ecclesiastical office because such a practice is contrary to Scripture.

11

The Office of the Church in Relation to Civil Government

We have considered aspects of the different offices that function within the church. But what about the calling of the church itself with respect to the civil government? What is the specific task of the church as seen in the functioning of the offices of minister of the gospel and the elder when it comes to the doings of the civil authorities? This question becomes urgent when concerned Christians notice that liberal churches speak up as if they represent *the* Christian position on issues of the day and support government policies that are clearly against biblical norms. Should conservative churches then not also address the powers that be? For example, one mainline church after another has openly supported same-sex marriage although God only instituted marriage as the union of male and female at the dawn of history. Should conservative churches remain silent or should they publicly oppose government policies that contradict biblical norms?

The question is urgent because already back in 2015 Pew Research reported that "a solid majority of white mainline Protestants (62%) now favor allowing gays and lesbians to wed, with just 33% opposed." A 2021 Gallup poll showed that American support for same-sex marriage is now at 70%. Virtually all Western nations have legalized same-sex marriage.[1] This is only an example. Other issues like abortion and the growing acceptance of transgender treatments can also be mentioned.

---

1 For these reports and further information see David Masci and Michael Lipka, "Where Christian Churches, Other Religions Stand on Gay Marriage." Found at https://www.pewresearch.org/fact-tank/2015/12/21/where-christian-churches-stand-on-gay-marriage/; Justin McCarthy, "Record-High 70% in U.S. Support Same-Sex Marriage." Found at https://news.gallup.com/poll/350486/record-high-support-same-sex-marriage.aspx?version=print; David Masci, Elizabeth Sciupac, and Michael Lipka, "Same-Sex Marriage Around the World." Found at https://www.pewforum.org/fact-sheet/gay-marriage-around-the-world/

The central issue that needs to be addressed is whether the church as a body has the biblical duty to officially engage government officials regarding planned legislation and to interact with them to oppose policies that run counter to biblical norms. There is pressure on churches to affirm these responsibilities as part of their official duty. After all, laws that violate biblical standards are not only harmful to the nation but also to the church for they undermine public morality. And public morals do have an influence on church members. Furthermore, can we let the distortion of biblical truth by liberal churches go unchallenged? In addressing this issue, we need first to consider the task of the church in the light of Scripture and then consider the implications. Next we will look at exceptional circumstances and come to some concluding remarks.

The Calling of the Church

Before the Lord Jesus ascended into heaven, he informed his disciples that all authority in heaven and on earth had been given to him. He then gave the church its commission in no uncertain terms. "Go and make disciples of all nations, baptizing them in the name of the Father and of the Son and of the Holy Spirit, and teaching them to obey everything I have commanded you. And surely I am with you always, to the very end of the age" (Matt. 28:19-20). For our purposes, two things can be noted. First, the task of the church is to preach the glad tidings of salvation in Jesus Christ so that those who hear may believe and be baptized. Second, it is also the task of the church to teach them "everything I have commanded you." This responsibility shows that preaching the gospel must include teaching the law and will of God. Those baptized need to know how to live the Christian life.

The teaching ministry of the church includes both the Sunday preaching, the weekly catechism class, and any additional special instruction that is given. Besides being instrumental in the process of personal sanctification, such instruction also equips and trains members of the church to function meaningfully in today's secular society as citizens of Christ's kingdom. After all, the ecclesiastical offices are Christ's gift to his people "to prepare God's people for works of service" not only within the church but also outside (cf. Eph. 4:12-16; 5:11-17). And therefore, for such teaching to be relevant, the current moral crisis in the Western world also needs to be addressed. Sermons, for example, cannot avoid speaking to issues from the public square that undermine God's institutions and good law for society as he has ordained it. At the same time, such preaching and teaching must be in complete accordance with the Word of God and not promote the personal opinion of the minister. The full gospel no more and no less is what is needed. In this way members of the church will be equipped with biblical norms to engage in the public debate about the issues of the day and be motivated to seek to influence decision making in politics where necessary. In this way they heed the apostolic demand: "Walk as children of light (for the fruit of light is found in all that is good and right and true), and try to discern what is pleasing to the Lord. Take no part in the unfruitful works of darkness, but instead expose them" (Eph 5:8–11). The church through its office bearers, in its official ministry, does not have to do what the members of the congregation are doing or should do.[2]

As a rule, it is therefore not the calling of the church as a corporate body to speak to the political issues of the day and attempt to influence the agenda of government. This is indeed the responsibility of the members of the church. They are the ones who are to carry the implications of the gospel into all of life, also into the political sphere. The church as corporate body does not normally have this responsibility. Its chief task is to preach the gospel and to equip the congregation for a life of service. It is not a political institution. This principle was dramatically displayed in the sixteenth century when Prince William of Orange fought courageously for the cause of Protestant Holland against the tyranny of Roman Catholic Spain. During that struggle he petitioned the Reformed Synod of Emden (1571) for its full and open support for the cause of the liberation of the Netherlands from the Spanish yoke. Although the synodical delegates were completely sympathetic to the cause of the prince, yet, as an ecclesiastical assembly they refused his request. Consistent with this refusal, the Synod of Dort (1574) decided that ecclesiastical assemblies could only deal with ecclesiastical matters.[3] This stipulation eventually ended up in the classic Reformed

---

2   A helpful resource is Tim J. R. Trumper, *Preaching and Politics: Engagement Without Compromise* (Eugene, OR: Wipf & Stock, 2009).

3   See the discussion in Cornelis Van Dam, *God and Government. Biblical Principles for Today: An Introduction and Resource* (Eugene, OR: Wipf & Stock, 2011), 49–50.

Church Order of the Synod of Dort (1618–19) which stated that ecclesiastical assemblies "shall deal with no other than ecclesiastical matters" (Art. 30). This is a good rule. The church does not have the authority or expertise to make all kinds of pronouncements on social and political issues.

It is, however, worthy of note that the Church Order of Dort did include an article which states that the office bearers of the church shall "endeavor by due respect and communication to secure and retain the favor of the authorities towards the church, so that the church of Christ may lead a quiet and peaceable life, godly and respectful in every way" (Art. 28).[4] Such communication has historically meant that synods would, for example, send to those in authority congratulations on a sovereign's birthday and expressions of condolences on the death of a prominent politician.[5] However, this article suggests that more than such actions can be undertaken. After all, in order that "the church of Christ may lead a quiet and peaceable life, godly and respectful in every way" (Church Order Art. 28), the state must make such conditions possible within their jurisdiction by enacting laws that are consistent with biblical norms. And so there may be situations in which churches need to address government authorities with their concerns. The Church Order adopted by the Free Reformed Churches of Australia correctly states that office bearers must "invoke the government to protect the ministry of the church." Local churches are often best situated to do that through their local Member of Parliament.[6]

Although the civil authorities and the church each have their own task and office, it is not possible for the church to wash its hands, so to speak, of all responsibility and say that what goes on in Parliament or Congress and the moral direction of our nation is really of no concern to the churches. This observation brings us to two exceptional situations which could warrant the church as a corporate body to be directly involved in the political issues of the day.

---

4   . *Book of Praise*, 653.
5   . In the history of the Reformed churches in the Netherlands, provision under this article of the Church Order has also meant that synods have made decisions respecting the spiritual care of those in prison and in the military and engaged local churches or synodical deputies for contact with the authorities to that end. See Bos, *De orde der kerk*, 104–5.
6   Article 27 as given and commented on in G. Van Rongen, *Decently and in Good Order*, reprint, 1986, Reformed Guardian (Kelmscott, W.A.: N.p., 2005), 46–48.

The Church's Involvement in Exceptional Circumstances

The Westminster Confession of Faith mentions these exceptions in Article 31. "Synods and councils are to handle, or conclude nothing, but that which is ecclesiastical: and are not to intermeddle with civil affairs which concern the commonwealth, *unless* by way of humble petition in cases extraordinary; or, by way of advice, for satisfaction of conscience, if they be thereunto required by the civil magistrate."[7] We need to consider each exception in turn.

The first exception entails that the church must confess and bear testimony to the lordship of Jesus Christ to the civil authorities when these magistrates are making decisions that directly affect the ministry of the church and could compromise the church's identity as "the pillar and foundation of the truth" (1 Tim 3:15). As a lampstand shining in a dark world (cf. Rev. 1:20), the church as an institution has no choice but to speak up when its ministry, identity, and well-being are directly threatened. A key purpose for the writing of the Belgic Confession was to testify to the authorities of the day what the persecuted church stood for so that room could be given to it in order that it could function in peace. As has happened more often in the history of the church, this testimony was sealed with the blood of martyrs.

Today the situation is different, but the church must be ever vigilant to defend the exercise of the true religion and be prepared to address the authorities if necessary. It has been correctly said that the church is the conscience of society.[8] That means the church should speak up when remaining silent would present a direct threat to itself and its biblical teaching, and, for that matter, would also present a danger to the well-being of society when immorality is promoted. For example, if a law were to be proposed which would forbid the denunciation of a specific sin, such as a homosexual lifestyle, the churches must consider whether they should lodge an official

---

7 *The Confession of Faith and Catechisms: The Westminster Confession of Faith and Catechisms Adopted by The Orthodox Presbyterian Church, with Proof Texts* (Willow Grove, PA: The Committee on Christian Education of the Orthodox Presbyterian Church, 2005), 146–47 (my emphasis).

8 So, for instance, John H. Redekop, *Politics Under God*, foreword by John A. Lapp (Waterloo, ON / Scottdale, PA: Herald Press, 2007), 150.

protest to the secular authorities. A public testimony of the biblical norms would be entirely appropriate. G. I. Williamson gave an example of a church speaking up when certain laws were passed trying to silence the biblical testimony of homosexual sin. He wrote that then "both in San Francisco and the State of New Jersey the Orthodox Presbyterian Church had no choice but to speak out—*to the State*—for satisfaction of conscience. It said to the State—and properly we maintain—that it must continue to denounce what the Bible denounces."[9] On a more local level, if city hall should approve a route for a Sunday Santa Claus parade which makes it difficult for church members to attend worship services, the consistory should consider engaging the civil authorities and seek a solution.

Moving beyond the church's public testimony to biblical norms and local protests, it is far better that members of the church get involved on the political front. This would avert the danger of a church as a corporate body becoming needlessly drawn into or too deeply involved in political issues about which it may lack expertise. Such involvement could damage the credibility of the churches. Political matters can be better dealt with without the official involvement of the church. In Canada, organizations like the Association of Reformed Political Action (ARPA), the Evangelical Fellowship, and the Christian Legal Fellowship are all on full alert to protect the place and mission of the church and the rights and freedoms of Christians. Other western nations probably have similar organizations. In any case, to remain with Canada in terms of an example, in 2021 the Supreme Court of Canada unanimously overturned a bad decision of the Ontario Court of Appeal and thus reaffirmed the independent jurisdiction of the church over matters of church discipline (membership in the church) and doctrine (how to deal with alleged heresy). This happy development to challenge a bad lower court decision was primarily due to the work of ARPA which had noticed this decision and had decided to do something about it by appealing it.[10] This example illustrates that the church need not get involved if there are committed Christians who are organized to do

---

9   G.I. Williamson, *The Westminster Confession of Faith: For Study Classes* (Phillipsburg, NJ: Presbyterian & Reformed, 1978), 327 (emphasis in the original).

10   The name of the case is *Ethiopian Orthodox Tewahedo Church et al. v. Aga et al.* See further ARPA, "Supreme Court Affirms the Exclusive Jurisdiction of the Church Over Doctrinal and Membership Questions." Found at https://arpacanada.ca/news/tag/aga/.

such work.

The other exception for churches to become politically involved, as mentioned by the Westminster Confession of Faith, is when the civil authorities request the input of a church on a current issue. The church then has the obligation to provide such input (cf. 1 Pet. 3:15). This can be of great help to the government. It is therefore understandable that a Reformed church federation can decide to provide official ways of communicating with the civil authorities. For example, the Reformed Churches (Liberated) in the Netherlands have deputies for contact with the governing authorities. Among their responsibilities, in accordance with their Church Order (Art. A5), is the duty to be vigilant about laws being prepared that would impact the confession and life of the church.[11] There is something to be said for having such synodically appointed deputies. They can be proactive in addressing the government on behalf of the churches with issues that directly affect the well-being of the church and its freedom to proclaim the gospel in fullness.

The Church's Prayers for and Obedience to Civil Authorities

It is obvious from what has been said so far that those in government need much wisdom and discretion. They not only require input from Christians on government policy and legislation, but they need our prayers as well. Offering such prayer is a biblical duty of the church. When discussing public worship, the apostle Paul instructed Timothy that "supplications, prayers, intercessions, and thanksgivings be made for all people, for kings and all who are in high positions, that we may lead a peaceful and quiet life, godly and dignified in every way" (1 Tim 2:1–2). How necessary this command is! Churches cannot expect to be able to function normally in a sin-broken world if the civil authorities are not able to do their duty to combat evil, exercise righteousness, and keep the peace among the citizens it governs. But to do this, those set above us need the prayers of God's

---

11 Gereformeerde Kerken vrijgemaakt, "Relatie kerk en overheid." Found in https://www.gkv.nl/deputaatschappen/relatie-kerk-en-overheid/; for Article A5 of the Church Order, see http://www.kerkrecht.nl/node/1106.

people when gathered in holy assembly. God desires a well-ordered society and the church has its part to play in the prayers it regularly offers in public worship. This responsibility cannot be minimized for God hears the prayers of the righteous and those prayers which he requests factor into his sovereign guidance of the authorities which he has set over us.

As we pray for those in authority, members of Christ's church are also obedient to them (Rom 13:1–7). Such obedience serves the cause of the proclamation and promotion of the gospel. The laws of the land, therefore, demand our compliance unless what is asked of us is against the Word of God. After all, "we must obey God rather than men" (Acts 5:29).

It is obviously very important that the church office bearers set a good example to the congregation when it comes to obeying government legislation. Article 28 of the classic Reformed Church Order mentioned earlier includes the provision that "all office-bearers are in duty bound to impress diligently and sincerely upon the whole congregation the obedience, love, and respect which are due to the civil authorities; they shall set a good example to the whole congregation in this matter."[12]

Setting a good example involves not only adhering to local fire regulations, but it also includes honoring all the legal obligations that come from the church's charitable status, including not engaging in political activity. Furthermore, obedience to those whom God has set above us means that office bearers report to the appropriate authorities any knowledge of criminal offenses committed, as well as reportable abuse cases. Being a good example involves obeying government emergency health orders as in the COVID-19 pandemic. It is critical for a church's witness to society that it shows itself credible in dealing seriously with the issues of the day as mandated by government and also exhibits Christian love for the neighbor in helping to combat the spread of sickness. Since we confess the seriousness of sin and the fallen state of the world, the church office bearers should be among the first to heed the call of government to confront the evils of the day with obeying legislation that seeks to combat it.[13]

---

12 *Book of Praise*, 653.
13 A very useful resource is Ray Pennings, *Church and Caesar: A Legal Primer for Church Office-Bearers* (Grand Rapids: Reformation Heritage Books / Free Reformed Publications, 2008).

Conclusion

The holy people of God, the Christian church, does not fit well within the current western culture that in several critical respects gives free reign to sin by opposing or undermining the creation ordinances of marriage, family, and the day of rest. We live in a society that is turning its back on the remaining vestiges of Christian influence bequeathed by previous generations. As such the Western world is ripe for God's judgment. Christians realize more and more that they are ultimately pilgrims and exiles in this world (1 Pet 2:11). But God has placed us in this world with a purpose. In Old Testament times, Jeremiah exhorted the Jewish exiles in Babylon to seek the welfare of the foreign country in which they now found themselves (Jer 29:7). Christians today have the same responsibility to the society and country in which they find themselves, or rather, in which God has placed them.

Furthermore, the church, as a corporate body with its office bearers, has a task. Its most important duty is to proclaim the gospel and so be a light, projecting the beacon of hope that is the gospel, in a dark world lost in sin. That gospel is the only ultimate solution to the ills and challenges of society. Government action and legislative ambitions will, in the end, not solve the problems of society for these problems all have a common root in sin. The church and its preachers must use all the opportunities that our current freedoms and liberties afford to be a salt and light in this world (cf. Matt 5:13–16). The testimony of the gospel alone can provide the salt to fight the spiritual and moral decay that is all around us. The good news alone can provide the light that actually penetrates the present darkness.

Although there are instances, as we have seen, when it may be appropriate for the church to testify publicly to the governing authorities on a particular issue, its primary duty is to proclaim the gospel and so equip believers to be agents for combating societal sins in the political realm and for shining the light of the good news in their homes and wherever the Lord has placed them in this world. The church's restricted responsibility to preach highlights the need for members of the church to project the claims of the gospel out into the world in which they live and work. Believers are part of the nation and share responsibility for its moral direction.

We need be a salt and light also in the political sphere and get involved in the processes that affect the present and future well-being of our country. After all, Christ's claims extend over all of life. And we should not be too easily discouraged if we do not have initial successes. Our Savior is triumphant Lord, seated at the right hand of God (Eph 1:20). He declared that "all authority in heaven and on earth has been given to me" (Matt 28:18). And our all-powerful Lord is on his way back to this world (Rev 22:12). So let us not grow weary and assume beforehand that our efforts as Christians are futile. Rather let us be encouraged by the opportunities that our sovereign Lord and Savior gives us and use them to his glory.

PART C

WOMEN IN SPECIAL SERVICE

CHAPTER 12

Culture and Biblical Authority: A Reminder from Luther

Due to the pressures of modernity and political correctness, first liberal and then conservative churches have proceeded to ordain women into ecclesiastical office. In other words, the momentum to change the qualifications from male ecclesiastical ordination to female, did not come from Scripture, but from the influence of the contemporary culture. Any decisive input from Scripture was marginal. This is the conclusion that Koen K. Lim reached on his study of women in ecclesiastical office in the Netherlands.[1] Given the clear biblical testimony on this issue and the long-standing consensus in the Christian church against female ecclesiastical ordination, there is reason to believe that current cultural influences such as egalitarianism were also the driving force toward female ordination elsewhere.

A purpose of this chapter is to show that the teaching of Scripture had indeed only marginal influence compared to the felt need to conform to current cultural expectations regarding the place of women. As subsequent chapters will show, there is no biblical justification for female ecclesiastical ordination, also not when we factor in the culture of the times that the Word of God came to us in written form. In this introductory chapter on the Bible and female ordination we will briefly consider how the authority of Scripture has been eroded when cultural norms are prioritized over the clear teaching of the Word of God. We will use the example of the decisions of the Reformed Churches in the Netherlands (Liberated) to open all the ecclesiastical offices to women at their Synod of Meppel in 2017. It is another major conservative church federation to fall under the spell of women's right to ordination.

---

1   Koen Kyungkeun Lim, *Het spoor van de vrouw in het ambt*, Theologie en Geschiedenis (Kampen: Kok, 2001), 288.

The Authority of Scripture

The momentum for change in the church has come from its leadership.[2] When typical church members read a faithful translation of Scripture, they see no justification for ordaining women into ecclesiastical office. To the contrary, the qualifications for the office of minister, elder, and deacon are clearly spelled out in the Bible and those qualifications include that those ordained must be male (1 Tim 3:1–13; Titus 1:5–9). But the leadership of many churches, the so-called elite intelligentsia, has ruled that what Scripture appears to say is not really what it means to say. Consequently, Scripture, in this case the qualifications for ecclesiastical office, are turned upside down. When Scripture clearly says that only males are to be ordained, today's self-proclaimed experts say that the ordination of both male and female is biblical. In this way the church is led into the bondage of the reigning cultural paradigm of our time and the church is no longer free in Christ to accept Scripture as it is written and meant to be taken in its plain sense.

There is a bitter irony about this new bondage in the Netherlands into which the Synod of Meppel led the churches because it took place in the 500th anniversary year of the great Reformation. This was a series of historic events that set the churches free from this type of captivity by asserting that Scripture alone (*sola Scriptura*) is the infallible rule for faith and the practices of the church.

Luther on Biblical Authority

One of Luther's most important contributions to the Reformation was his insistence on the absolute authority of God's Word which is to be understood and submitted to in its obvious meaning. That sounds familiar to us, but put in the context of Luther's time, it was revolutionary. By asserting the absolute authority and the clarity of Scripture, Luther took direct aim at the Roman Catholic teaching that only the pope and other ecclesiastical authorities could determine the meaning of the Bible. According to Rome, the Scriptures were obscure and needed the church to tell the

---

2 For a detailed study of this phenomenon in the Netherlands, see A. M. Lindeboom, *De theologen gingen voorop: eenvoudig verhaal van de ontmanteling van de Gereformeerde Kerken* (Kampen: J.H. Kok, 1987).

people what they meant. Thus God's people were kept in bondage to the "expertise" and authority of the church which taught them such "truths" as the sacrament of penance and the need for indulgences from the church in order to receive forgiveness.

Luther challenged all of that and more in his *The Bondage of the Will*. He attacked the Pope for maintaining that the Bible was not clear, and that Rome needed to tell the people what it meant. Luther went on to say that this is most pernicious "for it has led ungodly men to set themselves above the Scriptures and to fabricate whatever they pleased, until the Scriptures have been completely trampled down and we have been believing and teaching nothing but the dreams of madmen."[3] He further asserted that "those who deny that the Scriptures are quite clear and plain leave us nothing but darkness."[4]

By defending the absolute authority of Scripture and its clarity so that its obvious plain meaning could be accepted, Luther set many people free from the bondage of those who had set themselves up as authorities above the plain teaching of Scripture. Luther, however, realized that for the people to be truly free from such pseudo-authority the Bible had to be made available to the common people and translated into their language. All members of the church had to be able to read the Bible for themselves and become familiar with it so that they could embrace its teachings and reject heresy. Is not the Word a lamp before one's feet which is to illuminate the path we walk on (Ps 119:105)? Reading Scripture also makes one sensitive to the issues of the day and gives a biblical perspective. As Luther put it: "all spirits are to be tested in the presence of the church at the bar of Scripture."[5] No wonder Luther posted his Ninety-five Theses against Rome's teachings on the Castle Church door in Wittenberg to expose the false teachings of the church in the light of Scripture. And what a blessing for the church that he translated the Bible into the language of the people.

---

3   Luther, Martin, *Luther's Works*, ed. Jaroslav Pelikan, et al. (Saint Louis, MO: Concordia, 1955–2016), 33:90.
4   Luther, *Luther's Works*, 33:94.
5   Luther, *Luther's Works*, 33:91. "What is new in Luther is the notion of the absolute obedience to the Scriptures against any authorities; be they popes or councils." Heiko A. Oberman, *Luther: Man Between God and the Devil*, trans. Eileen Walliser-Schwarzbart (New Haven, CT: Yale University Press, 1989), 204.

Implications for Today

Luther set many in his generation free from the false teachings of Rome. The Word of God became the norm and had to be obeyed rather than the pronouncements of popes and councils which placed themselves above the Word. As children of the Reformation, we do well to remember that we are not to be in bondage to any teaching that opposes the clear instruction of the Word of God. Today, many look to contemporary authorities outside Scripture to address ethical and other issues on which the Bible is clear. Many look to science for objective truth on how the world began. But also the speculative theories of science on the origin of our planet need to be scrutinized in the light of God's normative and clear Word in its teaching about creation.[6] God used Luther to set his people free in the past from those authorities which placed themselves above Scripture. Also today we should not be in bondage to any authority which sets itself up over and against the clear teaching of God's Word.

An obvious potent force and authority that currently attacks and erodes the truth of Scripture is our godless egalitarian culture which acknowledges no norms except what humans desire for themselves and imagine their rights to be. This corrosive culture and the authority it wields in our society must not be allowed to enslave us and lead us to denying the clear teachings of the Word of God, also when dealing with qualifications for the offices in the church. Many biblical scholars, influenced more by the spirit of the times than by Scripture, are taking people into bondage on the issue of ecclesiastical ordination. This has most regrettably also happened in the Reformed Churches in the Netherlands (Liberated). They are slipping into the bondage of the powerful and seductive cultural spirits of our time and reinterpreting Scripture to make the qualifications for ecclesiastical office more agreeable to the current cultural norms. In the process, the authority of Scripture is undermined or denied, and it is sometimes made to say and mean the opposite of what God's Word plainly states.

For almost two thousand years, the Christian church in all its manifestations, has never opened up the ecclesiastical offices to women. But

---

6   See, e.g., Cornelis Van Dam, *In the Beginning: Listening to Genesis 1 and 2* (Grand Rapids, MI: Reformation Heritage Books, 2021), 26–58.

the sad reality is that the Reformed Churches in the Netherlands (Liberated) have now done this in their Synod held at Meppel (2017).[7] Their decisions on this issue is in effect a declaration that the church authorities, experts, and specialists of our time have now finally been able to see what the common people today and the church as a whole over the millennia have not been able to see; namely, that the apostolic qualifications for the offices can be ignored since they are culturally bound and no longer relevant for the church today. That sounds quite presumptuous, and it is. But it is also very sad. With this new understanding of Scripture, fallible creatures have declared null and void parts of God's Word, or made it say the opposite of what it plainly states. This approach will have ethical implications far beyond the issue of female ordination.[8] By acquiescing to this decision, churches are placing themselves in bondage to ecclesiastical authorities instead of Scripture. This was the bondage from which the sixteenth century Reformation had once set God's people free. And more recently it was also a bondage from which many of these Reformed churches had set themselves free in the ecclesiastical Liberation of 1944.[9]

It may be helpful to illustrate the dominant influence of contemporary culture on Synod Meppel's decisions by giving a brief look at the report that served Synod to justify their decisions.[10] The report does not present new arguments but largely reiterates arguments made by others who have admitted women to the ecclesiastical offices.

---

7 The synod decided on June 15–16 to open all ecclesiastical offices to women. The synod took this decision in steps by first approving female ordination to the office of deacon, then elder, and finally minister of the Word. On June 17, it also decided that as soon as a local consistory ratified the synodical decision, it could ordain women in these offices. *Acta GKv 2017*, Art. 18.

8 The issue of homosexual sin comes to mind. These Reformed churches exercise little or no discipline of those who live in homosexual relationships in spite of the fact that Scripture clearly condemns such relationships, e.g., in Romans 1. Indeed, according to Ad de Bruijne, professor of ethics and spirituality in Kampen, at the most only about a third of practicing homosexuals are kept from the Lord's Table. Ad de Bruijne, "Vriendschap voor christen-homo's," in *Open en kwetsbaar: christelijk debat over homoseksualiteit*, ed. Ad de Bruijne, TU-Bezinningsreeks 11 (Barneveld: Vuurbaak, 2012), 57–58.

9 For an introduction, see Cornelis Van Dam, ed., *The Liberation: Causes and Consequences. The Struggle in the Reformed Churches in The Netherlands in the 1940's* (Winnipeg: Premier, 1995).

10 A. Haan-Kamminga, et al., *Report of Deputies Male/Female and the Office: Serving Together* (2016). Available only in Dutch at https://www.gkv.nl/beleidsrapporten-generale-synode-meppel-2017/; the English translation seems to be no longer available on their website.

The Dominance of Culture

This report attaches great significance to culture, both in biblical times and now at the expense of the normativeness of the biblical text as God has given it to us. Those who wrote the report are, however, convinced that their recommendations are based on Scripture, and they emphatically deny that they are influenced by the demands of our current culture.[11] Without questioning the integrity of the deputies, this denial has some credibility issues within the context of the report. It is, for example, remarkable that the report states that the husband's authority over his wife is basically determined by the culture of that time and is thus not normative for today.[12] So what Scripture specifically says (e.g., 1 Pet 3:1), the report denies. It is also striking that among the grounds given for urging the churches to create room for women to show their gifts in proclamation, education, the pastorate, and diaconate, is the matter of our current culture. Since both men and women are now providing theological education and pastoral care, and since our current culture is strongly orientated to gender equality, these are reasons for female ordination in the offices of the church.[13] Today's societal culture demands it. Why can a woman be a judge in our society but not a minister? Such questions are raised in defense of female ordination in these Dutch churches.[14]

The report's use of culture in understanding and applying Scripture is a central feature and it is that emphasis on culture that undermines the ability of this report to give a sound interpretation of Scripture. The biblical text is not allowed to speak for itself. If Scripture needs to be read and understood, not by what the text plainly says, but through the lens of the culture of that time, we face some significant if not insurmountable obstacles to rightly understanding the Word. For unless you have an absolutely accurate picture of the culture of, for example, the time of Paul, you

---

11 Haan-Kamminga, et al., *Report of Deputies*, 61–62.
12 Haan-Kamminga, et al., *Report of Deputies*, 13, 15; cf., e.g., Wayne Grudem, "Wives Like Sarah, and the Husbands Who Honor Them: 1 Peter 3:1–7," in *Recovering Biblical Manhood and Womanhood: A Response to Evangelical Feminism*, ed. John Piper and Wayne Grudem (Wheaton IL: Crossway, 1991), 194–208.
13 Haan-Kamminga, et al., *Report of Deputies*, 68.
14 So, e.g., Myriam Klinker-de Klerck, *Als vrouwen het Woord doen: over schriftgezag, hermeneutiek en het waarom van de apostolische instructie aan vrouwen*, TU-Bezinningsreeks (Barneveld: Vuurbaak, 2011), 134.

will not be able to understand what God is saying to us today. This method of interpreting which places such a high premium on knowing the culture of biblical times so that it is absolutely essential for understanding what the text says has enormous consequences. When you stop to think this method through, then logically speaking it is only in our time with all the available resources of archaeological, cultural, and historical studies that we can finally find out what the Lord our God is actually teaching us in the apostle's writings. Such an attitude betrays human arrogance and is unwarranted. God is able to communicate to each generation what is necessary. The Word is clear for people from all times and places who read it.

It is of course true that the latest discoveries can help us to better understand Scripture. We can with thanks appreciate the additional information that archaeology and other fields of study have done to illumine the biblical text. But, God's Word is clear with respect to the intended basic meaning, not just to our generation but to all those who have preceded us as well. No reader of God's Word should be held hostage to the latest cultural studies in order to finally find out what God really meant to tell us about female ordination to ecclesiastical office. Yet this is essentially what this report says,

> and it admits that their recommendations mean a break with the past.[15]

In the chapters that follow on women and office, we will for the most part try to positively explain the biblical text within its context, but from time to time we will also illustrate how the method in the Dutch report that served at Synod Meppel 2017 is misguided and does injustice to Scripture. The report may be in tune with what is currently fashionable in biblical interpretation, but it is not faithful to God's Word. This reality is also evident to those outside the circle of Christianity.

Conclusion

In conclusion it can be noted, by way of example, that even a secular Jewish historian is not impressed with the so-called biblical arguments

---

15 Haan-Kamminga, et al., *Report of Deputies*, 61–62; see also Henk van den Belt, "Lessons from the Reformation for Hermeneutics Today," *Unio Cum Christo* 42 (2018): 99.

typically set forth for the ordination of women into ecclesiastical office. The Bible is simply too clear on the requirement for male ordination into ecclesiastical office. Here is what Yuval Noah Harari, professor at Hebrew University in Jerusalem, had to say in his book *Homo Deus* [Man is God] about the acceptance of gay marriage and female clergy. "Where did this acceptance originate? Not from reading the Bible." He then explains that it came from cultural forces such as Michel Foucault's *The History of Sexuality* or Donna Haraway's "A Cyborg Manifesto." But true believers cannot admit drawing their ethics from these people, "so they go back to the Bible . . . and make a very thorough search . . . until they find what they need: some maxim, parable or ruling that if interpreted creatively enough means that God blesses gay marriage and that women can be ordained to the priesthood. They then pretend the idea originated in the Bible, when in fact it originated with Foucault. The Bible is kept as a source of authority, even though it is no longer a true source of inspiration."[16]

Sometimes biblical scholars need to listen to those who have a better sense of what is going on in the current trends of interpreting Scripture even though they may not even be Christian.

---

16 Yuval Noah Harari, *Homo Deus: A Brief History of Tomorrow* (Toronto: Signal, 2015), 275–76, with thanks to the late Rev. Dick de Jong who alerted me to this passage.

13

CHAPTER 13   **Prophetesses in God's Service**

When the issue of female ordination into ecclesiastical office is discussed, one of the arguments raised in favor of their ordination is the fact that Scripture mentions prophetesses. If women could function as prophetesses in biblical times, why can they not be ordained in the church today? The name of Deborah often comes up in this connection. Do we not have an example here of a woman who was used by God in the official capacity of a judge, exercising authority over men, and as a prophetess, authoritatively speaking the Word of God? Could this not be an indicator that we are impoverishing the church today by denying talented females admission to the office of elder or minister? Indeed, Deborah is often used as a star precedent for female ecclesiastical ordination. Is such an understanding warranted? Besides Deborah, Scripture also mentions other prophetesses. The issues raised are important and we need to take a closer look, beginning with Deborah, but also considering others in the history of revelation in both the Old and New Testament, as well as in the time after Pentecost. In the process we will relate our findings to the current issues surrounding women in ecclesiastical office.

Prophetesses in the History of Revelation

Deborah

A primary rule for the correct interpretation and application of Scripture is to place the passage being discussed within its biblical context. Deborah lived in the days of the judges. This was a time characterized by Israel's repeated apostasy, followed by divine judgment, and the desperate cry of the nation for deliverance. God would repeatedly and graciously respond to Israel's pleas for help by raising up a judge who, equipped with the Holy Spirit, would rescue the people from their enemies. Prior to Deborah's time the LORD had raised up Othniel and Ehud to save his people.

However, after Ehud died, Israel again lapsed into sin and so the LORD sold them into the hands of Jabin king of Canaan, whose commander Sisera had 900 chariots at his disposal. He cruelly oppressed Israel for twenty years (Judg 4:2–3). The situation was critical. Danger was everywhere. Normal travel and therefore commerce was impossible, and villagers took refuge in walled cities (Judg 5:6–7). In these critical times Israel cried to the LORD for help (Judg 4:3). He heard their cry and used Deborah to give deliverance.

In God's Service

It is interesting to note how God introduced Deborah in the book of Judges and how he involved her for the salvation of his people. We read that "Deborah, a prophetess, the wife of Lappidoth, was judging Israel at that time. She used to sit under the Palm of Deborah between Ramah and Bethel in the hill country of Ephraim, and the people of Israel came up to her for judgment" (Judg 4:4–5). With the preceding two crises, the Hebrew expression "the LORD raised up a deliverer" (Judg 3:9, 15) was used. We also frequently read of the judges being empowered by the Spirit for their military task (Judg 3:10; 6:345; 11:29; 14:19; 15:14). Remarkably, these expressions are not used with Deborah. Rather she is introduced as a prophetess.

As a prophetess she was judging Israel and the Israelites came to her for judgment. What does this mean? One could imagine that she functioned as a judge and was resolving legal issues brought to her. However, this interpretation is unlikely. A judge in the book of Judges is a military leader who delivers Israel. When judge "so and so" judged Israel for so many years, then that expression means he *ruled* Israel for so many years (e.g. Judg 3:10; 10:2, 3 etc.). The NIV therefore translates that she "was leading Israel" (Judg 4:4). How was she leading Israel? She was a prophetess. People came to her "for judgment." Literally it says: "for the judgment" (Judg 4:5). In other words, in this time of national crisis, when Israelites "cried to the LORD for help" (Judg 4:3), they came to Deborah as prophetess for the judgment which she as prophetess could give, namely the judgment or answer of God in response to their cry for help. It is not surprising that the people went to her. After all, as a prophetess she was God's representative for the people.[1] She spoke God's Word.

_____

1   See Daniel I. Block, "Deborah Among the Judges: The Perspective of the Hebrew Historian," in
    Faith, Tradition, and History: Old Testament Historiography in Its Near Eastern Context, ed. A.

The times were extraordinary. After all, the normal way to receive God's judgment in a national emergency was for the leader of God's people to go to the high priest who had the Urim and Thummim "in the breastpiece of judgment" (Exod 28:30). God, through Moses, had given specific instructions in this regard (Num 27:21). The fact that the high priest was not consulted indicates that in the decadent time of the judges the priesthood did not function as God had intended. The degenerate state of Israel's religious life which would typify the days of Eli (cf. 1 Sam 2:12) was already a reality in the days of the judges (Judg 8:22–35; Judg 17–18).[2] In response to this sad state of affairs, God mercifully raised a prophetess, Deborah, and later he would send an unnamed prophet as well (Judg 6:8). People could thus still inquire of God by going to Deborah to seek a decision or judgment from God.[3] And they did. They were grievously suffering under the cruel oppression of Sisera, and God was moved to speak through Deborah.

As a result, she summoned Barak and gave him God's command to mobilize ten thousand men to defeat the foe (Judg 4:5–7). When he protested because he was afraid, Deborah assured him that she would accompany him. Her coming along as spokesperson for the LORD gave tangible expression to the fact that God himself would go with Barak and give him the victory.[4]

Deborah is never pictured as a military leader of Israel, a judge in the sense of Othniel or Gideon. She was a prophetess. It is therefore not surprising that there is no reference to her with respect to the battle. Although she gave leadership through her prophetic task, she is not described in Scripture as the judge who delivered Israel from Sisera. Rather, it is God who is specified as the deliverer of Israel (Judg 4:23) and he used another woman, Jael, to kill Sisera (Judg 4:21). Deborah's subordinate role as prophetess and not as a military leader is also evident from the fact that God did not send Deborah to head the troops into battle, but Barak. Furthermore, when Samuel would later mention deliverers of Israel (1 Sam 12:11), he did

---

R. Millard, J. K. Hoffmeier, and D. W. Baker (Winona Lake, IN: Eisenbrauns, 1995), 236–40.

2   Also see Cornelis Van Dam, *The Urim and Thummim: A Means of Revelation in Ancient Israel* (Winona Lake, IN: Eisenbrauns, 1997), 263–66.

3   Van Dam, *The Urim and Thummim*, 161–62.

4   Block, "Deborah Among the Judges," 249–51.

not mention Deborah, but he did name Barak, the commander. Similarly, Deborah is not mentioned with the heroes of faith in Hebrews 11. Several leaders are listed from the time of the judges, including Barak (v. 32), but not Deborah. All of this underlines her relatively modest role with respect to the deliverance of Israel.

Is Deborah a Precedent?

God raised up Deborah to be a prophetess in Israel when that nation found itself in dire straits. Deborah's function as a prophetess was an exception within an exceptional situation. The fact that she was also known as the wife of Lappidoth could indicate the ad hoc character of her office. People came to her in the current circumstances because God spoke through her; but, there is no record of her going out and prophesying among the people. Without taking anything away from her being a prophetess, it should not be forgotten that she is also identified as a married woman, indeed as "a mother in Israel" (Judg 5:7). Her prophetic office was not everything. She also fulfilled a woman's normal place in Israelite life.

Can Deborah function as an example and precedent for us to justify the ordination of women into the office of elder or minister? Taking into consideration all the factors mentioned earlier, the answer is clearly no. The situation in Israel was desperate and by way of exception God raised her up as a prophetess in Israel by endowing her with the gift of prophecy. In this way God enabled her to pass on God's command that Barak (and not Deborah) summon and head a military force against the enemy (Judg 4:6–7). The fact that God used a woman to make this clear was an implicit condemnation of the lack of male leadership in Israel. Furthermore, the need for Deborah to accompany Barak and to go with him to the battlefield (Judg 4:9–10) underlined how male leadership was completely missing in Israel. For a woman to need to goad a male to take charge and so in effect give leadership was akin to a disaster (cf. Isa 3:12). It showed that things had gone terribly wrong. Deborah is therefore not an example to be followed and her situation certainly provides no justification to open the leadership offices of the church to women. But God is sovereign, and he can do in extraordinary circumstances what we are not allowed to do.[5] He, therefore, did use Deborah in a special way for his service.

Besides Deborah, we will also consider Huldah, other Old Testament prophetesses, and Miriam as prophetess.

Huldah

The kingdom of Judah had been going through terrible times in the seventh century before Christ. The wicked king Amon had been murdered by his own servants and eight-year-old Josiah was placed on the throne (2 Kings 21:20–22:2). He feared the LORD and wanted to restore the true worship of God and repair the temple. In the course of renewing the temple, the Book of the Law was found in the house of the LORD. It had apparently been lost or hidden by a previous monarch who did not want to follow God's will. When this stunning find was reported to Josiah and he became aware of its demands (2 Chron 34:18–19), he tore his clothes for he realized that the LORD's anger against Jerusalem must be very great "because our fathers have not obeyed the words of this book, to do all that is written concerning us." The king therefore commanded Hilkiah, the high priest, and others to go and inquire of the LORD about what is written in this book "for me and for the people and for all Judah" (2 Kings 22:13). This was a matter of national significance. They went to the prophetess Huldah (2 Kings 22:14).

This sequence of events underlines the sad state of affairs in Judah. The priests had just rediscovered the Book of the Law, probably Deuteronomy (cf. Deut 29:21). When God needed to be consulted, the normal priestly means of revelation for matters of national importance, the high priestly Urim and Thummim was to be used (cf. Num 27:21). This did not happen, even though Hilkiah the priest should have known. Instead, Hilkiah and others who were sent by the king to inquire of the LORD went to the prophetess Huldah.[6] Why they did not go to Jeremiah or Zephaniah is not known. Perhaps they were not in Jerusalem or perhaps they were known as

---

5   This is the reasoning of John Calvin, *Commentaries on the Epistles to Timothy, Titus, and Philemon*, trans. William Pringle (Bellingham, WA: Logos Bible Software, 2010), 67 (commenting on 1 Tim 2:12).

6   See Van Dam, *The Urim and Thummim*, 251–52.

doomsayers and the hope was that Huldah would give a more favourable prophecy. In any case they went to "Huldah the prophetess, the wife of Shallum the son of Tikvah, son of Harhas, keeper of the wardrobe (now she lived in Jerusalem, in the Second Quarter)" (2 Kings 22:14). This last detail probably indicates that they visited her at her home.

Huldah's answer seems to have been given quickly and directly. It is noteworthy that in her response she said four times: "Thus says the LORD" or something similar (2 Kings 22:15–20). Let there be no mistake about it, this message comes from God! And the message was clear. God "will bring disaster upon this place and upon its inhabitants, all the words of the book that the king of Judah has read" (2 Kings 22:16). Judgment would come in accordance with the newly found Book of the Law which contained the covenant curses for disobedience (cf. Deut 28:15–26; 29:25–28). The prophetess thus confirmed the words of the newly found Scripture as the very Word of God. She also prophesied that Josiah would not see the disaster that God would bring over Jerusalem (2 Kings 22:23).

Clearly the times were desperate and as in the critical days of the judges when God used Deborah, the LORD now also used a woman. There are some similarities with Deborah. Besides the context of critical times, it is noteworthy that neither Deborah nor Huldah projected themselves into the public square. People came to them and sought them out—Deborah under her palm tree and Huldah at her home. These prophetesses did not seek the limelight. This reticence stands in stark contrast to men who were called to be prophets. Prophets like Jeremiah and Ezekiel, publicly and uninvited, proclaimed the Word of God. The prophetesses exercised their God-given task in such a way that they did not impede or obstruct male leadership.

Other Prophetesses

Another example of a prophetess is Isaiah's wife. She is called a prophetess (Isa 8:3), but it is not possible to determine whether she was called a prophetess because she was married to a prophet or because God had given her the office of a prophetess. Some have suggested that her designation as prophetess is due to the fact that the child she would bear was literally a prophecy, an incarnation of God's Word so to speak. After all, the child's name "Maher-shalal-hash-baz" forms the prophecy which Isaiah spoke for it means "quick to the plunder, swift to the spoil."[7] God's explanation of the name was: "the wealth of Damascus and the spoil of Samaria will be carried away before the king of Assyria" (Isa 8:4).

There are also references to the false prophetess, Noadiah (Neh 6:14), and those against whom Ezekiel prophesied (Ezek 13:17–23). However, since they are not God's prophets, they need not detain us.

Moving to the New Testament, Anna comes to mind. We read in Luke 2 that when Jesus was presented in the temple

> there was a prophetess Anna, the daughter of Phanuel, of the tribe of Asher. She was advanced in years, having lived with her husband seven years from when she was a virgin, and then as a widow until she was eighty-four. She did not depart from the temple, worshiping with fasting and prayer night and day. And coming up at that very hour she began to give thanks to God and to speak of him to all who were waiting for the redemption of Jerusalem. (Luke 2:36–38)

It is clear from this very brief reference that Anna's identity as a prophetess meant being in constant devotion in the temple. She did not go out on the streets to prophesy as prophets would normally be expected to do. Through the prophetic gift she recognized the Messiah in the temple, publicly praised God, and spoke to all who yearned for the coming of the Redeemer. At this very important occasion and at a critical juncture in God's self-revelation to his people Israel, God made sure that besides Simeon (Luke 2:25–35) also a woman was there at Christ's presentation in the temple. No part of God's people was excluded from meeting the Savior. Both male and female were represented.

We now go back to the Old Testament and consider Miriam, who is mentioned as a prophetess after the exodus from Egypt.

---

7   Young, *Isaiah*, 1:303; J. Alec Motyer, *The Prophecy of Isaiah* (Downers Grove, IL: InterVarsity, 1993), 90.

Miriam as Prophetess

After the Israelites had successfully crossed the Red Sea and the LORD had drowned the pursuing Egyptian forces, "Miriam the prophetess, the sister of Aaron, took a tambourine in her hand, and all the women went out after her with tambourines and dancing. And Miriam sang to them:

'Sing to the LORD, for he has triumphed gloriously;
the horse and his rider he has thrown into the sea'" (Exod 15:20–21).

Miriam is identified as "the prophetess." What does this mean? It is possible that Miriam received revelation from God (cf. Num 12:2, 6) as one would expect from a prophet (cf. Exod 7:1–2), but Scripture nowhere indicates that she publicly proclaimed new prophecy. The public prophetic act of this prophetess was singing with a musical instrument and exhorting praise to God. There are also indications elsewhere in Scripture that praising God and declaring his great deeds does indeed constitute prophesying. It is this activity that best defines her prophetic office. (Think also of our prophetic task as confessing God's name in the Heidelberg Catechism, Q.A. 32.)[8]

We see this close relationship between singing and making music and prophesying elsewhere as well. Take, for example, Saul. He met a procession of prophets with musical instruments prophesying and the Spirit came on him and he prophesied as well (1 Sam 10:5–11). This prophesying can best be understood as praising God.[9] Another example that can be mentioned is when David set apart some of the sons of Asaph, Heman and Jeduthun for the ministry of music in the temple. This ministry was a prophetic ministry for the singers are described as prophesying when they thanked and praised the LORD (1 Chron 25:1–3). Consistent with the nature of this musical ministry, the leaders of the temple song were called

---

8   Rashbam stated with respect to Miriam: "Anyone who offers praise to God or rebukes the people is called a prophet." Cited in Michael Carasik, ed. and trans., *The Commentator's Bible: The JPS Miqra'ot Gedolot: Exodus* (Philadelphia: Jewish Publication Society of America, 2005), 118. Also see William H. Propp, *Exodus 1–18*, AB 2 (New York: Doubleday, 1999), 546–47.

9   See, e.g., C. J. Goslinga, *Het eerste boek Samuël*, Commentaar op het Oude Testament (Kampen: Kok, 1968), 225; P. Kyle McCarter, Jr., *I Samuel*, Anchor Bible (Garden City, New York: Doubleday, 1980), 182.

seers or prophets (1 Chron 25:5; 2 Chron 35:15) and the poet Asaph was also called a seer or prophet (2 Chron 29:30).[10]

So, Miriam's prophetic task was seen in her music and singing ministry—an activity also associated with Deborah, the prophetess, when she, with Barak, sang a song extolling God's deliverance (Judg 5:1). Like Deborah, Miriam as prophetess also gave needed leadership to Israel, along with Moses and Aaron (Micah 6:4). Her leadership was for the women of Israel since they were the ones who followed her (Exod 15:20). In his sermon on Micah 6, Calvin noted that even though Miriam was a woman, God gave her this leadership role "in order that she might strengthen women." In his commentary on this passage, he noted that "it was an extraordinary thing, when God gave authority to a woman . . . no one may consider this singular precedent as a common rule."[11] It was an exceptional instance of leadership indeed, because when Miriam challenged the leadership of Moses, God punished her with leprosy (Num 12). Furthermore, Micah 6:4 is the only time that Miriam is mentioned as a leader along with Moses and Aaron. She is not mentioned in other places where the LORD mentions that he sent Moses and Aaron as leaders (Josh 24:5; 1 Sam 12:8; Ps 105:26). Her leadership in leading the women in singing at that one exceptional event cannot, therefore, function as an argument for ordaining women to the ruling and leadership offices of the church.

Conclusion

When considered over against the number of male prophets and the aggressive way in which they functioned, prophetesses were quite rare in Israel and they were generally not forward. God only raised them up in the most critical or dire circumstances and in this way highlighted the dearth of male leadership. The existence of female prophets in Israel did not signify divine endorsement for prophetesses as a normal model for God's people.[12] At the same time, the appearance of prophetesses did un-

---

10 See, e.g., Gary N. Knoppers, *1 Chronicles 10–29*, Anchor Bible (New York: Doubleday, 2004), 848.

11 John Calvin, *Sermons on the Book of Micah*, trans. Benjamin Wirt Farley (Phillipsburg: P&R, 2003), 318; John Calvin, *Commentaries on the Twelve Minor Prophets*, trans. John Owen (Bellingham, WA: Logos Bible Software, 2010), 3:333.

12 John Piper and Wayne Grudem, "An Overview of Central Concerns: Questions and Answers," in *Recovering Biblical Manhood and Womanhood: A Response to Evangelical Feminism*, ed. John

derline that God is sovereign and in special circumstances he did equip women with the prophetic office as well. There is absolutely nothing inferior about women as such that would prevent him from doing so. But it was not the normal role which God had in mind for women in ancient Israel.

Prophetesses in the Age of the Holy Spirit

We saw that prophetesses in ancient Israel were an exception to the general rule of male prophets and that their presence in the history of revelation does not justify opening the office of elder and minister of the Word to women today. But, one could ask, do we not now live in the age of the Spirit? The prophet Joel predicted that not only our sons but also our daughters will prophesy. Furthermore, the New Testament speaks of prophetesses in Christ's church. Does the reality of the Pentecost outpouring of the Holy Spirit not support admitting women into the offices of elder and minister? To answer that question we need to consider Joel's prophecy and its fulfillment as well as how prophets and prophetesses functioned in the church.

Joel's Prophecy

Through Joel, his prophet, God promised:
    And it shall come to pass afterward,
      that I will pour out my Spirit on all flesh;
your sons and your daughters shall prophesy,
    your old men shall dream dreams,
    and your young men will see visions.
Even on the male and female servants
    in those days I will pour out my Spirit (Joel 2:28–29).

It is clear that the gift of the Holy Spirit was promised to all, both male and female. On the day of Pentecost, the apostle Peter told those assembled that this prophecy was now being fulfilled (Acts 2:16–18). What is the meaning of everyone, male and female, prophesying? Does this, for example, mean that all will now be able to receive revelation, proclaim a new authoritative Word of God, and so contribute to the writing of the canonical Scripture,

Piper and Wayne Grudem (Wheaton IL: Crossway, 1991), 72.

as the Old Testament prophets did? Will everyone also be able to predict the future, as the Old Testament prophets did? When one considers the evidence of the New Testament, the answer to these questions is clearly no.

The apostles were the ones who had a task similar to that of the Old Testament prophets. They received revelation and spoke God's Word (cf. 2 Pet 1:20–21). Did the apostle Paul not write to the Thessalonians: "When you received the word of God, which you heard from us, you accepted it not as the word of men but as what it really is, the word of God, which is at work in you believers" (1 Thess 2:13; also see 4:8). Christ spoke through an apostle (cf. 2 Cor 13:3). The word of the Old Testament prophets and that spoken by the apostles are on the same level (2 Pet 3:2). We therefore accept the writings of the apostles as the very Word of God. They form part of Scripture.

What then was Joel predicting when he spoke of the Spirit being poured out on all people and enabling sons and daughters to prophesy? Joel's reference to the ability to function as a prophet is very general and covers all believers. Receiving new revelation from God is not referred to here. The context of the day of Pentecost indicates that Peter quoted this prophecy to explain why the believers filled with the Spirit were all "declaring the mighty works of God" in tongues or languages which all visitors to Jerusalem could understand (Acts 2:11). In other words, the prophesying here was equivalent to effectively communicating and declaring the wonders of God. This prophesying is therefore analogous to the prophesying that Miriam and the singers did in the temple, as noted earlier in this chapter. Moved by the Spirit, their compositions became part of Scripture.[13] Those at Pentecost were equipped by the outpouring of the Spirit to declare God's works and glory. According to God's promise, the Spirit would write God's Word on their hearts (Jer 31:33–34; cf. 2 Cor 3:3) and they would thus be enabled to pass it on. Here was the fulfillment of the wish of Moses: "Would that all the LORD's people were prophets, that the LORD would put his Spirit on them!" (Num 11:29). And so at Pentecost, God's people were all given the Spirit so that they could prophesy, even in different tongues or languages; that is, they could speak of God's salvation in Christ. Sub-

---

13 1 Chron 25:1–3 and, e.g., songs of Asaph such as Ps 73-83 and Jeduthun, Ps 39, 62, and 77.

sequent special outpourings of the Spirit resulted in similar instances of prophesying in tongues and extolling God's great deeds (Acts 10:46; 19:6).[14]

Later we read of Philip the evangelist who had "four unmarried daughters, who prophesied" (Acts 21:9). We are not told much about them. Noteworthy is that they are not actually called prophetesses, but they are characterized as having the gift of prophecy. That might indicate that they were blessed with the Pentecost gift of spreading the gospel and declaring God's wondrous acts of salvation as opposed to giving new revelation.[15]

The Pentecost outpouring of the Spirit "on all flesh" (Acts 2:17, 33) thus means in the first place that believers today are endowed with Christ's Spirit and thus share Christ's anointing, also as prophets and prophetesses (cf. Heidelberg Catechism, Q.A. 32). This identity enables all believers to do their prophetic calling. Believers have been entrusted with the Word of God (cf. Rom 3:2) and through the Spirit can now pass on God's Word to those around them (cf. 1 John 2:20, 27). The gospel can and should be communicated through believers in fullness. Thus they do their prophesying by confessing Christ to a world lost in sin (Matt 10:32–33; Mark 8:38).[16] However, when it comes to spreading the gospel in an official capacity, Christ specifically addressed the apostles to be his witnesses.[17] One cannot therefore use Joel's prophecy to justify female ordination, but it certainly supports female members of the church to be called prophetesses, as those enabled by the Spirit to declare the wonderful works of God in all of life.

Besides this general prophetic office of all believers made possible by the Pentecostal outpouring of the Spirit, there were also those with special prophetic gifts.

---

14 John van Eck, *Handelingen: de wereld in het geding*, Commentaar op het Nieuwe Testament. Derde Serie (Kampen: Kok, 2003), 66; D. G. Peterson, *The Acts of the Apostles*, Pillar New Testament Commentary (Grand Rapids, MI: Eerdmans, 2009), 141–42; R. Dean Anderson, *1 Korintiërs: orde op zaken in een jonge stadskerk*, Commentaar op het Nieuwe Testament, derde serie (Kampen: Kok, 2008), 172–73; Lenski, *The Interpretation of the Acts of the Apostles*, 74.

15 Lenski, *The Interpretation of the Acts of the Apostles*, 866; see also Peterson, *Acts*, 579–80.

16 Cf. Gaffin, *Perspectives on Pentecost*, 59. Gaffin is too restricted by his general definition of prophecy as inspired revelation that he does not recognize that Acts 2 speaks of the general prophetic office of believers. However, he does hesitate. He writes "apparently without exception." In the context, Acts 2 would be an exception to his idea that prophecy is a gift only given to some and it is a revelatory gift.

17 Acts 1:8; Mark 16:13; Luke 24:48; cf. Acts 13:31, 47; Col 1:23.

The Special Prophetic Gift

Subsequent to Pentecost, God raised up prophets in the apostolic period who passed on new revelation. In Acts 11, we read of prophets coming down from Jerusalem to Antioch. One of them, named Agabus, communicated the divine revelation that there would be a great famine and that Paul would be delivered into the hands of the Gentiles (Acts 11:28; 21:10–11). Prophets were active in Antioch (Acts 13:1) and Judas and Silas were also identified as prophets (Acts 15:32). The apostle Paul charged Timothy to wage the good warfare "in accordance with the prophecies previously made" about him (1 Tim 1:18; 4:14). These examples show that in the early Christian church the Lord endowed some with a special ability to prophesy. The apostle John was given this gift in great measure to write the book of Revelation (cf. Rev. 1:1–2; 22:7, 10, 18, 19).

The gift of prophecy was also found within the congregation of Corinth. The apostle Paul mentioned the ability to prophesy, along with other special gifts such as speaking in different kinds of tongues and the gift of healing and miraculous powers. The Spirit gave these gifts as he determined (1 Cor 12:1–11) and the apostle's exhortation to desire the gift of prophecy (1 Cor 14:1) should be read in that light.

The gift of tongues and prophecy are treated as complementary and belonging together in 1 Corinthians 14. This is not surprising since the two were linked on the day of Pentecost as well. Declaring the great deeds of God in different languages or tongues was a feature then and also later in Corinth (cf. 1 Cor 13:1; 14:9–12). However, not all could understand the languages spoken and so the gift of prophecy was more than the gift of tongues. "I want you all to speak in tongues, but even more to prophesy. The one who prophesies is greater than one who speaks in tongues, unless someone interprets, so that the church may be built up" (1 Cor 14:5; also see vv. 1 and 39).[18]

In 1 Corinthians 14 the gift of prophecy appears to have been similar to that experienced by the Old Testament prophets because divine rev-

---

18   Anderson, *1 Korintiërs*, 172–73.

elation was given through it.[19] This is evident from the close association of prophecy and revelation in this chapter. The apostle instructed: "Let two or three prophets speak, and let others weigh what is said. If a revelation is made to another sitting there, let the first be silent. For you can all prophesy one by one, so that all may learn and all be encouraged, and the spirits of prophets are subject to prophets" (1 Cor 14:29–32). These verses form part of the apostle Paul's instruction for orderly worship. Significantly, he earlier introduced this section by writing: "When you come together, each one has a hymn, a lesson, a revelation, a tongue, or an interpretation. Let all things be done for building up" (1 Cor 14:26). By including "revelation" he clearly alludes to prophesying as his subsequent instructions show (vv. 29–32).

The revelatory character of this prophecy is also seen by the manner in which the apostle closely associated the gift of prophesy with understanding "all mysteries." He wrote: "If I have prophetic powers, and understand all mysteries and all knowledge . . . but have not love, I am nothing" (1 Cor 13:2). A mystery is that which God needs to reveal. It is hidden to human beings. The apostle Paul considered himself to be a steward of God's mysteries (1 Cor 4:1) which means that God used him to reveal what would otherwise have been hidden. As he wrote to the Corinthians: "Behold! I tell you a mystery. We shall not all sleep, but we shall all be changed, in a moment, in the twinkling of an eye, at the last trumpet" (1 Cor 15:51–52). Similarly, he wrote to the Roman Christians: "I do not want you to be unaware of this mystery, brothers: a partial hardening has come upon Israel, until the fullness of the Gentiles has come in" (Rom 11:25–27).

The mystery of the gospel was made known by revelation to the apostles and prophets—in that order (Eph 3:3–5). These New Testament prophets, therefore, stand on the same line as the apostles in terms of receiving revelation. Richard Gaffin, emeritus professor at Westminster Theological Seminary, has shown in more detail than is possible here that the revelation given by the prophets in the New Testament church was

---

19 For this discussion, see Gaffin, *Perspectives on Pentecost*, 60–61; John Murray, *The Epistle to the Romans (2 Volumes in 1)*, reprint, 1965, New International Commentary on the New Testament (Grand Rapids: Eerdmans, 1968), 2:121–23. Anderson, *1 Korintiërs*, 174–77. Also see David E. Garland, *1 Corinthians*, Baker Exegetical Commentary on the New Testament (Grand Rapids. MI: Baker Academic, 2003), 582–83, 632.

indeed "on a par and of one piece with the inspired revelation received and proclaimed by Paul and the other apostles." Furthermore, revelation given through prophecy did not address "individualistic, purely localized interests, but concerns, along with apostolic revelation, the salvation in Christ with its rich and manifold implications for the faith and life of the church."[20] Thus, it is not difficult to see that "the one who prophesies speaks to people for their upbuilding and encouragement and consolation" (1 Cor 14:3).

One implication of prophets prophesying and passing on revelation from God was that, just as in the Old Testament, one had to be on guard against false prophecy. The words of those who claimed prophetic revelation had to be evaluated and weighed (1 Cor 14:29; 1 John 4:1; 1 Thess 5:20–21; cf. Rev 2:20). Another implication was that God used all true prophecy for building up the church. Indeed, the church is "built on the foundation of the apostles and prophets, Christ Jesus himself being the cornerstone" (Eph 2:20).[21]

The very fact that these prophets, along with the apostles, had a foundational purpose means that their function as conveyers of revelation was temporary. They served a one-time need for setting the foundations of the church in the beginning of "the last days" (Acts 2:17). Once that foundation had been established when God had given all the revelation that the church required, the need for apostles and prophets ceased (cf. 1 Cor 13:8).[22]

We noted earlier that Philip the evangelist "had four unmarried daughters, who prophesied" (Acts 21:9). If these women did have the special gift of divine prophecy,[23] it was a temporary gift to the church in this first period after Pentecost and it ceased to exist after the apostolic age. One can therefore not use the example of these four women as a reason for female ordination today. That was a unique situation in the history of the church. God no longer gives revelation to men or women and so this particular prophetic gift no longer exists and neither men nor women have

---

20 Gaffin, *Perspectives on Pentecost*, 62.
21 Gaffin, *Perspectives on Pentecost*, 95.
22 On the foundation character and cessation of the gift of prophecy, see Gaffin, *Perspectives on Pentecost*, 93–102.
23 So Anderson, *1 Korintiërs*, 174; as a possibility ("perhaps"), Gaffin, *Perspectives on Pentecost*, 59.

any task here. Consequently, there is on this point of the special prophetic gift, no reason to admit women to the ecclesiastical office of elder and minister.

Conclusion

The egalitarian spirit of our time urges us to ordain women into the offices of elder and minister. If we accept Scripture as authoritative, then we have to say no to that pressure that is also exerting its influence on churches with a Reformed name. However, forbidding women admittance to these offices does not in any way mean that women have no task in the church. They certainly do!

With respect to the prophetic task, both male and female are recipients of the promise of God that he will pour out his Spirit on his people and raise up prophets and prophetesses (Acts 2:17). *All* believers today have the full freedom and obligation to prophesy, that is, to bear witness to our Lord and Savior both in church and in society at large. One does not need to be ordained into an ecclesiastical office to fulfill one's prophetic task as Christians. All believers are under holy obligation to use one's prophetic gifts and talents both within and outside the church to the glory of our God. Again, think of the Heidelberg Catechism's biblical definition of a Christian which includes in part that "I am a member of Christ by faith and thus sharing in his anointing, so that I may as prophet confess his name" (Q.A. 32).

Summary

During the history of Old Testament Israel, the LORD graciously raised up prophetesses by way of exception because of the dire circumstances that his people faced. In this way God also exposed the lack of male leadership to the shame of those men who should have assumed a prominent role in guiding the people in the ways of the LORD. Prophetesses like Deborah, Huldah, and Anna did not thrust themselves into the public eye but were available for those who sought their counsel. With the outpouring of the Holy Spirit, God equipped all believers to prophesy, that is, to proclaim the wondrous works of God. This prophetic proclamation is what Miriam and others in Old Testament times had already been privileged to do with music and song. In the early Christian church God also enabled some believers, both male and female, to receive revelation through the gift of prophecy during the apostolic age after which time God ceased communicating with his people in this manner.

It is important to note that at no point in God's dealing with his people were women treated as inferior to men. Both male and female have been created in God's image and since the Day of Pentecost all believers are blessed with the Holy Spirit to be prophets and prophetesses attesting to God's salvation in Christ. But the divinely assigned tasks of male and female are different. Nevertheless, God is sovereign and in biblical times he made use of women outside their normal roles if that was needed for the well-being of his people. Today, living as we do in the final age, the age of the Holy Spirit, there are many opportunities for women to exercise their gifts for the upbuilding of the body of Christ without being ordained in ecclesiastical office. We shall see more on that issue in the next chapter.

CHAPTER 14   **Women Serving the Church: Divine Directives and Opportunities**

Scripture mentions women prophesying, teaching, and helping the work of the church in all sorts of ways. In discussions on female ecclesiastical ordination this fact is often raised in support of giving them official ecclesiastical status. We therefore need to consider the circumstances under which women used these gifts for the edification of the church. What is the picture that Scripture gives us with a view to whether they qualify for ordination? We need to take a closer look. We will first consider women and the gift of prophecy and teaching, as well as how women generally used their gifts for the cause of the gospel. Next we will consider whether women should be ordained for diaconal work and lastly come to some summary conclusions.

Silent and Prophesying Women

The most detailed discussion of prophesying is found in Paul's first letter to the Corinthians in chapter 14. We saw in the previous chapter of this book that the prophecy referred to in that correspondence consisted of receiving revelation from God. The apostle dealt with this special gift as well as speaking in tongues with a view to ensuring that all things were done for building up the church. Thus, to prophesy was better than speaking in tongues unless what was spoken in tongues was interpreted for the benefit of those who heard it. Prophecies however needed to be carefully weighed (1 Cor 14:29) for there was the danger of false prophets (cf. 1 John 4:1).

In that general context the apostle said: "As in all the churches of the saints, the women should keep silent in the churches. For they are not permitted to speak but should be in submission, as the Law also says" (1 Cor 14:33–34). From this passage it is clear that the requirement not to speak applies to all the churches and not just the one in Corinth. This prohibition is in accordance with "the Law." It probably refers to the first five books of the Old Testament which are traditionally called the Law (cf. Luke 24:44), with the creation account being specifically in view. After all, the apostle had appealed to creation earlier in regard to the relationship of men and women (1 Cor 11:8–9). The point is that when prophecies were being judged, women were not to speak. The demand for silence is repeated three times, underlining the importance of this prohibition. It is a general rule. "As in all the churches of the saints, the women should keep silent in the churches. For they are not permitted to speak . . . It is shameful for a woman to speak in church" (1 Cor 14:33b–34a, 35b).

This prohibition was obviously not a total ban for complete silence. We may assume that women sang psalms and hymns along with the men in holy worship (1 Cor 14:26). The point of being silent in the context of prophecies being judged is that the women should honor the place of their husbands. Each should consult with him about any questions she may have had when they were home and not raise these issues when in church (1 Cor 14:35). Her silence would indicate her willing submission to her husband and would furthermore acknowledge that women had no teaching authority in the church over the men (1 Tim 2:11–12), since evaluating prophecy would involve that function.[1]

In 1 Corinthians 11:5 we read, almost in passing, about women praying or prophesying. We may assume in light of 1 Corinthians 14 that here too the special gift of receiving revelation from God is referred to. It would be strange if such an incidental reference to prophesying was something completely different from what is discussed a few chapters later.[2] We are not specifically told whether this prophesying took place within or outside a church service.

The context of 1 Corinthians 11 would seem to indicate that the

---

1   Anderson, *1 Korintiërs*, 214–17; F. W. Grosheide, *Commentary on the First Epistle to the Corinthians*, in *1 Corinthians*, New International Commentary on the New Testament (Grand Rapids: Eerdmans, 1953), 341–43; Charles Hodge, *An Exposition of the First Epistle to the Corinthians*, reprint, 1857 (Grand Rapids, Michigan: Eerdmans, 1953), 304–5.
2   Anderson, *1 Korintiërs*, 148; Hodge, *1 Corinthians*, 207; see also Gaffin, *Perspectives on Pentecost*, 59.

prophesying took place outside the church. The apostle Paul had been dealing with issues not directly related to a church service. He continued without any indication that he was now speaking of a church service in addressing the matter of praying and prophesying and how to approach God. These activities were not restricted to a church service. It is only later, after this particular discussion (1 Cor 11:2–16), that the apostle made a clear transition to dealing with matters relating to worship services by writing: "But in the following instructions I do not commend you, because when you come together it is not for the better but for the worse. For, in the first place, when you come together as a church . . . When you come together" (1 Cor 11:17–18, 20). There are no such allusions to church worship in the preceding section. So it seems that the prophesying by women referred to earlier probably did not take place in church. Consequently, there is no contradiction between the apostle's acknowledgement of female prophesying and his command for women to be silent in church (1 Cor 14:34).[3]

We can also note that there is nothing about prophesying to indicate that it should be restricted to a church service (cf. Acts 21:10). Such female prophesying outside regular church services may also be inferred in the case of Philip's daughters (Acts 21:9).

Prophets giving divine revelation were part of the foundation of the church along with the apostles (Eph 2:20). As mentioned in the preceding chapter, since a foundation is only established once, there are no more inspired prophets or prophetesses today. Such prophesying and speaking in tongues as well as the manner in which they took place are therefore not normative for the church today. The cessation of this gift of prophecy (cf. 1 Cor 13:8) means that the reference to women prophesying in 1 Corinthians 11 has no direct bearing on the issue of whether women should be admitted to ecclesiastical office.

Women were also engaged in teaching in New Testament times. Would that provide a reason for female ecclesiastical ordination?

---

3   James Greenbury, "The Contribution of 1 Timothy 2:8–15 and 1 Corinthians 11:15 to the Discussion Concerning Women Speaking in Church," *Presbyterion* 44, no. 2 (2018): 66–69; Anderson, *1 Korintiërs*, 148, 151–54; Grosheide, *Commentary on the First Epistle to the Corinthians*, 251–52; R. C. H. Lenski, *First and Second Epistle to the Corinthians* (Minneapolis, MN: Augsburg Publishing House, 1963), 436–37.

Women Teaching

It is important to note that the gifts of prophecy and teaching were two distinctive gifts (Rom 12:6–7; 1 Cor 12:28; Eph 4:11). As we saw in the previous chapter, a prophet or prophetess received revelation by the inspiration of the Holy Spirit. God spoke directly through such a person and the words were therefore authoritative. Teachers cannot make that claim. Teaching or preaching explains the Word of God that has been entrusted to us. It interprets the text and derives its authority by being in harmony with Scripture.[4]

It is telling that God made use of female prophets in both ancient Israel and in the apostolic period of the Christian church, but he never used women in the main teaching offices of Israel, namely as priests (Lev 10:11; Deut. 33:10) or as elders (Deut 32:7; 1 Tim 3:2). These offices were reserved for men only. This pattern continued after Pentecost and it is also evident in Paul's instruction to Timothy on the limitations of women teaching in church.

"I do not permit a woman to teach"

The apostle wrote: "I do not permit a woman to teach or to exercise authority over a man; rather, she is to remain quiet. For Adam was formed first, then Eve" (1 Tim 2:12–13). This authoritative apostolic injunction occurs within the context of instructions for the church when gathered for worship. Since an elder (either teaching or ruling elder) is one who is "able to teach" (1 Tim 3:2; 5:17), this prohibition would exclude a woman from being ordained in that office since she is not permitted to teach in an official capacity in a church service.[5]

Modern scholarship disputes this traditional analysis in order to make room for women in office. This view is, for example, reflected in the report that laid the basis for the Reformed Churches in the Netherlands (Liberated) to open up all the offices to women.[6] It suggests that women

---

4   Also see Gaffin, *Perspectives on Pentecost*, 71–72.
5   For this traditional interpretation, see, e.g., Hendriksen, *The Pastoral Epistles*, 108–10.
6   Haan-Kamminga, et al., *Report of Deputies*, 19–20; see also the description of this position in Van Dam, *The Elder*, 208–9.

had to be silent because they lacked knowledge since it was not usual for women in the culture of Paul's time to be educated. So, when the apostle said: "let a woman learn quietly with all submissiveness" (1 Tim 2:11), he indicated that women were to be silent because they needed further instruction. That would also explain why the apostle did make use of gifted women such as Priscilla. The essence of the matter, according to this view, is that everyone is permitted to speak, but knowledge and insight are needed. Furthermore, it is incumbent on men and women to behave appropriately when speaking. What is appropriate is culturally determined and what was culturally fitting in the apostle's day is not necessarily culturally appropriate in our day. Thus the passages telling women to be silent (1 Cor 14:34 and 1 Tim 2:9–10) form no basis for keeping the ecclesiastical offices closed to women. Rather, according to this way of thinking as articulated in this report, these passages "contain a call to let oneself be educated in all modesty—something that pertains to both men and women—although that means something different for each of them as also determined by the culture of the time."[7]

Scripture, however, gives no indication that the women's lack of education was the reason that they were not able to teach or have authority over men. Rather the reason given is that God created Adam first and then Eve. In other words, the prohibition is not based on a passing cultural phenomenon, in this case their lack of education, but the apostle clearly justified it by the order in which God created male and female. He gave this as the reason. "I do not permit a woman to teach or to exercise authority over a man; rather, she is to remain quiet. *For* Adam was formed first, then Eve; and Adam was not deceived, but the woman was deceived and became a transgressor" (1 Tim 2:12–14, emphasis added). In other words, the reason for a woman to keep silent is based on creation, just as in 1 Corinthians 14:34 as we saw earlier in this chapter.[8]

---

7   Haan-Kamminga, et al., *Report of Deputies*, 20.
8   See further, G.H. Visscher, "1 Timothy 2:12–15. Is Paul's Injunction About Women Still Valid?" in *Correctly Handling the Word of Truth: Reformed Hermeneutics Today*, ed. Mees te Velde and Gerhard H. Visscher (Eugene, OR: Lucerna CRTS Publications; Wipf & Stock, 2014), 147–51; for detailed studies, Andreas J. Köstenberger and Thomas R. Schreiner, eds., *Women in the Church: An Interpretation and Application of 1 Timothy 2:9–15*, 3rd ed (Wheaton, IL: Crossway, 2016).

In view of the popularity of the New International Version of the Bible released in 2011, it needs to be noted that its revised translation of 1 Timothy 2:12 has yielded to the pressure of egalitarianism by translating the critical passage in such a way that women may exercise authority over men in church and so be ordained into office. The traditional rendering offered in the NIV (1984) translation states: "I do not permit a woman to teach or to have authority over a man" (1 Tim 2:12a). The NIV (2011) reads: "I do not permit a woman to teach or to assume authority over a man." The point is that one can conclude from this new translation that as long as women do not "assume" that authority on their own and apart from proper ecclesial authorization, they are free to exercise authority over men and thus be ordained into ecclesiastical office.[9]

Junia and the Apostles

Those seeking biblical justification for women in ecclesiastical office have also appealed to Paul's describing Andronicus and Junia as "outstanding among the apostles" (Rom 16:7 NIV). Since Junia is assumed to be a woman and since this translation identifies her as an apostle, these factors are then considered to be a biblical justification for women to be ordained in the teaching office of the church. After all, if a woman could be an apostle, surely she can be an elder or minister as well. There are however numerous difficulties with maintaining such reasoning.

In the first place, the translation that says that Andronicus and Junia were "outstanding among the apostles" is only one possible rendering. One can also translate the passage in question that "they are esteemed by the apostles" (footnote in NIV [2011]) or "are well known to the apostles" (ESV). These translations remove Junia's identity as an apostle and indeed may very well be preferable as reflected in recent Bible translations.[10]

---

9   See the analysis and conclusion in Denny Burk, "New and Old Departures in the Translation of *Authentein* in 1 Timothy 2:12," in *Women in the Church: An Interpretation and Application of 1 Timothy 2:9–15*, 3rd ed, ed. Andreas J. Köstenberger and Thomas R. Schreiner (Wheaton, IL: Crossway, 2016), 279–96.

10 For a summary of the debate and defense for the translation "well-known to the apostles" or something similar, see Michael Burer, "Rom 16:7 as 'Well Known to the Apostles': Further Defense and New Evidence," *Journal of the Evangelical Theological Society* 58 (2015): 731–56. The ESV (2016) and NET Bible (2005) render "well known to the apostles"; the Christian Standard Bible (2017) translates "noteworthy in the eyes of the apostles."

Let us suppose for the sake of argument that the translations that identify Andronicus and Junia as apostles is to be preferred. The question then needs to be asked what the word "apostle" means in this context. The term can mean different things. It does not need to refer to the apostolic office such as Paul had. The first meaning of the original Greek term (*apostolos*) is simply "messenger" or one who is "sent, dispatched."[11] Paul used it in this sense elsewhere. He wrote the Corinthian Christians concerning certain brothers, "they are messengers [*apostolos*] of the churches" (2 Cor 8:23). Epaphroditus he called a "messenger [*apostolos*]" (Philip 2:25). These translations of *apostolos* are not controversial. So why could Paul not have used this word with the sense of "messenger" in Romans 16:7 as well? When a passage like this is taken within the context of the apostle's clear directives for office bearers elsewhere, the apostolic office cannot be referred to here as an office which a female is entrusted with.

As if all the above is not enough to indicate that Romans 16:7 provides no basis for ecclesiastical office for women, there is another question that needs to be answered. Is it even certain that Junia was a woman? There has been considerable debate about this issue since the Greek original can signify either a male or female name, depending where one places the accent. Furthermore, there is the possibility that Junia reflects a masculine Hebrew personal name.[12] The prevailing consensus is that Junia was a woman, but such an identity is not indisputable.[13]

To conclude this part of the discussion, Romans 16:7 cannot be used to prove that there was a female apostle in the days of Paul. There are too many uncertainties to make this claim. Furthermore, to use Paul's writing in Romans 16:7 as a justification for an official female teaching role

---

11 Danker, *A Greek-English Lexicon of the New Testament*, 122; Franco Montanari, *The Brill Dictionary of Ancient Greek*, ed. Madeleine Goh and Chad Schroeder (Leiden, NL: Brill, 2015), 272.

12 Al Wolters, "IOYNIAN (Romans 16:7) and the Hebrew Name *Yĕḥunnī*," *Journal of Biblical Literature* 127 (2008): 397–408.

13 For the prevailing consensus, Wolters, "Romans 16:7," 397; an important defense for a female apostle is Eldon Jay Epp, *Junia: The First Woman Apostle*, foreword by Beverly Roberts Gaventa (Minneapolis: Fortress, 2005), but cf. Burer, "Rom 16:7," 731–56. For a recent summary of the evidence and discussion on Romans 16:7, see Thomas R. Schreiner, *Romans*, 2nd ed., Baker Exegetical Commentary on the New Testament (Grand Rapids, MI: Baker, 2018), 768–71.

in the church would be in stark contradiction to what the same inspired apostle wrote to Timothy as mentioned earlier.

Women as Teachers

Although, as noted above, women were not permitted to teach in an official capacity in a church service, outside such a service, capable women were encouraged to teach. There were no other restrictions on their use of this gift for the benefit of the gospel. The writings of the apostle Paul yield several examples. After Paul had informed Titus of the qualifications for the office of elder (Titus 1:5–9), he addressed different groups in the congregation. He first mentioned the duties of the older men "to be sober-minded, dignified, self-controlled, sound in faith, in love, and in steadfastness" (Titus 2:2). The apostle then continued that "older women likewise are to be reverent in behavior, not slanderers or slaves to much wine. They are to teach what is good, and so train young women to love their husbands and children" (Titus 2:3–5). After that the apostle addressed the younger men and slaves (Titus 2:6–10). There is no talk of office in Titus 2. Here the apostle gave instructions to the entire congregation. To seek justification for female ordination to ecclesiastical offices from the admonition that older women should be an example of Christian conduct to others and teach young women is simply not warranted.[14]

The obligation to teach is part of the general office of all believers, including women. This important responsibility comes from one's identity and duty as a Christian. Women are included in the general injunction: "you ought to be teachers" (Heb 5:12) and in the obligation to use a gift of teaching for the well-being of fellow believers (cf. Heb 10:24–25). Indeed, just like male members of the congregation, women should also share all the gifts they may have (Rom 12:6–8). "To each is given the manifestation of the Spirit for the common good" (1 Cor 12:7).

Women Using their Gifts for the Gospel

During the ministry of our Savior while on earth women used their gifts for the cause of the gospel. It is instructive to note how the Lord

---

14 Such justification was, e.g., sought in Haan-Kamminga, et al., *Report of Deputies*, 67.

Jesus accepted help from women and benefited from their loving service to him. Moved with love because the Lord Jesus had healed them, Mary Magdalene, Joanna, wife of Chuza, Herod's steward, Susanna, and many others provided for the Savior from their own resources (Luke 8:2–3). Women anointed him (Matt 26:6–13; Luke 7:37–38) and provided hospitality (Luke 10:38–40; John 12:2). Although the Lord Jesus valued the ministry of women and even allowed them to be the first witnesses of his resurrection (Matt 28:1–10), he never made a woman a leader. The leadership positions went to the disciples who were all male. This pattern continued after Christ's resurrection and ascension.

Women are mentioned as coworkers of Paul. The well-known example of Priscilla and Aquila comes to mind. This Christian couple had taken Apollos aside in Ephesus "and explained to him the way of God more accurately" (Acts 18:26). This was clearly private instruction and not official ecclesiastical work. It would have been work done "within the limits prescribed by Paul elsewhere"[15] and so Priscilla did not participate in this teaching as a female office bearer. Her teaching therefore proves nothing with respect to women in ecclesiastical office in the apostolic church. At the same time, the apostle Paul recognized the valuable work that Priscilla and Aquila did. He called them "my fellow workers in Christ Jesus, who risked their necks for my life" (Rom 16:3) and who opened their home for worship (1 Cor 16:19).

Another example concerns Euodia and Syntyche, women, whom Paul notes, "have labored side by side with me in the gospel" (Phil 4:3). Their task description is vague and general, but it does indicate that these women were coworkers with Paul. Since the verb expressing their work ("labored") is the same as that used to describe the contribution of the congregation as a whole (Phil 1:27), the efforts of these women most probably were similar to that of the local church and likely consisted in courageously bearing testimony to the faith and giving sacrificially of their financial resources to advance the cause of the gospel. It is far beyond the available evidence to speak of these women as church leaders or the like.[16]

---

15   "cf. 1 Cor 11:3–16; 14:33b–36; 1 Tim 2:8–15." John Murray, *Romans*, 2:228.
16   Andreas Köstenberger, "Women in the Pauline Mission," in *The Gospel to the Nations:*

Other instances of women using the opportunities for the work of gospel include Mary, mother of John, in whose home a prayer meeting was held (Acts 12:12), Lydia who extended hospitality to Paul and Silas by inviting them to stay at her home (Acts 16:15), Nympha in whose home a church met (Col 4:15), and Dorcas who was "full of good works and acts of charity" (Acts 9:36). Paul not only commended Phoebe but also other women to the church at Rome, namely, Mary; "workers in the Lord," Tryphaena, Tryphosa, and Persis; the mother of Rufus; and Julia and the sister of Nereus (Rom 16:6, 12–13, 15).

In short, apart from excluding women from ordained office in the church, Scripture gives women much room to use their gifts for the benefit of the gospel and expresses great appreciation for their doing so.

Furthermore, just like any member of the body of Christ, male or female, young or old, all are to use the gifts with which the Holy Spirit has endowed them (Rom 12:6–13; 1 Cor 12:4–30). Ultimately all such use of these gifts serve God's glory and the gospel. To be sure, some of these gifts have ceased, such as those of healing and speaking in tongues.[17] But the many gifts that remain need to be used by all members of the body of Christ. Peter commanded all those whom he addressed as "elect exiles," that is, all the Christians receiving his letter (1 Pet 1:1): "As each has received a gift, use it to serve one another, as good stewards of God's varied grace; whoever speaks, as one who speaks oracles of God; whoever serves, as one who serves by the strength that God supplies—in order that in everything God may be glorified through Jesus Christ" (1 Pet 4:10–11). Notice how the apostle Peter reminds us that all Christians are stewards. The gifts each one has received come from God and we are responsible to him to use them to the utmost for building up the body of Christ (Eph 4:12). The examples Peter gives underline the comprehensiveness of the gifts given to believers: speaking and serving. That covers everything. These two remind us that "whatever you do, in word or deed, do everything in the name of the Lord Jesus, giving thanks to God the Father through him" (Col 3:17). But one

---

Perspectives on Paul's Mission, ed. Peter Bolt and Mark Thompson (Leicester, UK; Downers Grove, IL: Apollos; InterVarsity Press, 2000), 233.

17 On the cessation of certain gifts of the Spirit, see, e.g., Anthony A. Hoekema, *Holy Spirit Baptism* (Grand Rapids: Eerdmans, 1972), 55–78; Gaffin, *Perspectives on Pentecost*, 89–116.

must be careful to do all in accordance with God's will for the gifts he has given. Christians are to speak "as one who speaks oracles of God" (1 Pet 4:11). There is to be no room for human speculation but God's wisdom is to be passed on.[18] It is obvious from the above that all members of the body, including women, young and old, have important contributions to make for the well-being of the church according to the gifts the Lord God has entrusted them with.

Deaconesses

It is affirmed by those who wish to ordain women in ecclesiastical office that Scripture speaks of women serving as deaconesses and so they should qualify for that ecclesiastical office today. We need to take a look. A recent example of such an affirmation was made by the Synod of Meppel (2017) of the Reformed Churches in the Netherlands (Liberated). This synod declared that "there are Scriptural grounds, next to men, also to call women to the ministry of mercy and therefore to the office of deacon." The biblical ground given was that "according to the testimony of Scripture, in apostolic times women shared in the office of the deacons (I Timothy 3:11, 5:9), and they too were called 'deacons' (Romans 16:1-2)."[19] Let us consider each of these passages in turn.

Wives or Deaconesses?

In 1 Timothy 3 the apostle Paul gave instructions on the qualifications necessary for being a deacon, including that he needed to be "the husband of one wife" (1 Tim 3:12). In the middle of the criteria for a male deacon and after noting, among other characteristics, that deacons must be dignified, he wrote; "women must likewise be dignified, not malicious gossips, but temperate, faithful in all things" (1 Tim 3:11 NASB).

So the question is: who are the "women" mentioned in this passage? Are they the wives of deacons (ESV) or are they female deacons (NIV

---

18 See on 1 Pet 4:10–11 Karen H. Jobes, *1 Peter*, Baker Exegetical Commentary on the New Testament (Grand Rapids, MI: Baker Academic, 2005), 281–82; P. H. R. van Houwelingen, *1 Petrus: Rondzend Brief Uit Babylon*, Commentaar Op Het Nieuwe Testament. Derde Serie (Kampen: Kok, 1991), 157–58.

19 *Acta GKv 2017*, Art. 18, Decision 4 (p. 38).

footnote)? The primary meaning of the Greek term in question (*gunē*) is "woman" and, if the context warrants, can also refer to a married woman and translate as "wife." The term signifies an adult female person and on its own cannot mean "deaconess" even though such a translation is sometimes suggested.

Those who wish to understand the women as deaconesses argue that the word "likewise" suggests that the apostle is moving from discussing deacons to deaconesses. However, it is just as likely that the apostle means that as deacons must be dignified, so should their wives. Furthermore, it seems odd to go on right after this passage to mention again the qualifications for male deacons in verses 12–13, as if this is a mere afterthought. Such a flip-flop from deacon to deaconess and back to deacon in such a short passage (1 Tim 3:8–13) is unnatural and unlikely. Furthermore, if the apostle had wanted his readers to know that he was now discussing female deacons, he would probably have been more specific and not used the term that can only be translated as "women" or "wives."

It seems best to understand the women as the wives of deacons. The passage concerns deacons and their qualifications. Those qualifications include that they have spouses who are supportive of the diaconal work. After all, these wives could be expected to be involved in one form or another in their husband's task as deacon by assisting him, especially when ministering to women.

There is no convincing basis to consider the women in 1 Timothy 3:11 as holding an official ordained office in the church. Not surprisingly, virtually all major English Bible translations prefer the rendering "women" or "wives" rather than deaconess or something similar.[20]

Enrolled Widows

Another passage adduced as evidence for female deacons is the apostle Paul's directive to Timothy: "Let a widow be enrolled if she is not less than sixty years of age, having been the wife of one husband, and having a reputation for good works: if she has brought up children, has shown

---

20 For a more detailed discussion on 1 Tim 3:11, see Van Dam, *The Deacon*, 81–83.

hospitality, has washed the feet of the saints, has cared for the afflicted, and has devoted herself to every good work" (1 Tim 5:9–10).

If the criteria for these widows are any indication, these women were probably enrolled to continue their service of good works for which they justly had the reputation. As needed, their work could include taking care of orphans, giving godly advice to young mothers (cf. Titus 2:3–5), and showing hospitality. The question is whether this service of love involved their being ordained as deaconesses.

Those favoring such an ordination argue that the Greek term for "enroll" can be understood as being selected for membership in a group with a special task. That task is then understood as an ordained office. Also, it is reasoned that since the apostle has mentioned qualifications for overseer (1 Tim 3:1–7) and for deacons (1 Tim 3:8–13) and discussed elders in 1 Timothy 5:17–19, he must also have been referring to ordained office when discussing enrolled widows in 1 Timothy 5.

These arguments however do not convince that a diaconal office is in view. The verb "to enroll" simply indicates making a selection for membership in a specific group.[21] It has nothing to do with being ordained or appointed to office. The text also makes no mention of this. Furthermore, it was not necessary for widows to be ordained to an ecclesiastical office to do their diaconal work. Since we must not draw conclusions that go beyond the biblical evidence, one must judge that there is insufficient evidence for deciding that these widows were ordained into diaconal office. These were unordained women who served the church with their labors of love. They can be an inspiration for female diaconal work in the church today.[22]

Who was Phoebe?

A passage often referred to in order to justify ordaining deaconesses is Romans 16:1–2 which reads: "I commend to you our sister Phoebe, a servant of the church at Cenchreae, that you may welcome her in the Lord in a way worthy of the saints, and help her in whatever she may need from you, for she has been a patron of many and of myself as well."

---

21 Danker, *A Greek-English Lexicon of the New Testament*, 520.
22 See further Van Dam, *The Deacon*, 84–87.

In this (ESV) and other translations, such as the NASB, NIV, and NET, Phoebe is described as a servant which translates the Greek term *diakonos*. This word has however also been translated as "deacon," (NIV [2011]) or "deaconness" (ESV footnote). Was Phoebe a servant or a female deacon or deaconness?

It is obviously not justifiable simply to reason that since the word can be translated as "deacon" therefore it should be in this instance. The word *diakonos* is used many times in the New Testament to indicate a person who is of assistance to someone and is therefore often translated as "servant" or something similar (e.g., Matt 20:26; 22:13; Rom 15:8). It is the context that must be decisive in determining whether the person in view is a deacon or more generally a servant or assistant.

There has been considerable debate, which we cannot enter into here, whether Phoebe was ordained in the diaconal office or simply a servant of the church. The fact that this debate continues shows that, at the end of the day, there is simply not enough information in Romans 16:1–2 to be able to conclude in any decisive manner that Phoebe was an ordained deaconess. The fact that the New Testament elsewhere gives male qualifications for the office of deacon (1 Tim 3:8–13) and nowhere else identifies a woman as a deacon underlines the dubiousness of concluding here that Phoebe must have been an ordained deaconess.[23]

Summary and Conclusions

Although Scripture does not permit the ordination of women into ecclesiastical office, there are, nevertheless, many opportunities for them to use their gifts for the upbuilding of the church. We have seen that during the apostolic age, God used women to pass on revelation by prophesying, apparently outside regular church services. Such prophesying was however a temporary gift and thus is not normative for the church today. Although women officially teaching in church was forbidden, this fact did not negate the obligation women had to use their gifts, including the gift of teaching, as opportunities presented themselves for the well-being of the church.

---

23 See further Van Dam, *The Deacon*, 77–81.

Such unofficial teaching also took place in the context of spreading the gospel as in the case of Priscilla.

There are many other possibilities for women to use their gifts. The Lord Jesus benefited from their support and hospitality. Women also functioned as coworkers of Paul by laboring at his side in his work of spreading the gospel. Widows used their gifts to take care of orphans, to show hospitality and to help young mothers. In short, like all members of the church, women were to use all their gifts for the upbuilding of God's people. The only limitation is not being ordained into ecclesiastical office. The requirements for the offices make it very clear that women are not included.

However, those who wish to see women admitted to ecclesiastical office will typically ask: But what then does Galatians 3:28 mean? "There is neither Jew nor Greek, there is neither slave nor free, there is no male and female, for you are all one in Christ Jesus." Does this passage not indicate that gender is no longer a factor for determining one's role in the church? In response it should be noted that Scripture must be interpreted with Scripture. Taken in isolation this text can be used to defend almost anything. But the context indicates that male and female are the same in terms of sharing fully in Christ's salvation (Gal 3:26–29). No one is excluded from that because of race, social standing, or gender.

It is not popular in our politically correct and egalitarian age to exclude women from ecclesiastical office. Christ however warned that the church can expect opposition from an unbelieving world (cf. John 15:18–19). The church must be obedient to the plain teaching of Scripture and if that means being counter-cultural and assigning different roles to men and women than what is customary in the society in which we live, so be it. We must be prepared to endure the possible scorn and ridicule, and even suffering (1 Pet 4:12–17). The biblical norms for office bearers as understood for millennia must be upheld in obedience to the head of the church.

PART D

EPILOGUE

15   **Retrospect and Prospect**

Having dealt with various aspects of being in God's holy service as Christians, male and female, and as office bearers, it may be helpful to step back for some closing reflections. Since our modern post-Christian society is justifiably often compared to the pagan world in which the early Christian church found itself, let us, consider how the first believers after Pentecost functioned and how the Christian church fared in its first centuries. Next we will consider how our situation today compares, what we can learn from this history, and what challenges we may face in the future.

The First Christians in a Pagan Society

Believers in the Lord Jesus Christ "were first called Christians" in Antioch (Acts 11:26). The passive ("were called") indicates that this designation was given by those who were not followers of Christ. Also elsewhere, an outsider, King Agrippa, is the one who used the term, probably with a hint of derision (Acts 26:28). The use of the name "Christian" by outsiders seems to indicate that it was meant in a derogatory sense, given by those who had no use for these people who were always talking about Christ, that criminal who was crucified outside Jerusalem. If you had that name, you could be expected to suffer society's derision and hostility (1 Pet 4:16). The first known use of the designation "Christians" within the circle of believers is in the second century by the church father Ignatius.[1]

Being a Christian in the first centuries after Pentecost was not easy. Immediately after the outpouring of the Holy Spirit, believers experienced the persecution and hatred of the Jewish establishment. Stephen was stoned to death, followed by the execution of James (Acts 7:58–60; 12:1–2).

---

1   See further detail in Bock, *Acts*, 416.

They were the first of many who would become martyrs for Christ. At first the Roman world considered Christians to be a Jewish sect. Since Judaism was tolerated, so initially were Christians. But that situation changed when it became obvious from Jewish hostility and the confession of Jesus as absolute Lord over one's entire life that Christians were a group apart from all others. By the time Peter sent his first letter in about AD 63, the mere fact that you identified as a Christian could make you subject to harassment or worse. He wrote to Christians scattered abroad: "If you are insulted for the name of Christ, you are blessed, because the spirit of glory and of God rests upon you... If anyone suffers as a Christian, let him not be ashamed, but let him glorify God in that name" (1 Pet 4:14, 16).

In view of the vast differences in worldview and worship between the typical citizen of the day and Christians, the Roman empire came to consider those of the Way (Acts 19:9) with suspicion. Although integrated into society, they were nevertheless separate with their own identity. They repudiated the worship of any god but their own and were therefore accused of atheism. They refused to worship the emperor and thus were considered treasonous and charged accordingly.[2] As the Lord Jesus predicted, persecution was often the lot of the early Christians (Matt 10:16–22). "If they persecuted me, they will also persecute you" (John 15:20). Although living in the world, Christians were distinct from it. Christ said: "If you were of the world, the world would love you as its own; but because you are not of the world, but I chose you out of the world, therefore the world hates you" (John 15:18–19). And so the early Christians found themselves marginalized, regarded with suspicion, and not really belonging to the society of which they were part.

And yet, at the end of the day, the head of the church, Jesus Christ, caused the Christian faith to triumph over paganism, superstition, and idol worship and those who were despised became leaders in the empire. Under Constantine (died AD 337), Christianity was officially tolerated and became more or less the imperial religion. What means did the Lord use to bring about such an astonishing development? How was such a dramatic

---

2   Pier Franco Beatrice, "Atheism, Accusation Of," in *Encyclopedia of Ancient Christianity*, Joseph T. Papa, Erik A. Koenke, and Eric E. Hewett (Downers Grove, IL: IVP Academic, 2014), 1:284–85; also see W.H.C. Frend, "Persecutions," in *Encyclopedia of Ancient Christianity*, Joseph T. Papa, Erik A. Koenke, and Eric E. Hewett (Downers Grove, IL: IVP Academic, 2014), 3:145–51.

turn of events possible? Historians have pointed to social and economic factors that facilitated the spread of Christianity such as the common language and the incredible Roman road network that bound the far-flung empire together and made the rapid spread of Christianity possible. However, ultimately all such factors would be irrelevant if it were not first of all for the faithful witness of individual Christians who spread the good news. God used ordinary Christians and their fearless testimony of the crucified Christ, who rose for the salvation of those who believe in him, to change the entire world in a manner unprecedented in ancient times.

The teaching of the Lord Jesus also pointed in this direction. Christ said that those who believe in him are the salt of the earth and the light of the world (Matt 5:13–14). Military force did not conquer the powers of darkness, but the faithful testimony of countless Christians simply and obediently living out their lives in faith did. As Gerald Sittser put it in his book *Resilient Faith*, the early Christians "immersed themselves in the culture as followers of Jesus, and agents of the kingdom, influencing it from within both as individuals and as a community."[3] To put it differently, to change the world God used young and old who honored their identity as sharing in Christ's anointing and exercising their office as prophet, priest, and king. In order better to appreciate how the Lord used the faithful testimony of ordinary Christians to actually change the culture and government of the Roman Empire, let us consider how God used their identity as prophets, priests, and kings in Christ.

Prophetic Testimony

Because of the prophetic testimony of God's people to Christ and their refusing to be silent, persecution resulted. After the Jews killed Stephen and intensified their persecution, many Christians fled from Jerusalem to escape (Acts 8:1). But they were not silenced. Those who were scattered travelled as far as Phoenicia, Cyprus, and Antioch "preaching the Lord Jesus. And the hand of the Lord was with them, and a great number who believed turned to the Lord" (Acts 11:20–21). It is striking how this growing Christian proclamation is described: "the word of God continued

---

3 Gerald L. Sittser, *Resilient Faith: How the Early Christian "Third Way" Changed the World* (Grand Rapids, MI: Brazos Press, 2019), 174, also see 101–8.

to increase" (Acts 6:7). This does not mean an increase of written revelation. Rather, this description underlines how the Word, the gospel, was so evident in the lives of the Christians that wherever they went, they visibly took the Word with them and so enlarged its impact. In this way "the word of God increased and multiplied" (Acts 12:24) and continued to "prevail mightily" (Acts 19:20). Indeed, "the word of God sounded forth" from the early Christians (1 Thess 1:8).

It is small wonder, seeing the zeal which believers had for the word of God and for Christ, that they were called Christians. They stood out because they were different and full of Christ, their Savior. Their testimony to him could not be suppressed. As Sittser noted: "[their] public contact was inherently evangelistic, as natural as neighborliness when walking a dog or companionship when joining a climbing or a quilting club is today."[4] When the seed of the Word is sown, in God's time it will germinate and bear fruit (cf. Isa 55:11).

But in order to fulfill their prophetic calling of confessing their Savior, they needed to be equipped. The reading and proclamation of the Word on the Lord's Day were important in that regard. This practice was of course already a reality in New Testament times (1 Tim 4:13–14; 2 Tim 4:1–2) and the post-apostolic church continued this practice during their worship services. For example, Justin Martyr (second century AD) wrote: "On the day which is called Sunday we have a common assembly of all who live in the cities or in the outlying districts, and the memoirs of the Apostles or the writings of the Prophets are read, as long as there is time." This reading was followed by an applicatory message.[5] Teaching the faith to equip the saints for their prophetic calling was also a major activity of the leaders in the church (Acts 11:26). An early example of a manual to train Christians in the faith is the *Didache* or The *Teaching of the Twelve Apostles* which begins with these telling words: "There are two ways, one of life, the other of death, and between the two ways there is a great difference."[6] From

---

4   Sittser, *Resilient Faith*, 112.
5   Thomas B. Falls, ed., *Saint Justin Martyr*, The Fathers of the Church (Washington, DC: The Catholic University of America Press, 1948), 106 (*First Apology*, chapter 67); for more examples, Valeriy A. Alikin, *The Earliest History of the Christian Gathering*, Supplements to Vigiliae Christianae (Leiden, NL; Boston, MA: Brill, 2010), 155–78.
6   Huub van de Sandt and David Flusser, *The Didache: Its Jewish Sources and Its Place in Early*

this and other early Christian sources it is clear that the church "developed a rigorous training program to form people in the faith, to prepare them for church membership, and to equip them to be effective witnesses in the empire."[7] This was a three-year program which immersed them in the Word of God and the central doctrines of the faith. It also included spiritual formation. Giving this type of intensive education to new believers was a top priority for the teachers of the day.[8] The development of such solid training was consistent with the apostolic command: "train yourself for godliness; for while bodily training is of some value, godliness is of value in every way, as it holds promise for the present life and also for the life to come" (1 Tim 4:7–8).

Priestly Service

Christians in the early history of the church showed their priestly identity in Christ by displaying love and compassion for their fellow human beings whom they recognized as also being made in God's image. Such an exhibition of love and care for others was very counter-cultural. The classical world had no religious or ethical motivation for helping those outside their immediate family. Those without family connections were in a precarious position if they became destitute or sick. There was no public provision for them. Even during the plagues, municipalities took no responsibility to bury the dead who were simply left on the streets. Within this context Christians demonstrated incredible love, not only for each other but even for their enemies.[9]

Such sacrificial love was evident during the great plague that swept through the Roman Empire in the mid-third century. It was a catastrophe of epic proportions which decimated the population. In some places those who died outnumbered the living. People were simply left to

---

Judaism and Christianity, vol. III.5 of *Jewish Traditions in Early Christian Literature*, Compendia Rerum Iudaicarum Ad Novum Testamentum (Assen: Van Gorcum, 2002), 10.

7   Sittser, *Resilient Faith*, 156; also see Alan Kreider, *The Patient Ferment of the Early Church: The Improbable Rise of Christianity in the Roman Empire* (Grand Rapids, MI: Baker Academic, 2016), 139–41, 156–84.

8   Clinton E. Arnold, "Early Church Catechesis and New Christian's Classes in Contemporary Evangelicalism," *Journal of the Evangelical Theological Society* 47 (2004): 43–51.

9   E.g., Gary B. Ferngren, *Medicine and Health Care in Early Christianity* (Baltimore, MD: Johns Hopkins University Press, 2009), 97–104, 132–38.

fend for themselves. The pagans abandoned the sick and threw the bodies of those who had succumbed out of their homes and on to the public alleys or streets. The response of Christians was radically different. In spite of persecution, they did what they could for the sick, often at the cost of their own life. Dionysius, bishop of Alexandria, wrote of elders, deacons, and church members helping the sick without regard for their own safety. Indicative of the tremendous devotion to show the love of Christ to others, Cyprian, bishop of Carthage, urged Christians in that city to help not only their fellow believers but also their persecutors and he organized the care of the sick for the entire city. No distinction was to be made between Christians and pagans.[10]

Christian compassion for their fellow citizens seemed boundless. Not only the sick but also the lives of orphans and unwanted children, left to the elements to die, were cared for in Christian orphanages that were being developed. Immediately after Pentecost, diaconal aid had already been organized and help continued to be extended to those in need, also outside the church.[11] Given the Christian ethos, it is not surprising that the origin of the hospital is distinctively Christian. It was Basil the Great, later bishop of Caesarea in Cappadocia, who established the first hospital in the Western world in about 369 AD.[12]

The zeal with which Christians showed their love for others in so many ways, and were consequently winning converts, was such an embarrassment to the pagans that Julian the Emperor even had to take note. He sent a letter to Arsacius, the high priest of Galatia, in which he lamented that "the Hellenic religion does not yet prosper as I desire" and observed that Christian "benevolence to strangers, their care for the graves of the dead and the pretended holiness of their lives that have done most to increase atheism [i.e. Christianity]. I believe we ought really and truly to practise every one of these virtues." He also noted that "it is disgraceful that, when no Jew ever has to beg, and the impious Galileans [Christians] support not only their own poor but ours as well, all men see that our

---

10 For this and other examples, see Ferngren, *Medicine and Health Care*, 118–19; Sittser, *Resilient Faith*, 146–48.
11 Van Dam, *The Deacon*, 96–98.
12 Ferngren, *Medicine and Health Care*, 124–27.

people lack aid from us." Such an embarrassing situation had to stop. So he made extra food available and among other orders, he commanded: "In every city establish frequent hostels in order that strangers may profit by our benevolence."[13]

But the Roman Empire could not compete with the love and compassion shown by Christians for each other and for those outside the fellowship of the saints. Pagan religion and culture simply did not provide the fundamentals for that kind of altruistic service. The Lord blessed the Christian witness. Their sacrificial service earned them not only the grudging respect of pagans, but it was also a compelling testimony of the reality of the gospel which God used to convert many to the faith.

Royal Authority and Power

The early Christians also showed that they participated in Christ's office as king in various ways. There was a regal dignity in the way they powerfully confessed Christ as Lord over all. The firm conviction with which they stood up for their Savior moved many pagan hearts to admiration. It also aroused interest in the Christian faith and conversions often followed.

Official persecution by Roman authorities was sporadic before AD 250 since Rome then did little to enforce the state religion. It was however, as Tertullian (ca. AD 160–225) made clear in his *Apology*, an offense in the empire simply to be a Christian. If accused and brought before a judge, you were even forbidden to defend yourself. The mere confession of the name of Christ was sufficient to convict you and only the specific denial of the name of the Savior was enough to secure your release. As the letter (ca. AD 112) of the Emperor Trajan to Pliny, the Younger, made clear, Christians were not to be the special object of persecution. However, if one was accused of being a Christian, then a trial should take place, and if convicted, one would be executed. Release from the charges was always possible if one denied being a Christian and gave proof by honoring the Roman gods.[14] Otherwise, con-

---

13 Julian Emperor of Rome, *The Works of the Emperor Julian: Volume 3*, trans. Wilmer Cavet Wright, Loeb Classical Library (Cambridge, MA: Harvard University Press, 1923), 66–73 (Letter 22).

14 Tertullian and Minucius Felix, *Tertullian's Apology and de Spectaculis*, eds G.P. Goold and W.C.A. Kerr, trans. T.R. Glover and Gerald H. Rendall, Loeb Classical Library (Cambridge, MA: Harvard University Press, 1931), 8–11 (Apology 2.1–20); Pliny, *Letters*, ed. T.E. Page, et al., trans. William

demned Christians were killed, sometimes by wild animals in an arena as sport for the pagan populace. Two examples of martyrs illustrate the point that simply being a Christian was enough to be condemned to death.

The elderly Polycarp, bishop of Smyrna, was arrested in about AD 167 during a local persecution against Christians which was probably incited by Jews. According to a contemporary eyewitness account, when those seeking him found him in a cottage, he offered his captors food and drink and asked time to pray before they took him away. This request was granted. His age and the regal courage and graciousness which he displayed made his captors beg him to save his life by denying his faith. "'Why, what harm is there in saying, "Caesar is Lord," and offering incense' (and other words to this effect), 'and thereby saving yourself?'" But he refused. Once in the arena, the proconsul repeatedly tried to persuade him to deny the faith. "Swear the oath, and I will release you; revile Christ." But Polycarp responded: "For eighty-six years I have been his servant, and he has done me no wrong. How can I blaspheme my King who saved me?" The proconsul tried again and again to dissuade Polycarp from his Christian faith, threatening him with wild beasts and fire. To which Polycarp responded: "You threaten with a fire that burns only briefly and after just a little while is extinguished, for you are ignorant of the fire of the coming judgment and eternal punishment, which is reserved for the ungodly. But why do you delay? Come, do what you wish." The proconsul's herald proclaimed three times to the entire arena: "Polycarp has confessed that he is a Christian." The crowds were in a great hurry to gather wood, with the Jews being especially zealous. He was tied to a stake to be burned alive as "a burnt offering prepared and acceptable to God." He prayed to God, thanking him to be counted worthy to be a martyr and to be received "in your presence today, as a rich and acceptable sacrifice." When his prayer was finished, the fire was lit.[15]

Another early famous martyr was Vibia Perpetua, a young twenty-two year-old noblewoman who was married and had an infant whom she nursed. She and her pregnant slave Felicity were arrested for their faith in AD 203. While in prison awaiting death, Perpetua kept a diary. She re-

---

Melmoth, The Loeb Classical Library (London: William Heinemann, 1931), 2:407 (Letter 97).

15 The quotations are from *The Martyrdom of Polycarp*, §§ 8–12, 14 as found in Holmes, *The Apostolic Fathers*, 233–40; the precise date of Polycarp's martyrdom is contested; cf. Holmes, *The Apostolic Fathers*, 223.

corded how before being jailed her anguished pagan father pleaded with her to renounce her faith. "I said: 'Father, do you see that container over there, for instance—a jug or something?' And he said: 'Yes, I do.' And I said to him: 'It can't be called anything other than it is, can it?' And he said: 'No.' 'So too, I can't call myself anything other than I am: a Christian.'" During her imprisonment, she had a hearing. Her father tried again to dissuade her from maintaining her faith. "My daughter, have pity on my white hairs! Show some compassion to your father, if I deserve to be called father by you... Look at your son, who won't be able to live if you die. Don't flaunt your insistence, or you'll destroy us all." Out of devotion he kissed her hands and flung himself at her feet. She wrote: "I comforted him, saying: 'At the tribunal things will go as God wills: for you must know we are no longer in our own hands, but in God's.' He left me, grief stricken." At the tribunal her father again tried to dissuade her. The governor, Hilarianus, who was the judge in her case, sided with the father and pleaded that she renounce her faith. "'Perform the ritual for the Emperor's welfare.' And I answered: 'I will not perform it.' Hilarianus: 'You are a Christian then?' And I answered: 'I am a Christian.'" She was condemned "to the beasts of the arena." "And joyful we went back to prison." She knew herself safe in God's hands. "I knew I should have to fight not against wild beasts but against the Fiend; but I knew the victory would be mine."[16]

Tertullian, a contemporary of Perpetua, describes how both Perpetua and Felicitas, who had in the meantime given birth, conducted themselves. "The day of their victory shone forth, and they proceeded from the prison into the amphitheatre, as if to an assembly, joyous and of brilliant countenances; if perchance shrinking, it was with joy, and not with fear."[17] The day of their death was the day of their victory!

---

16 The quotations are from *Passio Sanctarum Perpetuae et Felicitatis* (§§ 3, 5, 10) as found in translation in Peter Dronke, *Women Writers of the Middle Ages: A Critical Study of Texts from Perpetua (†203) to Marguerite Porete (†310)* (Cambridge, UK: Cambridge University Press, 1984), 1–4.

17 The quotation is from §6.1 of the *Passio* as found in Tertullian, "The Martyrdom of Perpetua and Felicitas," in *Ante-Nicene Fathers, Volume III: Latin Christianity: Its Founder Tertullian*, eds Alexander Roberts, James Donaldson, and A. Cleveland Coxe, trans. Peter Holmes (Buffalo, NY: Christian Literature Company, 1885), 704; for parts of the *Passio* obviously not written by Perpetua being attributed to Tertullian, see E. Romero Pose, "Perpetua and Felicitas," in *Encyclopedia of Ancient Christianity*, Joseph T. Papa, Erik A. Koenke, and Eric E. Hewett (Downers Grove, IL: IVP Academic, 2014), 3:144.

Such devotion to the cause of Christ was, however, not always exhibited. When Emperor Decius issued an empire-wide edict in January AD 250 that everyone had to offer pagan sacrifices to show their loyalty to the Roman gods, many Christians could not stand up to the pressure and offered the required sacrifices. But, many also stood firm and became martyrs. Decius's religious policy was a failure and ended with his death in AD 251. Subsequent attempts to crush the church also failed.[18] Although there were lapses, even significant ones in times of persecution, nevertheless, the overwhelming message which pagans received from Christians was their faithfulness to their Savior, no matter the cost.

In regally standing up to paganism and its gods, Christians showed that they shared Christ's royal office as those who would defy the foe. They realized that their struggle was not "against flesh and blood, but against the rulers, against the authorities, against the cosmic powers over this present darkness, against the spiritual forces of evil in the heavenly places" (Eph 6:12). Armed with the sword of the Spirit, God's Word, strengthened in the Spirit by their prayerful walk with God, and showing in every possible way the gospel of love and peace, they were able to extinguish the flaming arrows of the evil one (cf. Eph 6:13–18).

The unquestioning dedication and loyalty to the Lord confounded the enemy. They simply could not comprehend what made Christians behave the way they did—even dying for the faith. But those who took the trouble to seriously investigate, experienced God's mercy and converted to the faith. They realized that a martyr's death was a triumph over the evil one (cf. Matt 16:24–26). Indeed, historians agree that every public martyrdom of Christians was a successful opportunity for the church to gain converts.[19] The human army of Jesus Christ gradually increased in number until in the days of Constantine, the Empire officially became Christian.

That fact that individual Christians faithfully exercised their office as prophets, priests, and kings determined the identity of the church as a "a chosen race, a royal priesthood, a holy nation" (1 Pet 2:9). This identity of the early Christian church as a whole, merits some reflection.

---

18 Frend, "Persecutions," 3:148–51.
19 Kreider, *The Patient Ferment*, 51.

"A Chosen Race, a Royal Priesthood, a Holy Nation"

The new "Israel of God" (Gal 6:16), the Christian church, functioned in a real way as a nation, a holy people with their own distinct identity. The apostle Peter reminded the Christians dispersed throughout Pontus, Galatia, Cappadocia, Asia, and Bithynia (1 Pet 1:2) that as believers they now had status as a special people. They were not just scattered individuals. He told them: "You are a chosen race, a royal priesthood, a holy nation, a people for his own possession, that you may proclaim the excellencies of him who called you out of darkness into his marvelous light. Once you were not a people, but now you are God's people; once you had not received mercy, but now you have received mercy" (1 Pet 2:9–10). This unique identity as a holy nation, scattered throughout the empire, and yet united as God's special creation and possession, puzzled the Roman authorities. They did not really know what to do with this phenomenon—the Christian church.

As a royal priesthood and a holy nation, the early Christian church was completely counter-cultural. This becomes obvious, for example, from a letter written, probably in the late second century AD, to a certain Diognetus who had asked what Christianity was all about. In describing Christians, this anonymous letter states in part:

> They live in their own countries, but only as aliens; they participate in everything as citizens, and endure everything as foreigners. Every foreign land is their fatherland, and every fatherland is foreign . . . They love everyone, and by everyone they are persecuted. They are unknown, yet they are condemned; they are put to death, yet they are brought to life. They are poor, yet they make many rich; they are in need of everything, yet they abound in everything. They are dishonored, yet they are glorified in their dishonor; they are slandered, yet they are vindicated. They are cursed, yet they bless; they are insulted, yet they offer respect. When they do good, they are punished as evildoers; when they are punished, they rejoice as brought to life. By the Jews they are assaulted as foreigners, and by the Greeks they are persecuted, yet those who hate them are unable to give a reason for their hostility.[20]

---

20   *The Letter to Diognetus* §5.5, 11–17 as found in Holmes, *The Apostolic Fathers*, 542.

Notice how when they are punished, "they rejoice." This is a key characteristic of the early Christian church.

This joy was already evident at the very beginning, at the day of Pentecost. As they shared fellowship and food they had "glad and generous hearts." Their joy included praising God and being looked on favorably by all the people (Acts 2:46–47). Joy characterized the apostle Paul's letter to the Philippian believers even though he wrote it from prison (Phil 1:17–18). "Even if I am to be poured out as a drink offering upon the sacrificial offering of your faith, I am glad and rejoice with you all. Likewise you also should be glad and rejoice with me" (Phil 1:17–18). "Rejoice in the Lord always; again I will say rejoice" (Phil 4:4). That joy continued to be shown in the church, as we, for example, saw with Perpetua's martyrdom. She endured it with joy. So while pagan society as a whole may grumble and mutter about lesser matters, Christians strived to show their joy in the Lord, regardless what their present circumstances may have been like.

This joy was coupled with enormous patience. The apostle John described his Christian identity as being a "partner in the tribulation and the kingdom and the patient endurance that are in Jesus" (Rev 1:9). It was this patient endurance for which the Lord had commended the churches at Ephesus, Thyatira, and Philadelphia (Rev 2:2–3, 19; 3:10). It was through enduring patiently that victory was assured as the conclusion of Christ's letters to these churches indicate. Alan Kreider in his study on patience in the early church also noted that the church fathers consistently underscored the need for patience and even considered it crucial for their well-being and growth.[21] He compared the influence of Christian testimony to a process of fermentation, a gradual unstoppable energy. Christians living lives of patient ferment meant that the gospel slowly but surely took hold where Christians lived. The church did not grow because of concerted evangelistic efforts. "Rather, it was primarily because the Christians and their churches lived by a habitus that attracted others. The Christians' focus was not on 'saving' people or recruiting them; it was on living faithfully." The growth of the church was considered to be God's work and not that of the members of the church. "So they did not engage in frantic action

---

21   Kreider, *The Patient Ferment*, 13–36.

to save those who were not baptized; instead they entrusted the outsiders to God."[22] The church was patient and lived their faith trusting that God would use their everyday testimony to attract and draw others in.

It is striking that the church did not make a concerted use of their worship services to evangelize. Because of persecution, starting with that of Nero in 68 AD, churches across the empire began to prohibit outsiders to join them in worship which became secret. The fear that some might attend in order to spy on them and report them to the authorities caused churches to keep their worship services hidden. By the late second century the exclusion of outsiders from worship was widespread. Christians were of course far from being shy about their faith. They spread the gospel by patient personal contacts and lifestyle evangelism but not by their church services. "We do not speak great things but we live them," Cyprian said in the mid-third century.[23]

Christians lived and shared their faith with anyone whom God put in their life's path. They formed a nation which was not defined by race or ethnicity, but by being born again as children of Father in heaven. The outpouring of the Holy Spirit on the day of Pentecost brought with it a foretaste of the realization of the promise of a reunited humanity. God had shattered the initial unity of the human race in punishing the sin of the Tower of Babel by destroying their ability to understand each other (Gen 11:1–9). But at Pentecost, the judgmental confusion of tongues was being reversed and replaced with the miracle that those of different languages and backgrounds could understand the gospel. Regardless of one's ethnic or linguistic background, "we hear them telling in our own tongues the mighty works of God" (Acts 2:11). All believers were citizens of the heavenly Zion of which Psalm 87 spoke. The apostle John saw the redeemed, the church, "a great multitude that no one could number, from every nation, from all tribes and peoples and languages, standing before the throne and before the lamb" (Rev 7:9).

In the meantime, this people of God, this in a sense invisible nation, is spread over the whole earth. They are all different, racially, socially,

---

22 Kreider, *The Patient Ferment*, 129–30.
23 Kreider, *The Patient Ferment*, 11–14, 135.

culturally, but they are one in Christ. There is, therefore, as the apostle Paul wrote to the Galatians, "neither Jew nor Greek, neither slave nor free, there is no male and female, for you are all one in Christ Jesus" (Gal 3:28; also Col 3:11). This unity overrides the diversity in importance. All God's children have a common citizenship. No matter the background or ethnicity, Christians can say: "our citizenship is in heaven" (Phil 3:20), the Jerusalem above, "she is our mother" (Gal 4:26). This sense of the overriding unity among diverse Christians was also experienced and reflected in the early Christian church. The church is even called "this new race [*genos*]" in the letter to Diognetus which was mentioned earlier.[24]

Through their simple testimony of consistent Christian living, believers in the first centuries after Pentecost jolted the empire. They were like a growing invisible nation that showed that their first loyalty was to their risen Savior. Eventually, God used their witness to overturn the pagan social order. Are there lessons here for us today?

Being Christian in Neo-Pagan Times

Current Western culture is slowly but surely heading toward a post-Christian neo-paganism. The Christian faith and its values are increasingly marginalized and rejected. A culture that used to be predominantly influenced by biblical values is being transformed into one that has very little patience with its past, denies it, and even overturns its norms. For example, protection for divinely given life has been removed with unfettered abortion; the institution of marriage is being sabotaged by state-sanctioned same-sex unions; and a person's biological birth sex can be medically overturned by one's perceived gender identity. While the powers that be promote essentially pagan norms for a largely self-centered therapeutic society, Christians find themselves isolated and seemingly out of place in their own country.

Of course, an advantage of this state of affairs is that we are in effect constantly reminded that as Christians we are ultimately not of this world, but that "our citizenship is in heaven, and from it we await a Savior,

---

24 *The Letter to Diognetus* §1.1 as found in Holmes, *The Apostolic Fathers*, 534–35.

the Lord Jesus Christ" (Phil 3:20). Just as the early Christian church, we are a nation of citizens who belong to "a better country" (Heb 11:16); a nation that transcends national boundaries; the innumerable multitude that the Lord is gathering from all peoples and tongues (Rev 7:9).

How are we to respond as believers living in a Western society that is renouncing its Christian past? Since we appear to be heading to a situation that is somewhat similar to what the early Christians found themselves in, can we learn from their testimony and the manner in which Christianity spread so rapidly? The dispersing of the early Christian faith was facilitated by an excellent transportation and communication network coupled with a common language that bound the empire together. We have the same advantage for disseminating the Christian faith today with the incredible possibilities of the internet and the widespread use of the English language. The global village of today shares some of the same salutary features as the Roman Empire did for the early Christians.

To be sure there are significant differences. One is the fact that in the West the Christian faith is not a novelty about which people may be curious to know more about. It may, therefore, be more difficult to reach a society that is consciously jettisoning its Christian heritage than to reach one for whom the Christian faith is brand new. Yet, there are lessons to be had from those first centuries after Pentecost.

The most important takeaway from a consideration of the growth of the early church is a reaffirmation of the central importance of every Christian simply living out their faith as those who share Christ's anointing as prophet, priest, and king. Just as the faithful testimony of ordinary Christians to the risen Christ in their everyday walk and talk made all the difference in the first centuries after Pentecost, so too in our day, the Lord will bless the steadfast witness of Christians to the Lord Jesus today. This reality has several important implications that we need to consider: the place of worship and instruction, the need to be counter-cultural, and the necessary willingness to count the cost of being a Christian in an increasingly hostile environment.

The Critical Place of Worship and Instruction

The life and growth of the Christian church was fueled by the Spirit's use of the Word of God in worship and instruction. The Sunday gatherings were worship services in which the reading and proclamation of the Word had an important place. Timothy had to devote himself "to the public reading of Scripture, to exhortation, to teaching" (1 Tim 4:13). Since God's Word is "able to make you wise for salvation through faith in Jesus Christ" and since it is "profitable for teaching, for reproof, for correction, and for training in righteousness" (2 Tim 3:15, 16), the great significance of preaching in the context of worship is indisputable. As we have already noted above, the early Christian church understood.

With the Word of God read and proclaimed occupying a prominent place in their meetings on the Lord's Day, the focus was on worshipping God who is in heaven and listening to him and his salvation. As Sittser noted, early Christians "saw themselves not primarily as consumers who attended worship to hear a good sermon and sing a few familiar songs but as beholders of the unspeakable glory of God." Worship "ushered them into the very presence of God" so that they were prepared "to return to the ordinary life of market, home, and neighborhood as disciples of Jesus."[25] In other words, as Kreider put it, worship was "the energizing center of Christian communal life." Through their worship services "God changed them and strengthened them to cope with precarious realities and daunting problems of daily living."[26] Our worship services today should do no less. The only way to ensure this blessing is by keeping the proclamation of the whole Word of God central. Nothing should diminish its primary importance.

We have seen that the early Christian worship service was not trying to be seeker-friendly. Indeed, non-Christians were often excluded from their services. But the Sunday worship services were critical for the growth of the church. In those services Christians were informed, equipped, and encouraged to live the faith joyfully so that they were prepared to defend and explain the gospel "to anyone who asks you for a reason for the hope

---

25   Sittser, *Resilient Faith*, 174.
26   Kreider, *The Patient Ferment*, 185–86.

that is in you" (1 Pet 3:15). Those attracted to the faith, while not always admitted to the worship services, were offered instruction in the Word of God. Indeed, the teaching ministry was called "hearing the Word."[27] The instruction of those new to the faith was an extremely important feature of the growth of the early church as noted above. In terms of the factors that enabled the church to grow, the worship service had a relatively modest place. The increase of the church in the post-apostolic period was by the personal testimony and lifestyles of Christians. Neighbors, fellow workers, and people whom Christians met in the course of the day became interested in the gospel from the behavior, talk, and joy displayed by Christians. This interest was followed up with biblical instruction.

As Reformed churches we are blessed with a long tradition of solid catechetical instruction that ultimately goes back to the early church. This practice must continue for the health and, as God wills, for the expansion of the church. We should, however, be aware of the fact that we no longer live in a culture that is familiar with the Bible. In the education that the churches give to non-Christians absolutely nothing, or very little, can be assumed. In that respect our situation today is much closer to the time of the early church than, for example, to the nineteenth century Victorian era when Bible knowledge was widespread. Another important aspect of catechetical teaching in Reformed churches that should continue to be honored is the systematic preaching and teaching of biblical doctrine as summarized in the Heidelberg Catechism in the afternoon worship services.

The Holy Spirit enables the church to grow through the agency of the Word of God proclaimed in church and exhibited by Christians in their daily life. It is not, for example, our activism or special programs, however beneficial they may be, that will suddenly make the church increase. If the example of the early Christian church is of value, any church growth will primarily be by our daily patient and faithful testimony that exhibits the fruits of the Spirit. One consequence of this reality is that we should not worry too much about whether our church services will attract outsiders. Unbelievers are not normally drawn to biblical preaching. However, as *public* worship services, they should obviously be as understandable as

---

27   Noted in Kreider, *The Patient Ferment*, 152.

possible for any non-believer who may attend. And then they will hopefully notice that God is really in our midst (cf. 1 Cor 14:25)! They will see something totally different from the worldly culture with which they are familiar. It may cause them to stop and think about the reality of God. A church service is profoundly counter-cultural. Indeed, so is the Christian faith.

Christianity is Counter-Cultural

A common mistake which many churches make is trying to make themselves appealing to non-believers. As a result, they profile a culture of entertainment for their worship services or build a following after a popular personality. But if one wishes to be entertained, the world offers plenty of choice. And if a popular personality has created a following, the audience will disperse when such an individual leaves the stage. The temptation to lower the cultural threshold for the outsider can lead to an accommodation that makes the faith almost unrecognizable as the true and robust Christian faith. The other possibility of seeking accommodation to a worldly culture is that the gospel becomes so hidden within the cultural packaging as to be almost invisible. The clear call to believe and repent and the need to subject all of life to Jesus as Lord is then no longer heard.[28]

Kreider put it well: "Unlike many churches today, the third-century churches… did not try to grow by making people feel welcome and included. Civic paganism did that. In contrast, the churches were hard to enter. They didn't grow because of their cultural accessibility; they grew because they required commitment to an unpopular God who didn't require people to perform cultic acts correctly but instead equipped them to live in a way that was richly unconventional."[29]

Non-Christians in the pagan culture of the Roman world and the neo-pagan one of our day can be drawn to a totally different worldview and the culture that Christianity offers if they know enough about it to realize the enormous benefits of true freedom and joy in Christ being offered. After all, what at bottom does a pagan or neo-pagan culture really have to give? Justin Martyr in his *First Apology* pictured the life of the non-Chris-

---

28   See also Sittser, *Resilient Faith*, 177.
29   Kreider, *The Patient Ferment*, 149.

tian as one in bondage "characterized by addictive practices in four primal areas: sexual ethics, marred by fornication; the occult, trapped by magical arts; wealth and possessions, distorted by competitive acquisitiveness; and violence and xenophobia, filled with hatred and murder toward people of different tribes and customs."[30] This summary of what was written in the second century AD still rings true today.

It is a current reality that churches which have tried to keep in step with the evolving secular culture are churches that are most susceptible to losing large numbers of members. Two Reformed examples come to mind. Both have been trying to keep abreast of the current societal culture by ordaining women to ecclesiastical office even though this practice is contrary to the explicit teaching of Scripture that the offices are for males only (1 Tim 3:1–7; Titus 1:5–9). The Christian Reformed Church in North America began to open the door to women in office in 1992 and actually did so in 1996. But from 1992 the membership of that church has been steadily shrinking—a 25 percent decline between1992–2018.[31] Similarly, the Reformed Churches Liberated in the Netherlands saw their membership decline significantly after deciding to admit females to ecclesiastical office in 2017. The last figures available (for 2020) saw a record 2,262 leave from a total membership of about 112,000. The preceding years were not much better.[32] To be sure, Christianity is on the whole declining in the Western world, but could that phenomenon not be traced to the abandonment of biblical faithfulness in mainline churches? Recent studies would support that notion and, remarkably, conservative churches that want to be faithful to Scripture are either stable or growing.[33] Also, maintaining an identity

---

30 As summarized in Kreider, *The Patient Ferment*, 143.

31 Nathan Stripp, "CRC Membership Decline Correlates with Calvin Enrollment," *Calvin University Chimes*, 26 April 2018. https://calvinchimes.org/2018/04/26/membership-in-the-crc-in-decline/.

32 Eline Kuijper, "Gereformeerde Kerken vrijgemaakt verliezen in 2020 recordaantal leden," *Nederlands Dagblad*, 5 May 2021; Sjirk Kuijper, "Mensen, kerken en trouw," *Nederlands Dagblad*, 8 May 2021.

33 For the decline in American mainline churches, but less change in evangelical or historically black churches, see Pew Research Center, *America's Changing Religious Landscape*, Report (2015), 20; for a detailed study focussing on southern Ontario, but also incorporating many other studies, David Millard Haskell, Kevin N. Flatt, and Stephanie Burgoyne, "Theology Matters: Comparing the Traits of Growing and Declining Mainline Protestant Church Attendees and Clergy," *Review of Religious Research* 58 (2016): 515–41.

that is distinct from the larger culture contributes to their growth.[34]

The decline in churches that cater to current secular culture reminds us that those who are spiritually restless and seeking meaning with a new focus for their life are not looking for more of the same culture which they are already familiar with. They are looking for something totally different—something that will give them true freedom, purpose and the peace that surpasses all understanding. That is the biblical Christian faith and it is completely counter-cultural and at odds with the current neo-pagan norms. That means being a Christian comes with the price of discipleship. Just as the early Christians had to count the cost, so do we.

Counting the Cost

Our situation today as Christians is obviously not the same as in the days of the Roman Empire. We have freedoms unheard of in classical times. Furthermore, those living in the Western world do not suffer the same kind of persecution that Christians did in the centuries after Pentecost. That can change of course. Christians suffer enormously in countries like North Korea, China, and some Muslim-majority nations. There is no guarantee that Christians will not experience oppression and jail time in the West. It has, as a matter of fact, already happened. Although legal issues are sometimes difficult to disentangle, it remains a fact that long-time pro-life activists have been jailed from time to time, sometimes repeatedly for minor offenses.[35] A Canadian father who objected to the decision of his fourteen year-old daughter to undergo medical treatments to become a male had to endure six months in jail.[36] In Finland, the Prosecutor General has brought criminal charges against a politician and a church leader for holding to the biblical view on sex and marriage.[37] Such developments

---

34 As noted in Haskell, Flatt, and Burgoyne, "Theology Matters," 539 with reference to the study of Canadian evangelical churches S. Reimer and M. Wilkinson, *A Culture of Faith* (2015), 55–62.

35 See, e.g., for Canada, Kaiden McIntyree and Peter Bowal, "The Story of Linda Gibbons." Found in https://www.lawnow.org/the-story-of-linda-gibbons/ (dated January 4, 2017).

36 Erin Perse, "Father Jailed After Referring to Biological Female Child as His Daughter." Found at https://thepostmillennial.com/rob-hoogland-canada-prisoner-of-conscience (dated at March 16, 2021).

37 . Julian Mann, "A Finnish Politician is Facing Jail for Her Biblical Beliefs." at https://www.christiantoday.com/article/a.finnish.politician.is.facing.jail.for.her.biblical.beliefs.could.the.same.happen.here/136755.htm (May 5, 2021).

would have been unthinkable just a few decades ago when Christian influence on Western society was stronger.

Yet, to be oppressed for being a Christian is in a sense normal. Christ warned that those who believed in him would face hostility and persecution (John 15:19–20), but he also said: "Blessed are those who are persecuted because of righteousness, for theirs is the kingdom of heaven" (Matt 5:10). The Lord God will give the necessary faith and courage for his children who trust in him so that they can stand up to the challenges of an unbelieving culture. As he blessed the first Christians who put their trust in him and confessed him regardless of the consequences, he will also bless us today when we meet opposition and even persecution.

In a pagan culture, only true Christianity will survive. As Derek Thomas perceptively noted: "Sooner or later, nominal Christianity will accommodate itself to the pagan culture; it will adopt its values and conform to its levels of acceptability... The result will be that such Christianity will itself become increasingly pagan."[38]

Are we prepared to pay the price of being a Christian? It is noteworthy that when the empire-wide Decian persecution started, Cyprian to his horror saw how quickly many denied the faith even though Scripture had said that there would be oppression. "Immediately at the first words of the threatening enemy a very large number of the brethren betrayed their faith, and were laid low not by the attack of persecution, rather they laid themselves low by their voluntary lapse."[39] There were obviously several factors contributing to this abandonment of the faith, but the main one seems to have been an unsound relationship to the world. Cyprian lamented the worldliness as seen in materialism, vanity, intermarriage, and worldly clergy. When faced with a choice for or against Christ, they choose the way of least resistance. The church was simply not prepared and its leadership had not made the church ready for oppression.[40] This is a sober

---

38 Derek W.H. Thomas, *Acts*, Reformed Expository Commentary (Phillipsburg, NJ: P&R Publishing, 2011), 324.

39 Saint Cyprian, *The Lapsed*, trans. and ed. Roy J. Deferrari, The Fathers of the Church (Washington, DC: Catholic University of America Press, 1958), 62 (Chapter 7).

40 For more on this see Fred M. Williams, "Reaction to Persecution: A Lesson from the Early Church," *Trinity Journal* 6 (1977): 34–43.

reminder for us to be prepared. The apostle Paul warned that "all who desire to live a godly life in Christ Jesus will be persecuted" (2 Tim 3:12).

This warning implies that Christians should have a visible presence. An invisible Christian cannot be harassed. It is noteworthy that in his high priestly prayer Christ did not pray for the Father to take believers out of the world that hates them but that they be kept safe from the clutches of the evil one. They belong to the Son, and Satan must not have them (John 17:14–15). To that end, Christ also prayed: "Sanctify them in the truth; your word is truth" (John 17:17). With this petition our Savior asked the Father to confirm our separateness from the world as Christians since we are to be consecrated, sanctified, to holy service in accordance with the word of truth, the Scriptures. With the agency of the Spirit, the Word is to be our guide for holy living and for developing a godly culture that challenges the decadent one of this passing age. Living counter-culturally, that calls into question and disputes the dominant sinful norms and provides a godly alternative, will evoke a response from the evil one. That can even include possible persecution. But we must not hold back on that account. Early Christians, like the apostles, even rejoiced "that they were counted worthy to suffer dishonor for the name" of Christ (Acts 5:41). Peter also exhorted: "Rejoice insofar as you share Christ's sufferings" (1 Pet 4:13). The point is that suffering should not be a reason for bitterness, but as evidence that our reward will be great in heaven (Matt 5:11–12).

In this context it is good to remember that the thriving and growth of Christianity does not depend on being in a society that has a Christian heritage. The history of the last centuries of what has been called Christendom has shown an overall steady decline of biblical Christianity in the Western world. But the history of the early Christian church shows that the church can flourish within a hostile environment. The same can be said, for instance, of the current flourishing of Christianity within China in spite of the attempts of the communist dictatorship to crush it.[41]

---

41 For a recent collection of essays showing the dramatic changes currently taking place, often in ways analogous to the early church, see the special issue of *Religions* Francis K.G. Lim, ed., *New Developments in Christianity in China* (Basel, CH: MDPI, 2020); also available at https://www.mdpi.com/journal/religions.

In Conclusion

Christians today face challenges not unlike those that the early Christian church had to contend with in the first centuries after Pentecost. But like them, we can be encouraged by the fact that the Lord, who equipped his people in the past to stand up to the wiles of Satan and to testify to his name and salvation, has promised to do the same today. On his departure into heaven, he declared: "I am with you always to the end of the age" (Matt 24:20). The outpouring of the Spirit on the day of Pentecost was a fulfillment of that promise.

The Lord made it clear that he expects his people to use the gifts and abilities he has given them in his service. The gifts vary, but the responsibility to use them is the same (Matt 25:14–30). However, all Christians share in common the gift of the enabling Spirit so that they may also share in Christ's anointing in his prophetic, priestly, and royal offices. We have seen how Christ showed some important ways in which we can exercise the responsibilities given to us and how the early Christian church gives us examples. It may be useful, in conclusion, to summarize some highlights.

In fulfilling our prophetic office, we need to simply confess that we are Christians and let the chips fall where they may. Identifying with Christ and the Good News is foolishness to an unbelieving world, but it is the power of new life for those who believe (Rom 1:16; 1 Cor 1:18). That has ramifications and consequences in all of life. Similarly, as those sharing Christ's priestly office, we exhibit the love and compassion he has shown to others by being considerate, charitable, helping the poor, and following government health guidelines during a pandemic. In this way we give ourselves wholeheartedly in a sacrificial life of thanksgiving. At the same time, we show that we belong to the victorious King by sharing his royal office. We denounce sin in our own life and in the life of our nation. We detest the evil one and his demons but show compassion to those enslaved by sin and try to show them the freedom of the gospel.

When we seek to live up to Christ's expectations for our life, then our testimony has impact. Christ said that Christians are the salt of the earth (Matt 5:13). Salt seeks to preserve and fights deterioration and decay. But it acts very slowly and almost unnoticeably. A little at a time. If our witness to the truth of the gospel does not bear immediate fruit we must not be disappointed, but patient. You cannot rush the effects of being salt of the earth. Believers are also "the light of the world" with the mandate "let your light shine before others, so that they may see your good works and give glory to your Father who is in heaven" (Matt 5:14, 16). By showing the light of the gospel through our walk and talk, we also give hope to the despairing. The apostle Paul characterized children of God as being "in the midst of a crooked and twisted generation, among whom you shine as lights in the world, holding fast to the word of life" (Phil 2:15). "Walk as children of light" (Eph 5:8), indeed, as those sharing in the anointing of *the* light of the world, Jesus Christ (John 8:12).

The example of the early Christian church underlined the importance of exercising patience. Christ said that a Christian witness and life works like leaven. "The kingdom of heaven is like leaven that a woman took and hid in three measures of flour, till it was all leavened" (Matt 13:34). Leaven has an effect through slow fermentation. It also takes time and patience for the effects of the gospel to be felt. This is good to keep in mind lest we become too easily discouraged. After all, as we have seen, a dominant characteristic of a Christian must be joy—a joy in the Lord whose promises will all be fulfilled!

Appendix:
Original Publication Information

This book is a composite of new writing and the revision of some earlier writings. The lead numbers that follow represent the corresponding chapter in this book and where an earlier version of material found in this chapter was first published.

2. "Who is this Woman?" *Clarion* 69 (2020) 132-35, 163-66.

3. "Saved through Childbearing" *Clarion* (2018) 3-5.

4. "The Calling of Husband and Father" *Clarion* (2020) 330-33.

5. "Calvin and the Reformation of Ecclesiastical Offices" is a revised version of a public lecture given on February 23, 2012 in Anyang, South Korea on the occasion of the Second School Day of the Theological Academy of the Independent Reformed Church. It has been published in both Korean and English respectively in *Reformation of Liturgy and Offices by Calvin* (2012) and in *Diakonia* 26:2-3 (2012) 42-49.

6. This chapter incorporates: "The Preacher as Priest" *Clarion* 57 (2008) 590-93.

7. A revised version of a presentation on April 14, 2016 at a combined Council Meeting of the Canadian Reformed Church and the United Reformed Church in Dunnville, ON, organized by the United Reformed Church.

8. "Elders – A Treasure to Cherish" *Clarion* 57 (2008) 550-552.

9. "Aspiring, preparing and equipping for the office of elder: Is Special Training Required?" *Diakonia* 28:1 (2014), 14-20.

10. "Congregational Involvement in Electing to Office" incorporates "Slippery Slope?" *Clarion* 60.10 (2011) 234-236.

12-14   These chapters incorporate in some form:

"Prophetesses, Then and Now" *Clarion* 62 (2013) 91-92, 122-124, 146-148.

"Dutch Report on Women in Ecclesiastical Office" *Clarion* 66 (2017) 70-73.

"Our Sister Churches Open all Ecclesiastical Offices to Women" *Clarion* 66 (2017) 394-397.

"Dutch Decision on Female Ordination to the Office of Elder Weighed and Found Wanting" *Clarion* 66 (2017) 423-426.

"The Justification for Female Ministers in our Sister Churches" *Clarion* (2017) 502-504.

"How Convincing is Synod Meppel's Evidence for Female Ordination as Deaconesses?" *Clarion* 66 (2017) 527-529.

15   This chapter includes:

"Early Christians and their Prophetic Testimony" *Clarion* 70:15 (2021) 433-35.

"Early Christians in Priestly and Royal Service" *Clarion* 70:16 (2021) 460-63.

"Early Christians: a Chosen Race, a Royal Priesthood, a Holy Nation" *Clarion* 70:17 (2021) 491-93.

"Being a Christian in Neo-Pagan Times" *Clarion* 70:18 (2021) 519-522.

"The Cost of Being a Christian" *Clarion* 70:19 (2021) 543-546

Select Bibliography

Bavinck, Herman. *Reformed Dogmatics*. 4 vols. Edited by John Bolt. Translated by John Vriend. Grand Rapids, MI: Baker Academic, 2003–8.

Beeke, Joel, "Catechism Preaching." *Puritan Reformed Journal* 7 (2015): 215–42.

Blamires, Harry. *The Christian Mind*. London, UK: SPCK, 1966.

Blamires, Harry. *Recovering the Christian Mind: Meeting the challenge of Secularism*. Downers Grove, IL: InterVarsity, 1988.

Boekenstein, William, and Steven Swets, eds., *Faithful and Fruitful: Essays for Elders and Deacons.* With a foreward by Michael Brown. Reformed Fellowship Inc., 2019.

The Book of Church Order of the Orthodox Presbyterian Church. Willow Grove, PA: The Committee on Christian Education of the Orthodox Presbyterian Church, 2011.

Book of Praise: Anglo-Genevan Psalter. Winnipeg, MB: Premier, 2014.

Brakel, Wilhelmus à. *The Christian's Reasonable Service*. Edited by Joel R. Beeke. Translated by Bartel Elshout. Grand Rapids, MI: Reformation Heritage Books, 1992–95.

Brown, Michael, ed. *Called to Serve: Essays for Elders and Deacons.* Grandville, MI: Reformed Fellowship, 2006.

Calvin, John. *Institutes of the Christian Religion*. Edited by John T. McNeill. Translated by Ford Lewis Battles. Library of Christian Classics. Philadelphia, PA: Westminster, 1960.

Clowney, Edmund P. *Called to the Ministry*. Chicago: Inter-Varsity Press, 1964.

De Jong, Peter Y. "Comments on Catechetical Preaching (1)." *Mid-America Journal of Theology* 1, no. 2 (1985): 155–89; 2, no. 2 (1986): 149–70; 3, no. 1 (1987): 89–134.

DeRidder, Richard, trans & comp. *The Church Orders of the Sixteenth Century Reformed Churches of the Netherlands: Together with Their Social, Political, and Ecclesiastical Context.* With the assistance of Peter H. Jonker and Leonard Verduin. Grand Rapid, MI: Calvin Theological Seminary, 1987.

Eyres, Lawrence R. *The Elders of the Church.* Phillipsburg, NJ: Presbyterian and Reformed, 1975.

Ferngren, Gary B. *Medicine and Health Care in Early Christianity.* Baltimore, MD: Johns Hopkins University Press, 2009.

Folkerts, F.H. "Women's Voting Right in the Church." *Lux Mundi* 14, no. 2 (1995): 2–7.

Free Church of Scotland Board of Ministry. *Elders and Deacons in the Free Church: A Study Guide for Office Bearers.*

Gaffin, Richard B., Jr. *Perspectives on Pentecost: Studies in New Testament Teaching on the Gifts of the Holy Spirit.* Phillipsburg, NJ: Presbyterian and Reformed, 1979.

Goodykoontz, Harry G. *The Minister in the Reformed Tradition.* Richmond, VA: John Knox Press, 1963.

Gootjes, Nicolaas H. "Catechism Preaching." In *Teaching and Preaching the Word: Studies in Dogmatics and Homiletics*, edited and compiled by Cornelis Van Dam, 383–409. Winnipeg, MB: Premier, 2010.

Henderson, Robert W. *The Teaching Office in the Reformed Tradition.* Philadelphia: Westminster Press, 1962.

Hendriks, A. N. "The Place and Significance of the Offices in the Congregation of Christ." *Diakonia* 4, no. 2 (1990): 31–38.

Hendriks, A. N. "Preaching from the Catechism." *Diakonia* 1, no. 3 (1988): 2–8.

Hoekema, Anthony A. *Holy Spirit Baptism.* Grand Rapids: Eerdmans, 1972.

Hyde, Daniel R. "The Principle and Practice of Preaching in the Heidelberg Catechism." *Puritan Reformed Journal* 1 (2009): 97–117.

Kreider, Alan. *The Patient Ferment of the Early Church: The Improbable Rise of Christianity in the Roman Empire.* Grand Rapids, MI: Baker Academic, 2016.

McKee, Elsie Anne. *Elders and the Plural Ministry: The Role of Exegetical History in Illuminating John Calvin's Theology.* Travaux d'Humanisme et Renaissance. Geneva: Librairie Droz, 1988.

McKee, Elsie Anne. *John Calvin on the Diaconate and Liturgical Almsgiving.* Travaux d'Humanisme et Renaissance. Geneva: Librairie Droz, 1984.

Murray, David P. "Serious Preaching in a Comedy Culture." *Puritan Reformed Journal* 3, no. 1 (2011): 328–38.

Parker, T.H.L. *John Calvin: A Biography.* Philadelphia: Westminster, 1975.

Payne, Jon D. "Hipster or Herald?" *Modern Reformation* 22, no. 4 (2013): 10–13.

Pearcey, Nancy. *Total Truth: Liberating Christianity from its Cultural Captivity.* Foreword by Phillip E. Johnson. Wheaton, IL: Crossway, 2005.

Pennings, Ray. *Church and Caesar: A Legal Primer for Church Office-Bearers.* Grand Rapids: Reformation Heritage Books / Free Reformed Publications, 2008.

Piper, John. *Brothers, We Are not Professionals: A Plea for Radical Ministry.* Nashville, TN: Broadman & Holman, 2002.

Piper, John, and Wayne Grudem, editors. *Recovering Biblical Manhood and Womanhood: A Response to Evangelical Feminism.* Wheaton IL: Crossway, 1991.

Schilder, Klaas. *Christ and Culture.* Translated by William Helder and Albert H. Oosterhoff; annotated by Jochem Douma; foreword by Richard J. Mouw. Hamilton, ON: Lucerna, 2016.

Sietsma, K. *The Idea of Office.* Jordan Station, ON: Paideia Press, 1985.

Sinnema, Donald. "The Second Sunday Service in the Early Dutch Reformed Tradition." *Calvin Theological Journal* 32 (1997): 298–333.

Sittser, Gerald L. *Resilient Faith: How the Early Christian "Third Way" Changed the World*. Grand Rapids, MI: Brazos Press, 2019.

Tripp, Paul David. *Awe: Why It Matters for Everything We Think, Say, and Do*. Wheaton, IL: Crossway, 2015.

Trumper, Tim J. R. *Preaching and Politics: Engagement without Compromise*. Eugene, OR: Wipf & Stock, 2009.

Van Dam, Cornelis. *The Deacon: Biblical Foundations for Today's Ministry of Mercy*. Grand Rapids, MI: Reformation Heritage Books, 2016.

Van Dam, Cornelis. *The Elder: Today's Ministry Rooted in All of Scripture*. Phillipsburg, NJ: P&R, 2009.

Van Dam, Cornelis. *God and Government. Biblical Principles for Today: An Introduction and Resource*. Eugene, OR: Wipf & Stock, 2011.

Van Dam, Cornelis. *Worship Matters: Essays on Public Worship*. With a contribution by Arjan De Visser. Reformed Perspective Press; Lucerna CRTS Publications, 2021.

van de Sandt, Huub, and David Flusser. *The Didache: Its Jewish Sources and Its Place in Early Judaism and Christianity*. Vol. III.5 of *Jewish Traditions in Early Christian Literature*. Compendia Rerum Iudaicarum Ad Novum Testamentum. Assen: Van Gorcum, 2002.

Van Dellen, Idzerd, and Martin Monsma. *The Church Order Commentary*. Grand Rapids: Zondervan, 1941.

Van Oene, W. W. J. *With Common Consent: A Practical Guide to the Use of the Church Order of the Canadian Reformed Churches*. Winnipeg: Premier, 1990.

Van Rongen, G. *Decently and in Good Order*. 1986. Reformed Guardian. Kelmscott, W.A.: N.p., 2005.

Visscher, G.H. "1 Timothy 2:12–15. Is Paul's Injunction about Women Still Valid?" In *Correctly Handling the Word of Truth: Reformed Hermeneutics Today*, edited by Mees te Velde and Gerhard H. Visscher, 142–54. Eugene, OR: Lucerna CRTS Publications; Wipf & Stock, 2014.

Selective Index of Biblical Texts

www.ingramcontent.com/pod-product-compliance
Lightning Source LLC
Chambersburg PA
CBHW070918120626
46546CB00001B/308